Table of Contents

Copyright ©
Copyright Protection

Your Free Bonus Gift!

As a small token of thanks for buying this book, I would like to offer a **FREE** bonus gift to all my readers. I am offering a **FREE** online VBA macros course called ***How to Record Macros in Excel***.

In this **FREE** course you will learn:

- How to record a macro to eliminate manual repetitive Excel tasks
- How to execute a macro by:
  - ➢ Using the Macro Dialog Box
  - ➢ Using the Visual Basic Editor
  - ➢ Clicking a button
  - ➢ Clicking a shape

Once you have completed the course you will be able to:

- ➢ Automate Excel tasks easily
- ➢ Save valuable time
- ➢ Advance your Excel skills

You can register for this **FREE** online VBA course by entering the link below to your web browser.

https://bit.ly/2JLFosd

Chapter 1: Introduction to Microsoft Office 365

1.1 What is Microsoft Office 365?

Microsoft Office 365 is a cloud-based suite of productivity applications offered by Microsoft. It includes popular software like Word, Excel, PowerPoint, Outlook, OneNote, Teams, and more. Unlike the traditional Microsoft Office suite that you install on your computer, Office 365 allows you to access and work on your files from anywhere with an internet connection. It also provides collaborative features, making it easy for multiple users to work together on the same documents simultaneously.

1.2 The Evolution of Microsoft Office 365

Before the emergence of cloud computing, Microsoft Office was available as a standalone suite of applications distributed on physical media such as CDs and DVDs. With Office 365's introduction in 2011, Microsoft transformed its traditional desktop software into a cloud-based offering, catering to the changing needs of modern workplaces and users who sought greater flexibility and collaboration capabilities.

1.3 Key Components of Microsoft Office 365

1.3.1 Office Applications

The core of Microsoft Office 365 comprises familiar applications used for productivity and document management. These include:

- **Microsoft Word**: A word processing application used for creating, editing, and formatting documents.

- **Microsoft Excel**: A powerful spreadsheet application for data analysis, calculations, and visualisation.

- **Microsoft PowerPoint**: A presentation software used to create visually engaging slideshows.

- **Microsoft Outlook**: An email client that helps manage emails, calendars, contacts, and tasks.

- **Microsoft OneNote**: A digital notebook for capturing and organising notes, drawings, and other content.

- **Microsoft Access**: A database management system to manage data and analyse large amounts of information efficiently.

1.3.2 Microsoft Teams

Microsoft Teams is a collaborative platform that facilitates real-time communication and teamwork. It combines chat, video conferencing, file sharing, and app integration, making it an essential tool for remote and in-person collaboration within organisations.

1.3.3 OneDrive

OneDrive is Microsoft's cloud storage service that allows users to store and access files from any device with an internet connection. It seamlessly integrates with Office applications, enabling easy sharing and collaboration on documents.

1.4 Features and Benefits of Microsoft Office 365

1.4.1 Accessibility and Mobility

Office 365's cloud-based nature enables users to access their files and applications from virtually anywhere with internet connectivity. This flexibility empowers users to work on their projects using different devices, such as computers, tablets, or smartphones, ensuring productivity on the go.

1.4.2 Real-time Collaboration

One of the most significant advantages of Office 365 is its robust collaboration capabilities. Multiple users can work simultaneously on the same document, spreadsheet, or presentation, and changes are reflected in real-time, streamlining group projects and enhancing teamwork.

1.4.3 Automatic Updates and Latest Features

With an Office 365 subscription, users always have access to the latest versions of the applications. Microsoft regularly releases updates, improvements, and new features to enhance user experience and security.

1.4.4 Security and Compliance

Microsoft prioritises the security of Office 365 users' data. The platform adheres to industry-standard security practices and offers built-in compliance features to meet various regulatory requirements.

1.5 Use Cases for Microsoft Office 365

1.5.1 Personal Use

Office 365 offers subscription plans tailored for individuals, making it suitable for students, freelancers, and anyone seeking the latest Office applications with cloud benefits and continuous updates.

1.5.2 Small and Medium-sized Businesses (SMBs)

For SMBs, Office 365 provides a cost-effective solution for essential productivity tools and collaboration services, allowing seamless communication and file sharing among team members.

1.5.3 Enterprises and Organisations

Large enterprises benefit from the advanced features of Office 365, such as robust security, compliance capabilities, and centralised administration tools that enable IT departments to manage users and resources efficiently.

1.6 Benefits of Office 365

Microsoft Office 365 offers a wide array of benefits for individuals, businesses, and organisations of all sizes. As a cloud-based suite of productivity tools, Office 365 introduces a new level of flexibility, collaboration, and convenience that traditional software cannot match. In this chapter, we will explore the key advantages of using Office 365 and how it enhances productivity and efficiency across various use cases.

1.6.1 Accessibility and Mobility

One of the primary advantages of Office 365 is its accessibility and mobility. As a cloud-based service, Office 365 allows users to access their files, applications, and tools from virtually anywhere with an internet connection. Whether you are working from your office, home, or on the go, you can log in to your Office 365 account on any device and continue your work seamlessly. This flexibility empowers users to stay productive, collaborate with others, and respond to critical tasks even when they are away from their primary workspace.

1.6.2 Real-time Collaboration

Collaboration lies at the heart of Office 365, and it excels in enabling real-time teamwork. With applications like Microsoft Word, Excel, and PowerPoint, multiple users can work together on the same document simultaneously. Changes made by one collaborator are instantly visible to others, allowing for seamless co-authoring and eliminating the need to manage different versions of files. Whether you are brainstorming ideas with colleagues, conducting a virtual meeting, or editing a presentation with team members, Office 365's collaborative features foster efficiency and enhance productivity.

1.6.3 Automatic Updates and Latest Features

Office 365 subscribers enjoy the benefit of automatic updates and access to the latest features. Unlike traditional software, where you might need to purchase a new version to access the latest improvements, Office 365 is continually updated by Microsoft. Subscribers receive regular updates that include bug fixes, security patches, and enhancements to the existing features. This ensures that users always have access to the most up-to-date and efficient tools, providing a smooth and hassle-free experience.

1.6.4 Seamless Integration with Cloud Services

Office 365 seamlessly integrates with Microsoft's cloud services, most notably with OneDrive and SharePoint. OneDrive offers secure cloud storage, allowing users to save their files and documents in the cloud, ensuring easy access and sharing across devices. SharePoint, on the other hand, enables collaborative content management, making it a powerful tool for businesses and organisations to create intranets, team sites, and document libraries. This integration enhances data security, facilitates efficient file sharing, and streamlines document management across teams.

1.6.5 Enhanced Communication and Collaboration with Teams

Microsoft Teams, a central component of Office 365, revolutionises communication and collaboration within organisations. Teams is a unified platform that combines chat, video conferencing, file sharing, and app integration. It allows team members to communicate and collaborate in real-time, irrespective of their physical location. With features like channels, private chats, and screen sharing, Teams fosters efficient and effective teamwork, making it an invaluable tool for remote and hybrid work environments.

1.6.6 Advanced Security and Compliance

Microsoft prioritises the security and privacy of Office 365 users' data. The platform adheres to industry-standard security practices, offering robust measures to safeguard against data breaches, malware, and unauthorised access. Additionally, Office 365 includes compliance features that help organisations meet industry-specific regulations and standards, making it suitable for businesses in various sectors, including finance, healthcare, and government.

Microsoft Office 365 offers a host of benefits that revolutionise the way individuals and organisations approach productivity and collaboration. With its cloud-based infrastructure, real-time collaboration, automatic updates, and seamless integration with other cloud services, Office 365 empowers users to work efficiently and stay connected in today's fast-paced and interconnected world. From personal use to small businesses and large enterprises, Office 365 continues to be a driving force behind enhanced productivity, streamlined workflows, and successful teamwork.

1.7 Different Subscription Plans of Microsoft Office 365

Microsoft Office 365 offers a range of subscription plans tailored to meet the diverse needs of individuals, families, small businesses, and enterprises. Each plan provides access to a set of Office applications and cloud-based services, ensuring that users can choose the one that best aligns with their requirements and budget. In this section, we will explore the key features and target audiences of various Office 365 subscription plans.

1.7.1 Office 365 Personal

Office 365 Personal is designed for individual use and offers a comprehensive set of Office applications and cloud services. With this plan, subscribers can install Office on one PC or Mac and one tablet, making it suitable for users who work primarily on a single device and require the full suite of Office apps for productivity. Office 365 Personal includes applications such as Word, Excel, PowerPoint, Outlook, OneNote, and Publisher (Windows only), as well as 1 TB of OneDrive cloud storage. This subscription plan is ideal for students, freelancers, and anyone who wants the power of Office on their personal devices.

1.7.2 Office 365 Home

Office 365 Home is geared towards families and households. It offers all the features of Office 365 Personal but expands the installation to cover up to six users across multiple devices. Each user can install Office on their PC or Mac, tablet, and smartphone, ensuring that everyone in the household can access and use Office applications on their preferred devices. Office 365 Home comes with 1 TB of OneDrive storage per user, making it a cost-effective solution for families who need individual Office accounts and cloud storage for all their members.

1.7.3 Office 365 Business

Office 365 Business plans cater to small and medium-sized businesses (SMBs) and offer essential Office applications and services to enhance productivity and collaboration. These plans come with business-class email hosting using Exchange Online, allowing users to have a professional email address with their domain name. Depending on the specific plan, subscribers may also get access to additional applications like SharePoint and Microsoft Teams for seamless teamwork and content management. Office 365 Business is available in different tiers, allowing businesses to choose the plan that aligns with their team size and requirements.

1.7.4 Office 365 Enterprise

Office 365 Enterprise plans are designed for large organisations and corporations. They provide advanced features, security measures, and compliance capabilities, making them suitable for enterprises with complex IT requirements and stringent data regulations. Office 365 Enterprise includes all the features of Office 365 Business and adds additional security layers, enterprise-grade email protection, and advanced data loss prevention tools. With these plans, organisations can enforce policies, manage users at scale, and ensure data security across the entire organisation.

1.7.5 Office 365 Education

Office 365 Education is a specialised offering for educational institutions, including schools, colleges, and universities. It enables educators, students, and staff to access Office applications and cloud services for educational purposes. Office 365 Education includes collaborative tools like Microsoft Teams, making it an invaluable platform for virtual classrooms, online assignments, and group projects. Microsoft also offers Office 365 A1 for free to educational institutions, providing basic features and services at no cost.

Microsoft Office 365 offers a variety of subscription plans to cater to the diverse needs of users, businesses, and educational institutions. Whether it's for personal use, family, small business, or enterprise, there's a plan that suits everyone. From individual productivity to seamless collaboration, Office 365 subscription plans provide the essential tools and services to enhance productivity and drive success across different scenarios. Users can choose the most suitable plan based on the number of users, device installations, and additional features required, ensuring they get the most out of their Office 365 experience.

1.8 Getting Started with Office 365

Getting started with Microsoft Office 365 is a straightforward process that involves setting up an account, choosing the right subscription plan, and accessing the suite of Office applications and cloud services. In this section, we will walk you through the step-by-step instructions to get started with Office 365 and provide some essential data to help you make informed decisions.

Step 1: Choose the Right Subscription Plan

Before you can begin using Office 365, you need to select the subscription plan that best suits your needs. Microsoft offers various plans for individuals, families, businesses, and educational institutions. To make an informed decision, consider the following factors:

- **Number of Users**: Determine how many users will need access to Office 365 applications and services. For personal use, Office 365 Personal might be sufficient, while Office 365 Home is ideal for families with multiple users.

- **Device Installations**: Assess the number of devices (PCs, Macs, tablets, smartphones) you need to install Office on for each user. Office 365 Personal allows installation on one PC/Mac and one tablet, while Office 365 Home extends it to multiple devices per user.

- **Business Needs**: If you're a small business or enterprise, consider Office 365 Business or Enterprise plans, depending on the size of your organisation and the additional features required.

- **Educational Use**: Educational institutions can opt for Office 365 Education plans, tailored for students, teachers, and staff.

Step 2: Create a Microsoft Account

To use Office 365, you need a Microsoft account. If you don't have one, follow these steps to create an account:

1. Go to the Microsoft account creation page (https://account.microsoft.com/).

2. Click on "Create one" to set up a new account.

3. Enter your email address (or create a new one) and follow the on-screen instructions to complete the registration process.

Step 3: Choose a Subscription Plan

After creating your Microsoft account, visit the official Office 365 website (https://www.microsoft.com/en-us/microsoft-365) and explore the available subscription plans. Compare the features and pricing to find the plan that best matches your requirements.

Step 4: Purchase and Activate Office 365

Once you've chosen the subscription plan, follow these steps to purchase and activate Office 365:

1. Click on the "Buy now" or "Subscribe" button next to the plan you want.

2. You'll be prompted to log in with your Microsoft account. Enter your credentials to proceed.

3. Choose the payment method and provide the necessary details for billing.

4. Complete the payment process to purchase the subscription.

5. After the purchase, you'll receive an email with instructions on how to activate Office 365.

6. Follow the activation steps provided in the email to set up Office 365 on your devices.

Step 5: Access Office Applications and Cloud Services

After activation, you can start using Office 365 applications and services. Here's how to access them:

1. On your PC or Mac, open a web browser and go to https://www.office.com/.

2. Sign in with your Microsoft account credentials.

3. From the Office portal, you can access Office applications such as Word, Excel, PowerPoint, Outlook, and more.

4. To use cloud services like OneDrive, click on the "OneDrive" icon, and start storing and sharing your files in the cloud.

Getting started with Microsoft Office 365 involves selecting the right subscription plan, creating a Microsoft account, purchasing, and activating the subscription, and accessing the Office applications and cloud services. With the various plans available, users can choose the one that aligns with their needs and budget, ensuring they have the power of Office 365 at their fingertips for enhanced productivity and collaboration.

Chapter 2: Microsoft Word

Microsoft Word is a versatile word processing application developed by Microsoft, and it is a part of the Microsoft Office suite. It is widely regarded as one of the most popular and essential software tools for creating, editing, and formatting various types of documents. Launched in 1983, Microsoft Word has evolved over the years, introducing numerous features that cater to the needs of individuals, students, professionals, and businesses. In this chapter, we will explore what Microsoft Word is, its key features, and the diverse range of applications for which it is used.

2.1 What is Microsoft Word?

Microsoft Word is a word processing software that enables users to compose, edit, format, and save textual content in electronic documents. Unlike traditional typewriters, Microsoft Word offers a digital platform that empowers users to create and manage documents efficiently. The user-friendly interface, along with a wide array of formatting tools and features, allows for easy customisation and professional-looking documents. From simple letters and memos to complex reports and publications, Microsoft Word is the go-to application for crafting a variety of written materials.

2.2 Key Features of Microsoft Word

Below are the main features and benefits of Microsoft Word:

2.2.1 Document Creation

Microsoft Word provides a blank canvas where users can start typing their content, allowing for seamless document creation from scratch.

2.2.2 Editing and Proofreading

The application offers a comprehensive set of editing tools, including spell check, grammar check, thesaurus, and track changes, enabling users to review and improve their content.

2.2.3 Formatting

Microsoft Word offers extensive formatting options to customise the appearance of text, such as font styles, sizes, colours, alignment, indents, and line spacing.

2.2.4 Page Layout

Users can control the layout of their documents, adjusting margins, headers, footers, page orientation (portrait or landscape), and page breaks.

2.2.5 Inserting Media

Microsoft Word allows the insertion of images, shapes, charts, tables, hyperlinks, and other multimedia elements to enhance the visual appeal and information presentation of the document.

2.2.6 Collaboration

With real-time collaboration features, multiple users can work simultaneously on the same document, making it ideal for team projects and group work.

2.2.7 Templates

Microsoft Word offers a wide range of pre-designed templates for various document types, such as resumes, flyers, newsletters, and more, saving users time and effort.

2.3 Applications of Microsoft Word

2.3.1 Personal Use

Microsoft Word is commonly used by individuals for personal projects, such as writing letters, creating resumes, designing invitations, and making to-do lists.

2.3.2 Academic and Educational Purposes

Students and educators use Microsoft Word for writing essays, research papers, reports, and creating study materials.

2.3.3 Business and Professional Documentation

In the business world, Microsoft Word is the go-to application for creating official documents like business letters, reports, proposals, contracts, and invoices.

2.3.4 Publishing and Content Creation

Authors, bloggers, and content creators use Microsoft Word to draft and edit their written content before publishing it on various platforms.

2.3.5 Collaboration and Teamwork

Microsoft Word's collaboration features make it an essential tool for group projects, allowing team members to contribute to a document simultaneously.

2.4 Creating a New Document in Microsoft Word

Microsoft Word provides a straightforward and intuitive interface for creating documents. In this section, we will walk you through the step-by-step process of creating a new document in Microsoft Word.

2.4.1 Creating a New Document

Step 1: Launch Microsoft Word

- Open Microsoft Word on your computer by clicking on the Word icon or searching for "Microsoft Word" in your operating system's search bar.

Step 2: Choose a Blank Document or Template

- After opening Word, you will see the Start screen. Here, you can choose to create a new blank document or select from a variety of templates. If you prefer a blank document, click on "Blank document".

Step 3: Start Typing

- A blank document will appear on the screen. Start typing your content directly into the document. Word automatically saves your document as you work, so there's no need to worry about losing your progress.

Step 4: Save the Document

- To save your document with a specific name and location on your computer, go to the "File" tab in the top left corner, click on "Save As," and choose a location and filename for your document. Click "Save" to confirm.

2.5 Formatting Text and Paragraphs on Microsoft Word

Microsoft Word offers a wide range of formatting options to customise the appearance of text and paragraphs in your documents. In this section, we will guide you through the step-by-step process of formatting text and paragraphs to make your documents visually appealing and professional.

2.5.1 Formatting Text

Step 1: Select Text

- To format specific text, start by selecting the portion of text you want to modify. Click and drag your cursor over the text to highlight it.

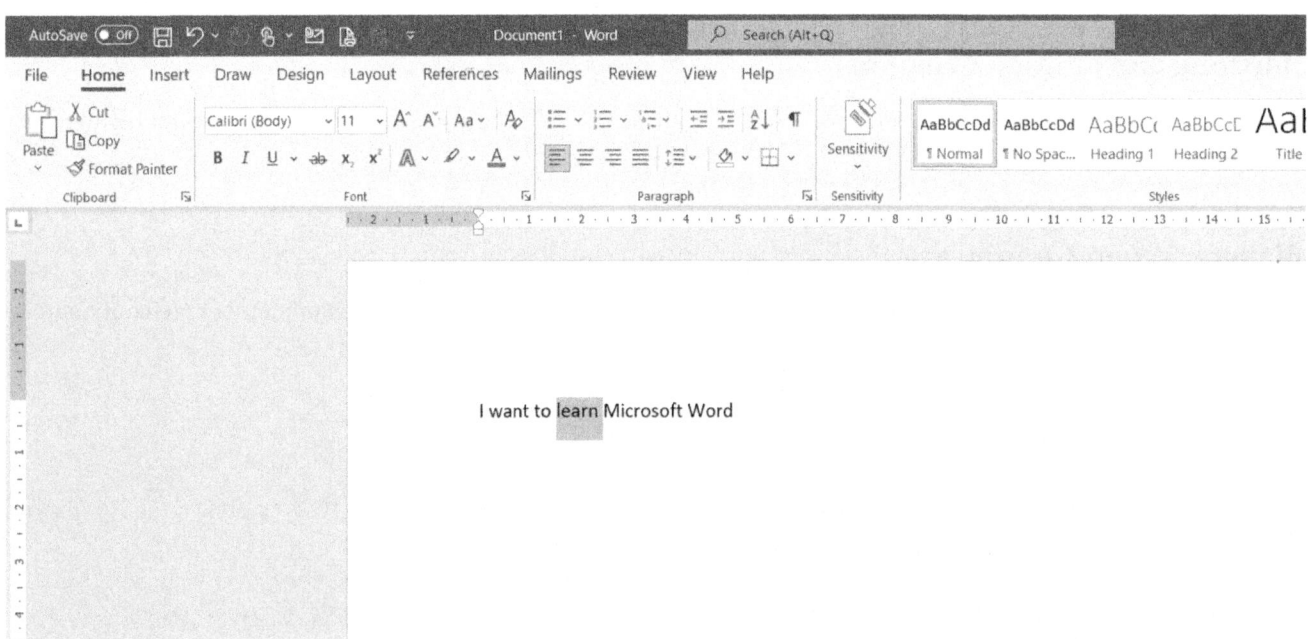

Step 2: Font Styles and Sizes

- In the "Home" tab of the top menu, you will find various options to format your text. The "Font" group allows you to change the font style and size. Click the drop-down menus to select the desired font and size for your text.

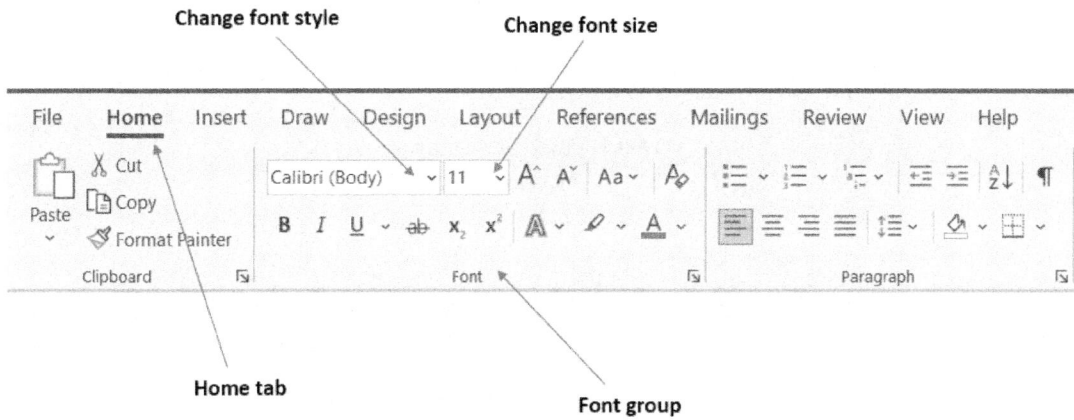

Step 3: Bold, Italic, and Underline

- The "Font" group also contains buttons for bold (B), italic (I), and underline (U). Click on these buttons to apply the respective formatting to the selected text.

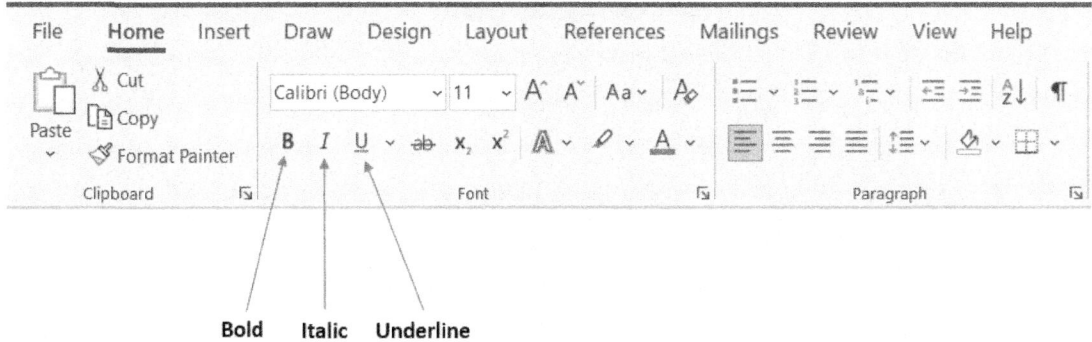

Step 4: Font Colour

- To change the colour of your text, click the "Font Colour" button (A with a coloured underline) in the "Font" group. Select a colour from the drop-down menu or choose "More Colours" for a wider colour selection.

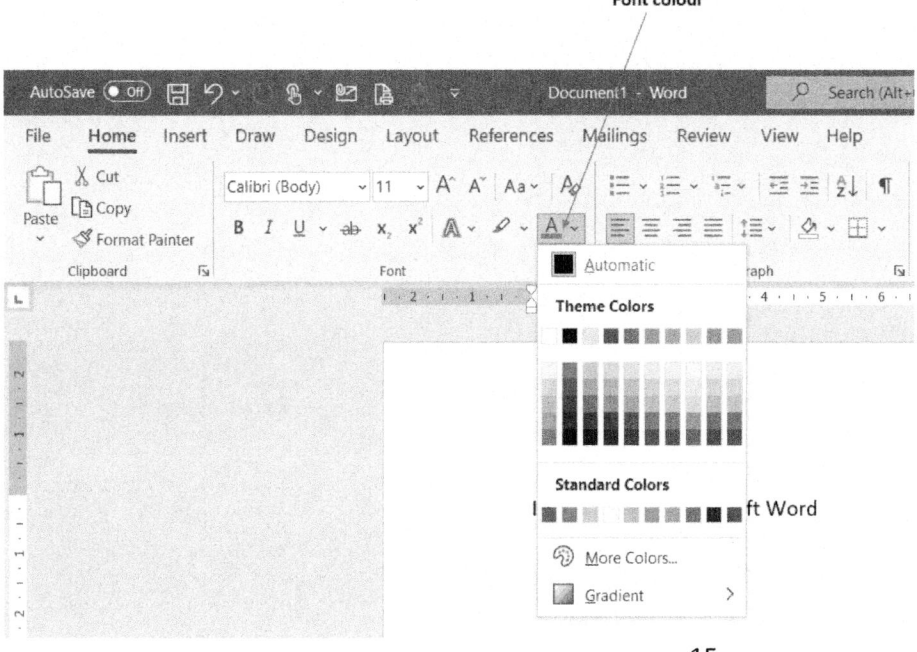

Step 5: Text Highlighting

- The "Text Highlight Color" button (highlighter icon) allows you to add a coloured background to your selected text. Click the button and choose a highlight colour from the drop-down menu.

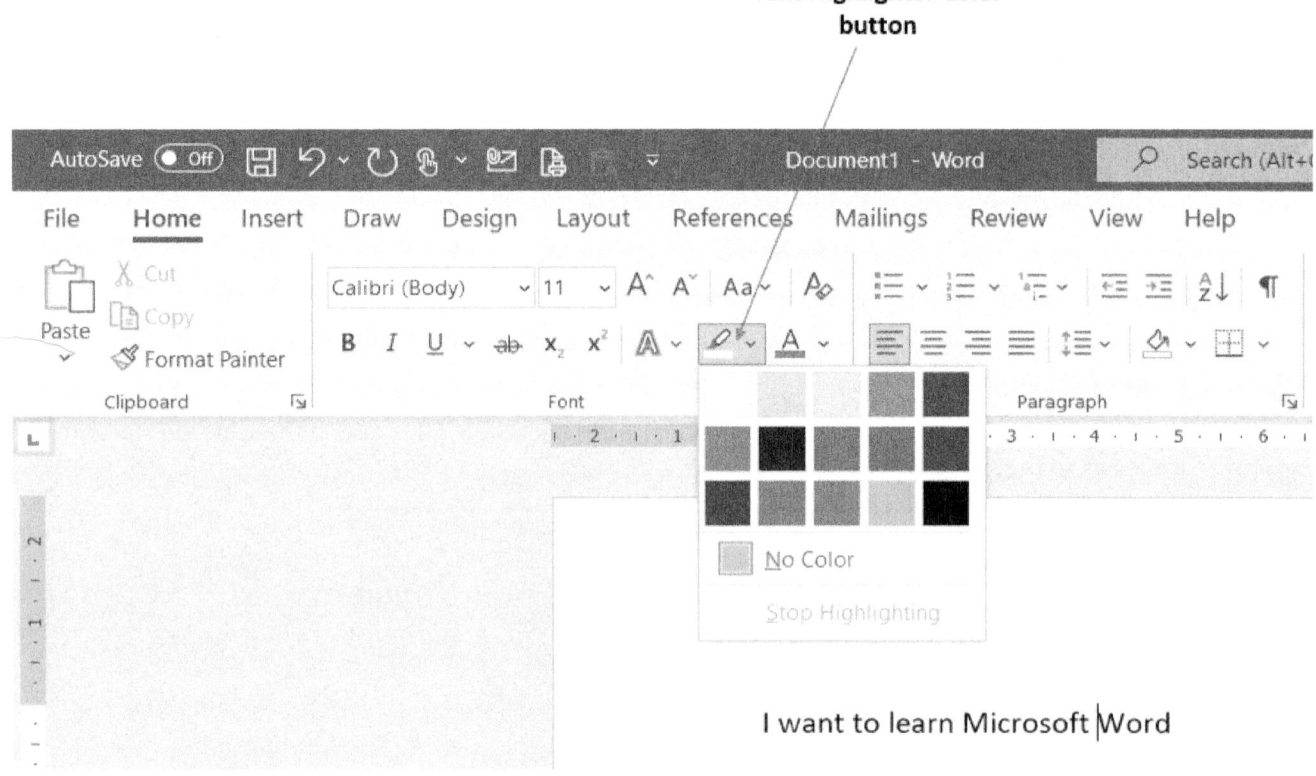

2.5.2 Formatting Paragraphs

Step 1: Adjust Alignment

- The "Paragraph" group in the "Home" tab provides alignment options for your paragraphs. You can choose left alignment, centre alignment, right alignment, or justified alignment for your text.

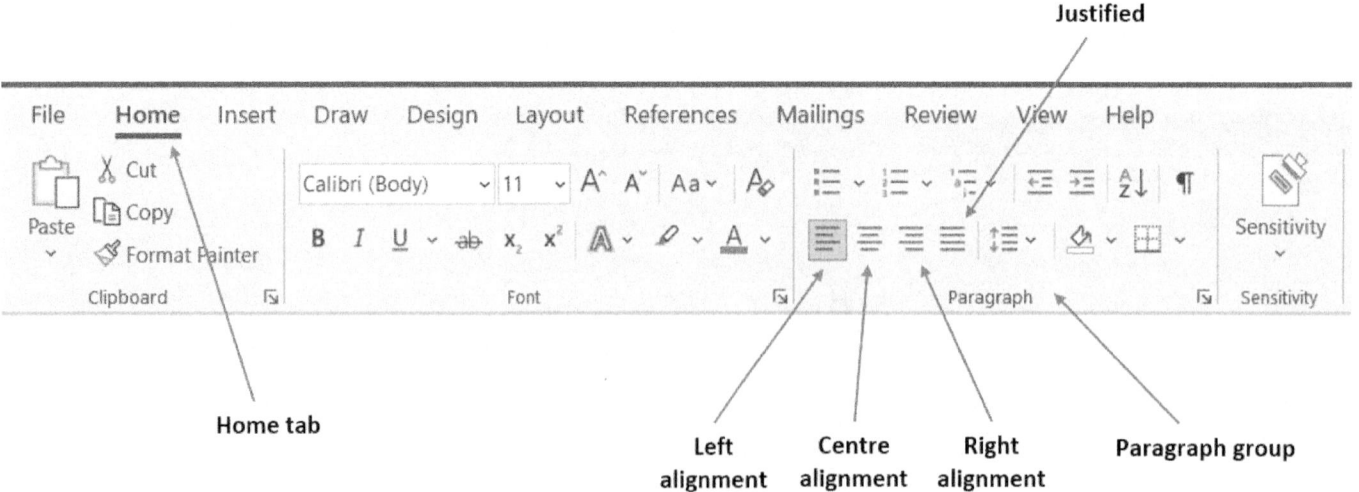

Step 2: Indentation

- To adjust the indentation of paragraphs, use the "Increase Indent" and "Decrease Indent" buttons in the "Paragraph" group. These buttons move the entire paragraph inward or outward.

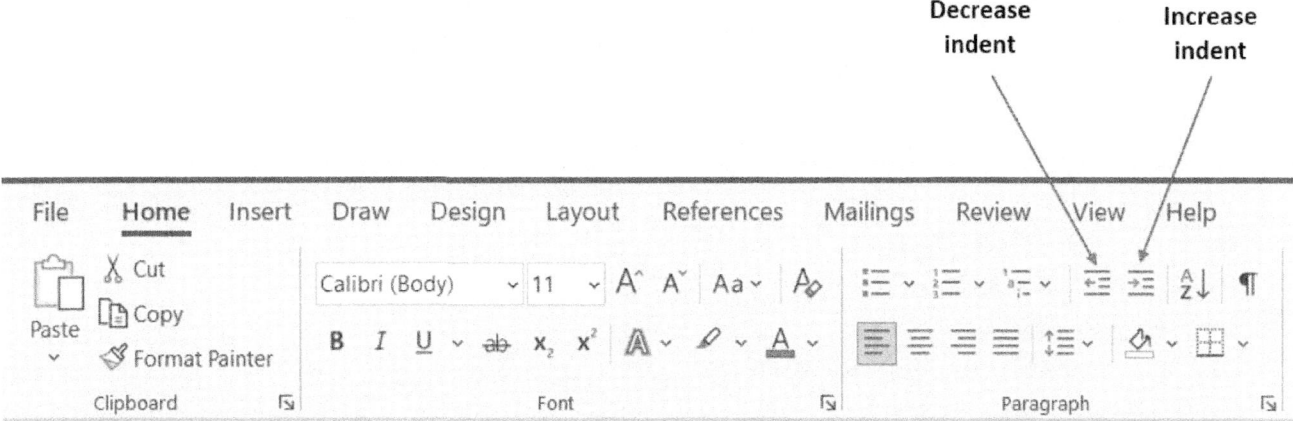

Step 3: Line Spacing

- In the "Paragraph" group, you'll find the line spacing options. Click the drop-down menu to choose single spacing, 1.5-line spacing, double spacing, or customise the spacing as needed.

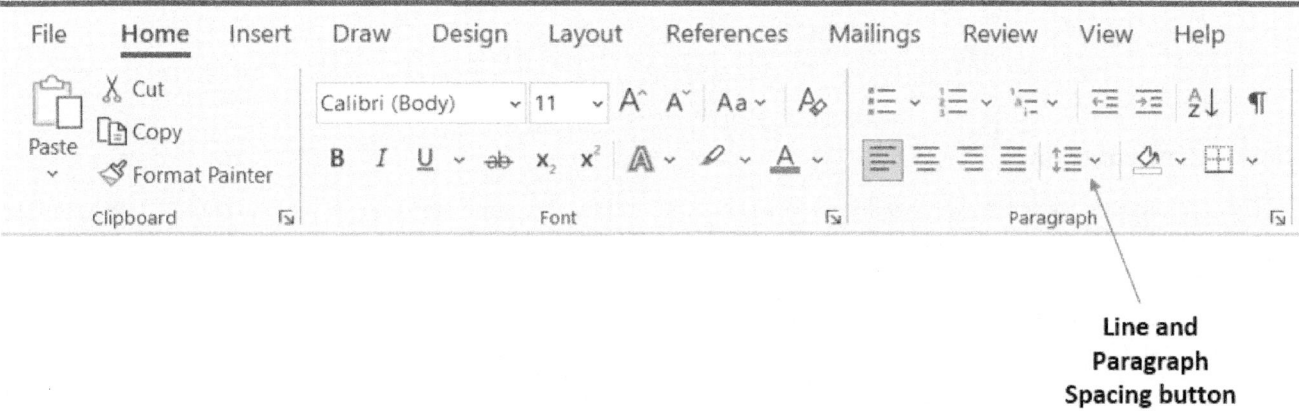

Step 4: First Line Indentation

- If you need to create a first-line indent (often used in academic or professional writing), click on the small arrow at the bottom-right corner of the "Paragraph" group to open the Paragraph dialog box.

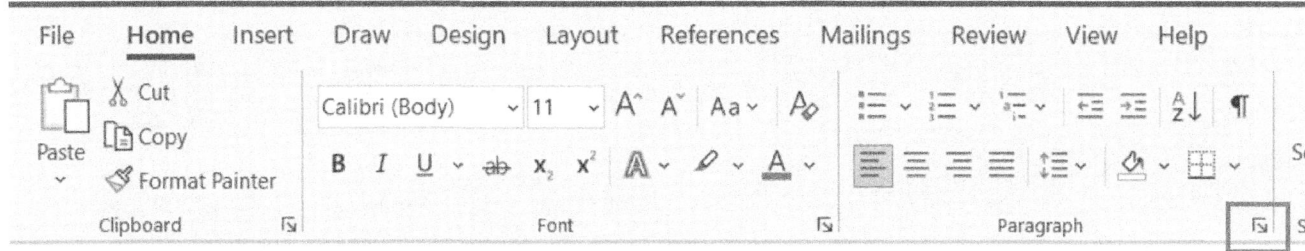

- Under the "Indentation" section, enter the value for "Special" and choose "First line".

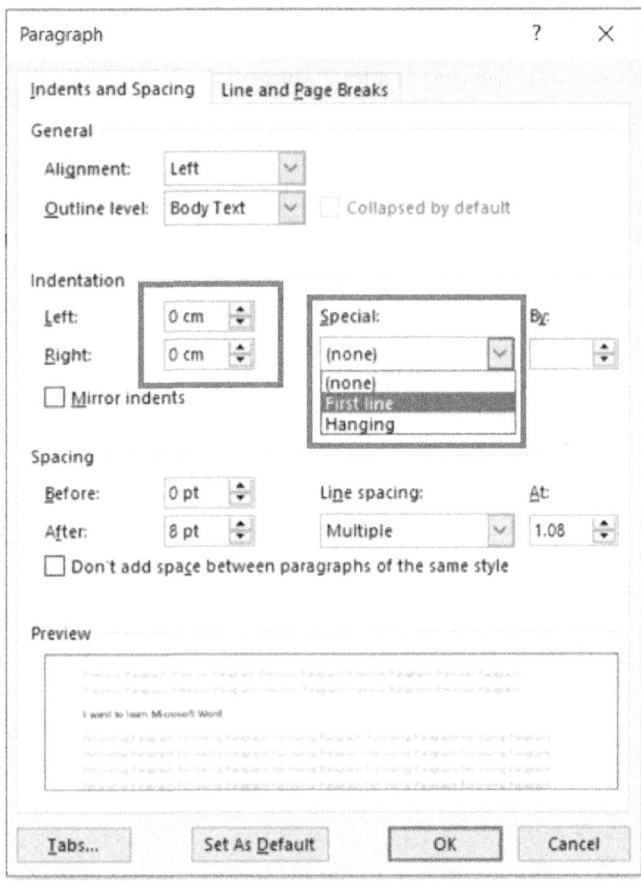

Step 5: Hanging Indentation

- To create a hanging indent (often used in reference lists), follow the same steps as above but choose "Hanging" in the "Special" section.

2.5.3 Clear Formatting

If you need to remove any formatting applied to text or paragraphs and revert to the default styles, select the text, and click the "Clear All Formatting" button (eraser icon) in the "Font" group.

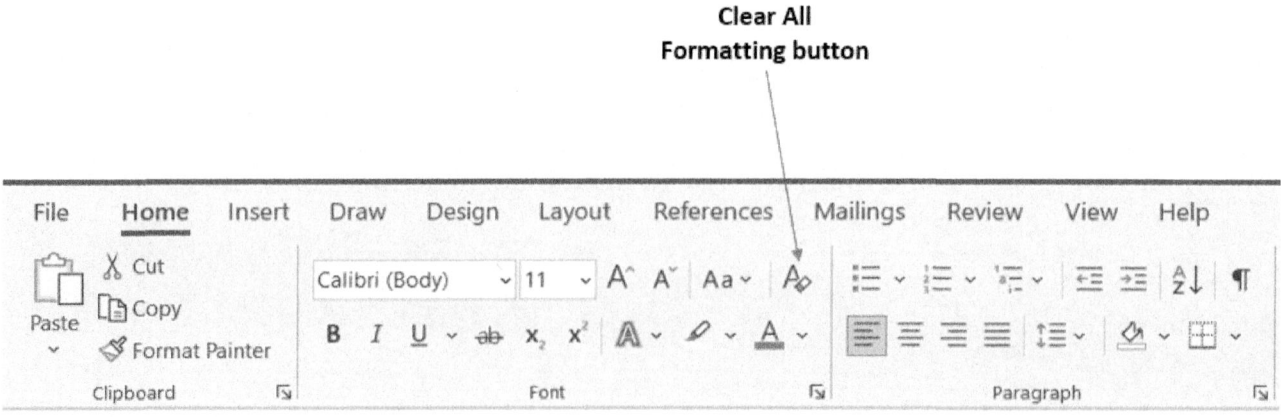

Microsoft Word's comprehensive set of formatting options allows you to customise text and paragraphs in your documents with ease. Whether you need to change font styles, apply bold and italics, adjust alignment, or create indents, Word provides the tools to make your documents look polished and professional. By following the step-by-step instructions in this section, you can effectively format your text and paragraphs to suit your specific document requirements.

2.6 Creating Tables and Charts in Microsoft Word

Microsoft Word allows beginners to create tables and charts to organise data and present it visually. In this section, we will provide step-by-step instructions on how to create a table and a chart in Microsoft Word.

2.6.1 Creating a Table

Step 1: Open Microsoft Word

- Launch Microsoft Word on your computer by clicking on the Word icon or searching for "Microsoft Word" in your operating system's search bar.

Step 2: Insert a Table

- In the Word document, place your cursor where you want to insert the table. Go to the "Insert" tab in the top menu and click on the "Table" button. Choose the number of rows and columns you want for your table by hovering over the grid.

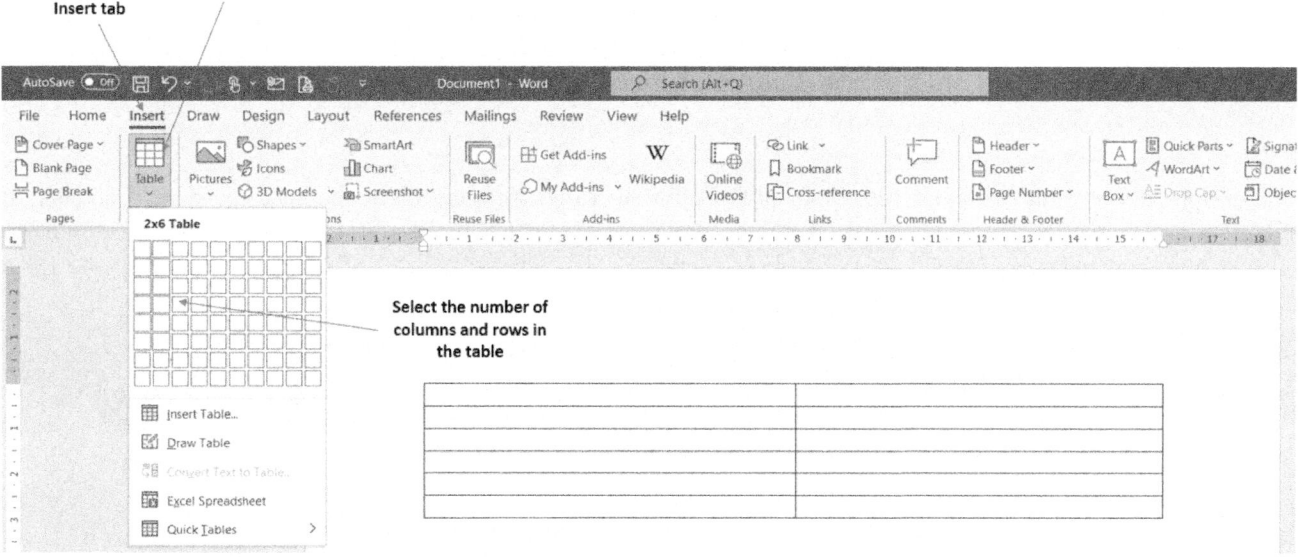

- Sample Data: Let's create a simple table to track monthly expenses.

Expense	Amount
Rent	1,000
Groceries	300
Utilities	200
Transportation	150
Entertainment	100

Step 3: Enter Data into the Table

- Once the table is inserted, you can start entering data into the cells. Click on each cell and type the appropriate information.

Step 4: Formatting the Table

- To format the table, you can use the Table Design and Layout options that appear when the table is selected. Change the font size, colour, and add borders to make the table visually appealing.

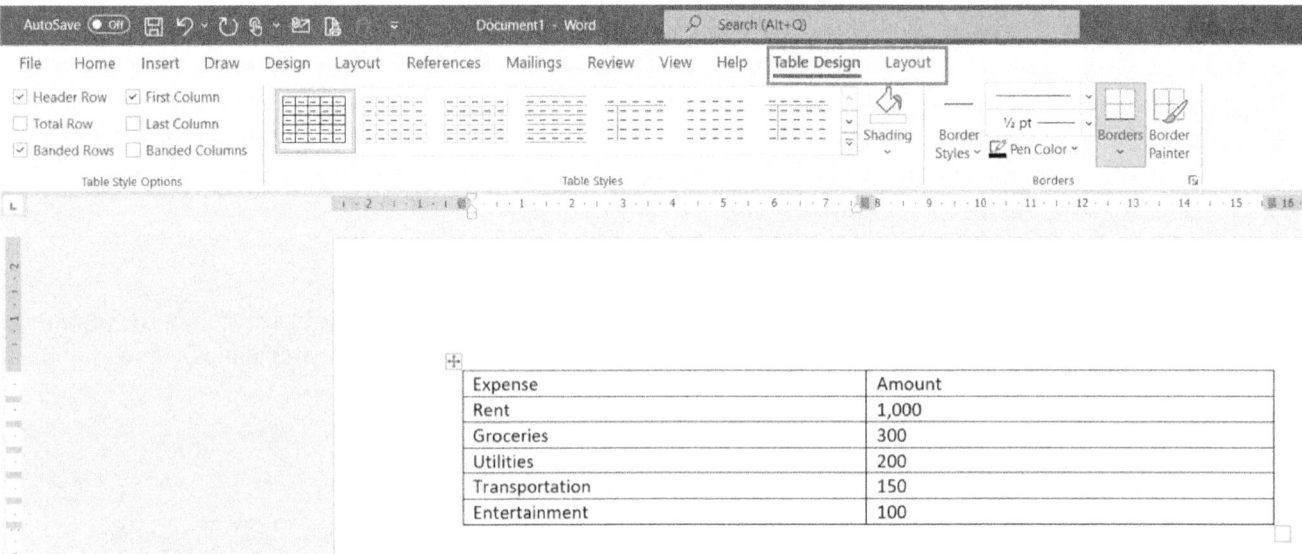

- For example, if you want to change the colour of the table headings, first highlight the headings, and then click on "Table Design" in the top menu. Next, click the drop-down menu in the "Shading" button and choose the colour you want the headings to be from the list of available colours.

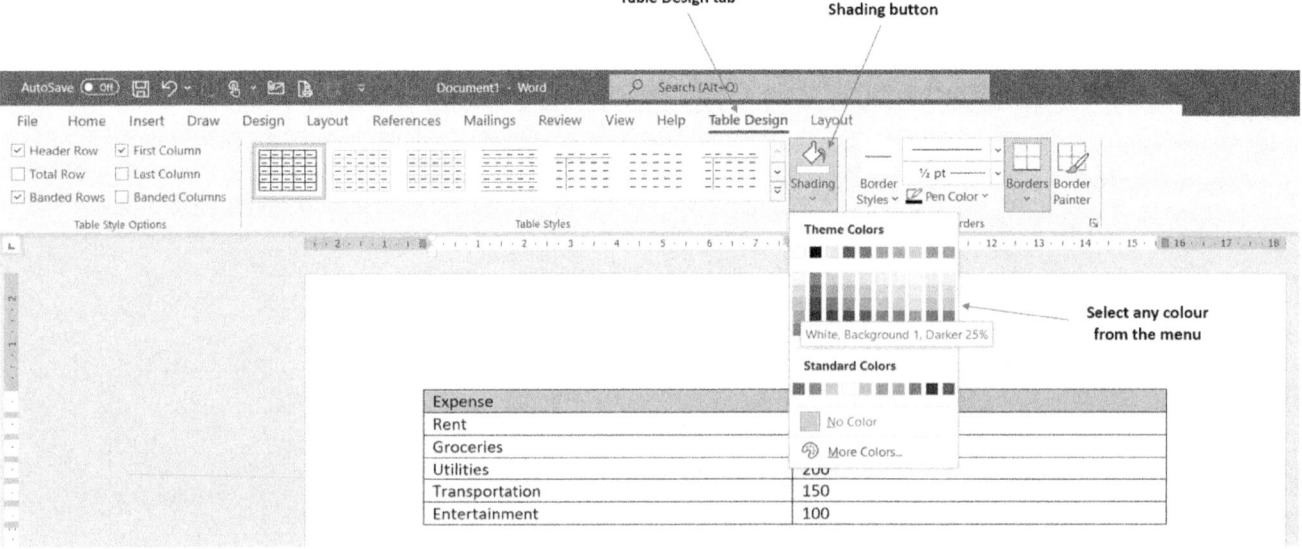

2.6.2 Creating a Chart

Step 1: Go to the "Insert" Tab

- Navigate to the "Insert" tab in the top menu to find the "Chart" button.

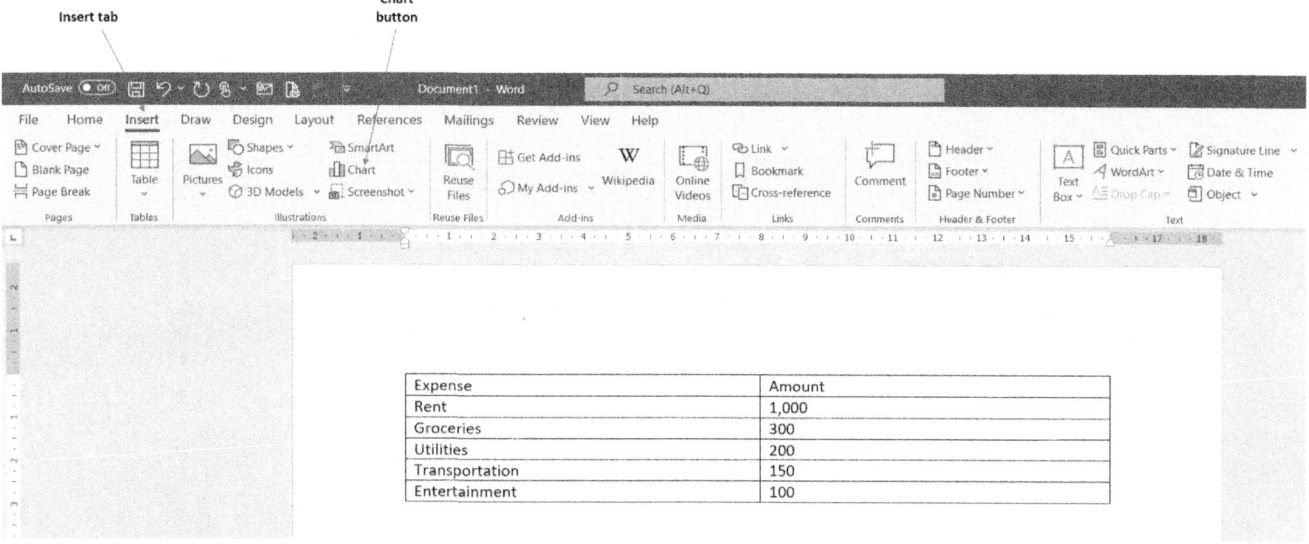

Expense	Amount
Rent	1,000
Groceries	300
Utilities	200
Transportation	150
Entertainment	100

Step 2: Choose the Chart Type

- Click on the chart type you want to create. In this example, we'll select a "Column Chart".

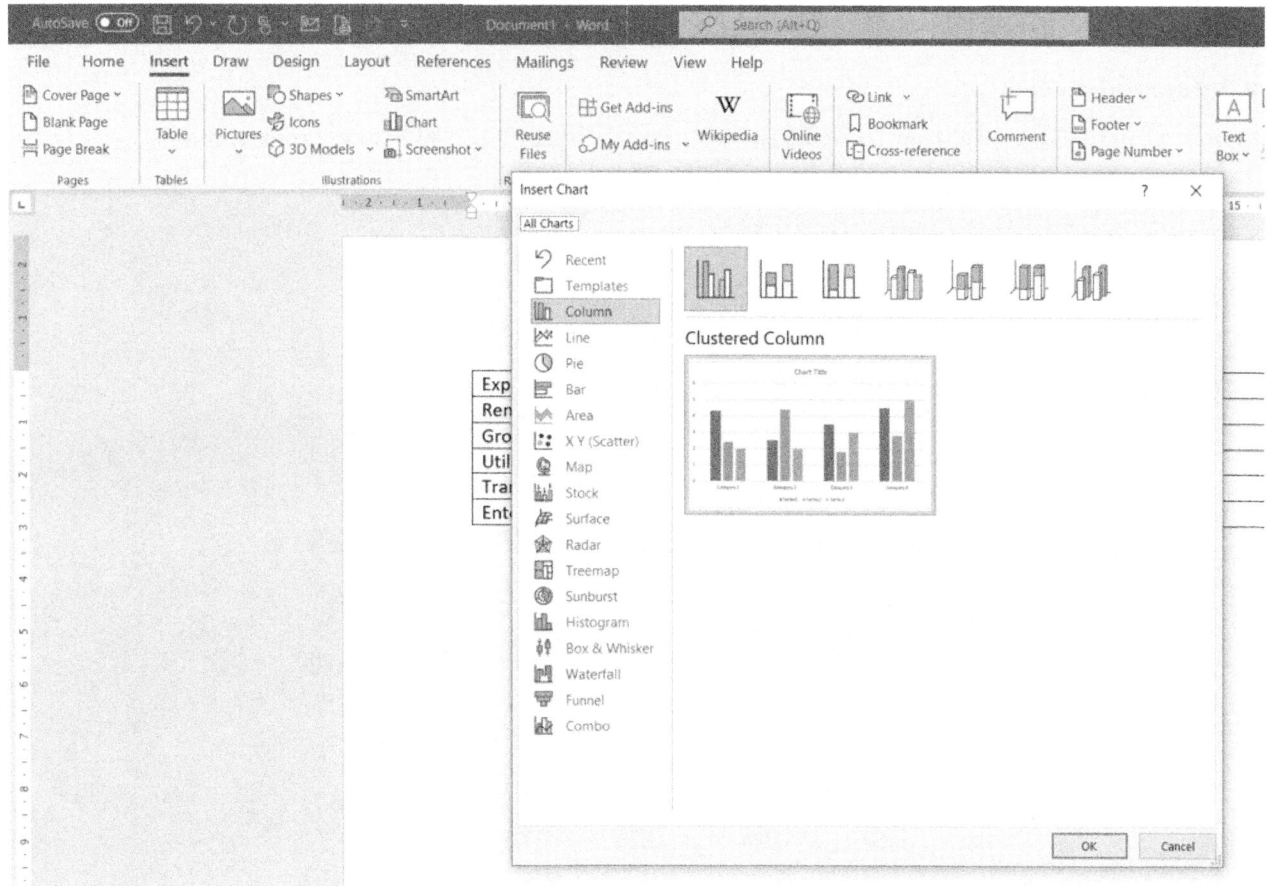

Step 3: Insert your data

- Insert your data over the default data in the spreadsheet. To delete any columns in the default data that are not needed, simply select the columns and then right-click the mouse and select "Delete" from the menu.

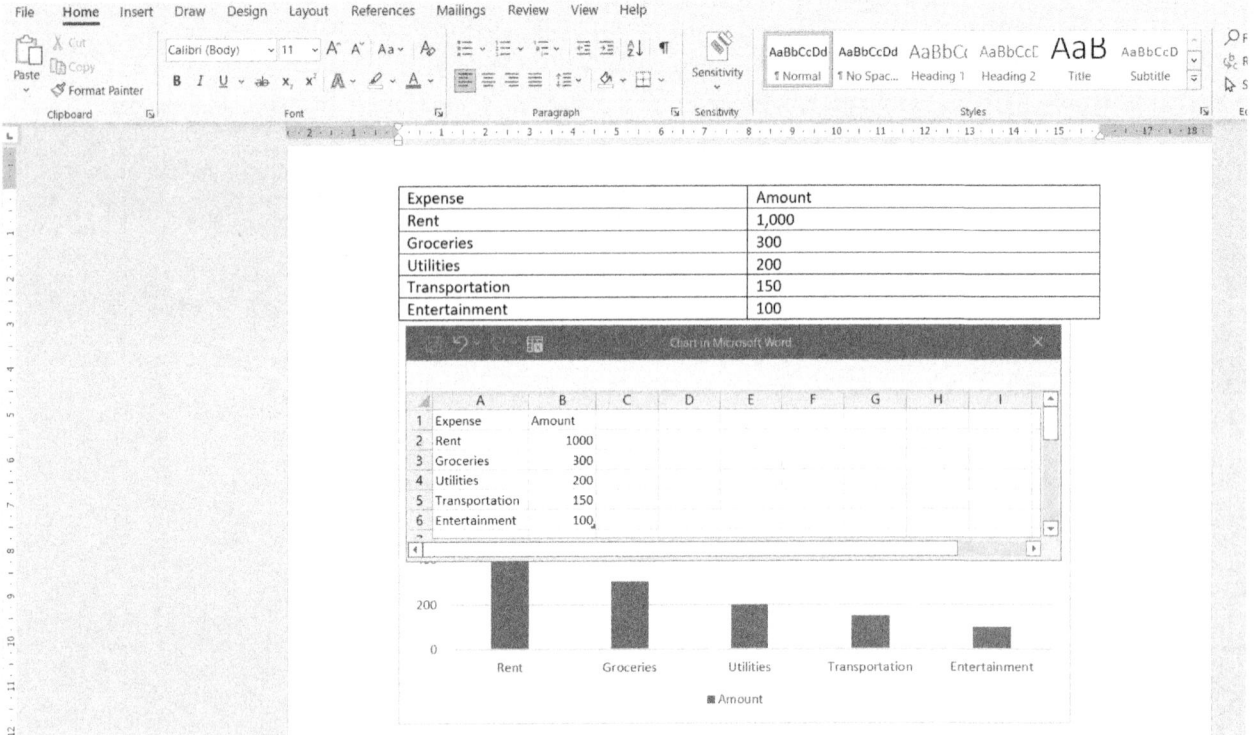

Step 4: Close the spreadsheet

- Click on the "X" in the upper right corner of the spreadsheet to close it once you have entered your data.

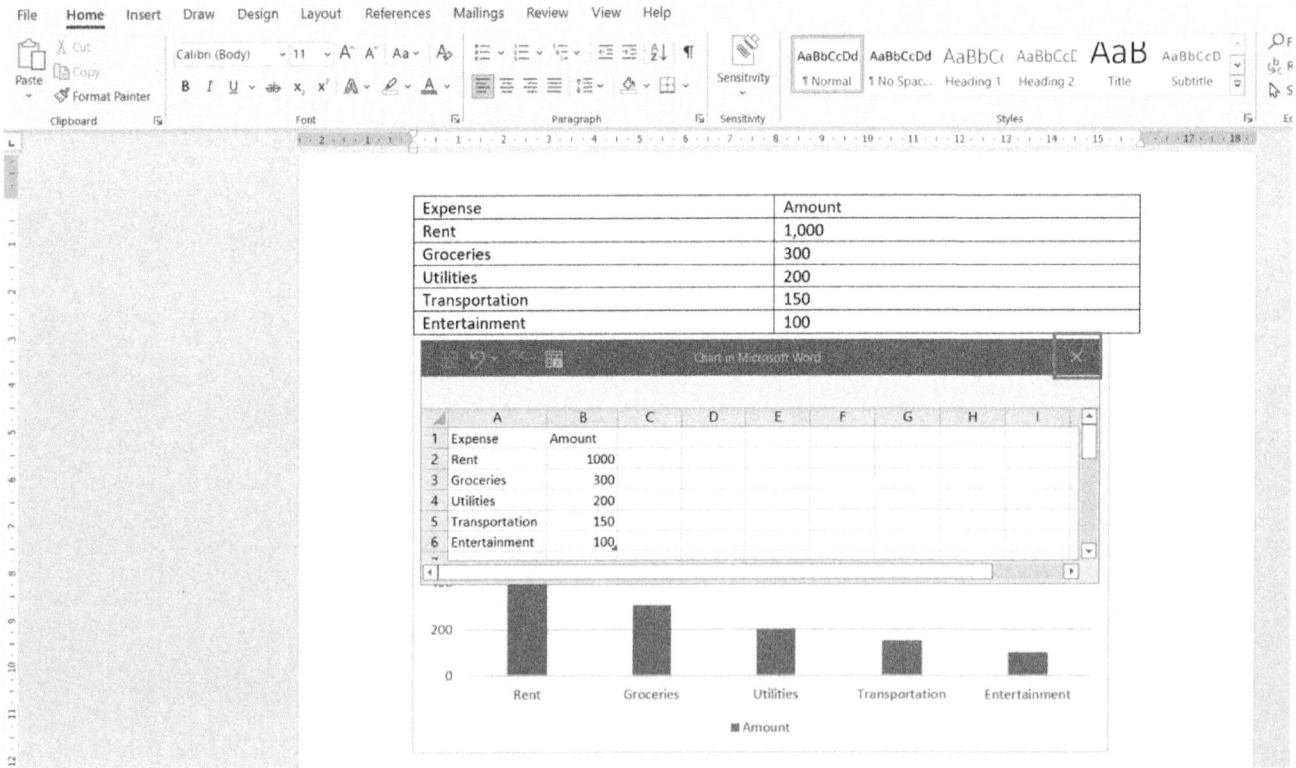

Step 5: Customise the Chart

- After inserting the chart with the correct data, you can customise it further. Click on the chart to reveal the "Chart Elements" (plus sign) and "Chart Styles" (paintbrush) buttons.

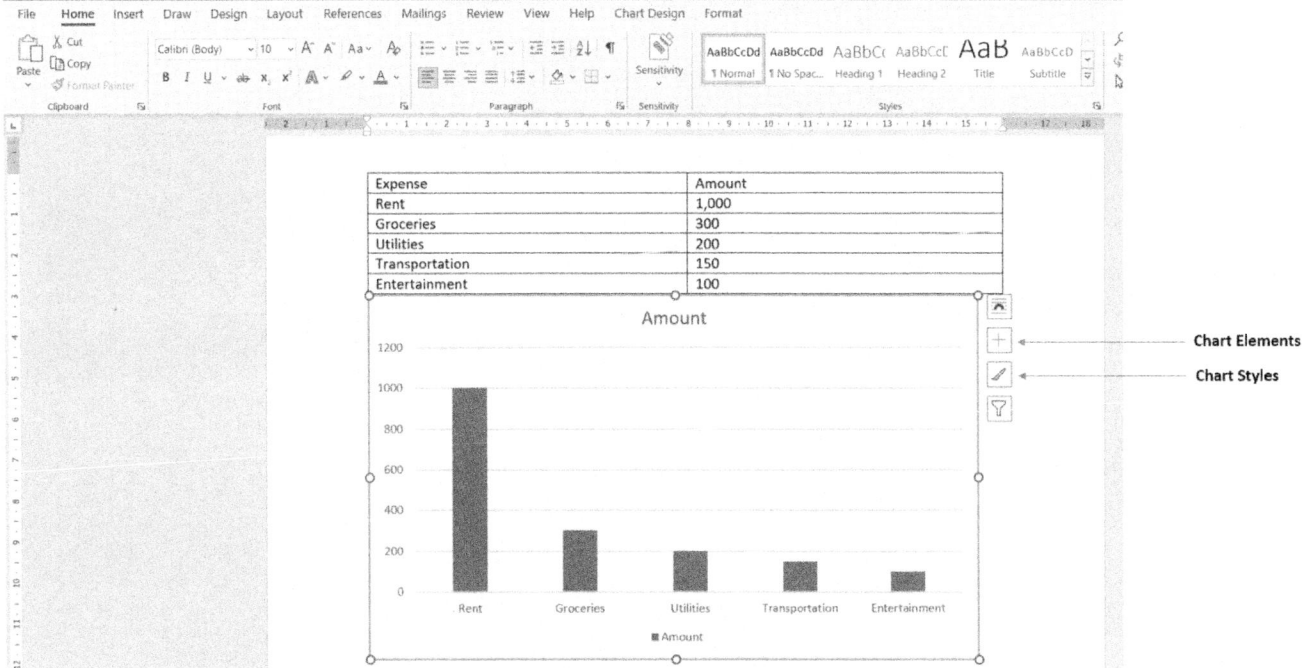

Step 6: Add Data Labels

- To add data labels to the chart, click on the chart, go to "Chart Elements," and select "Data Labels". The data labels will display the values above each column in the chart.

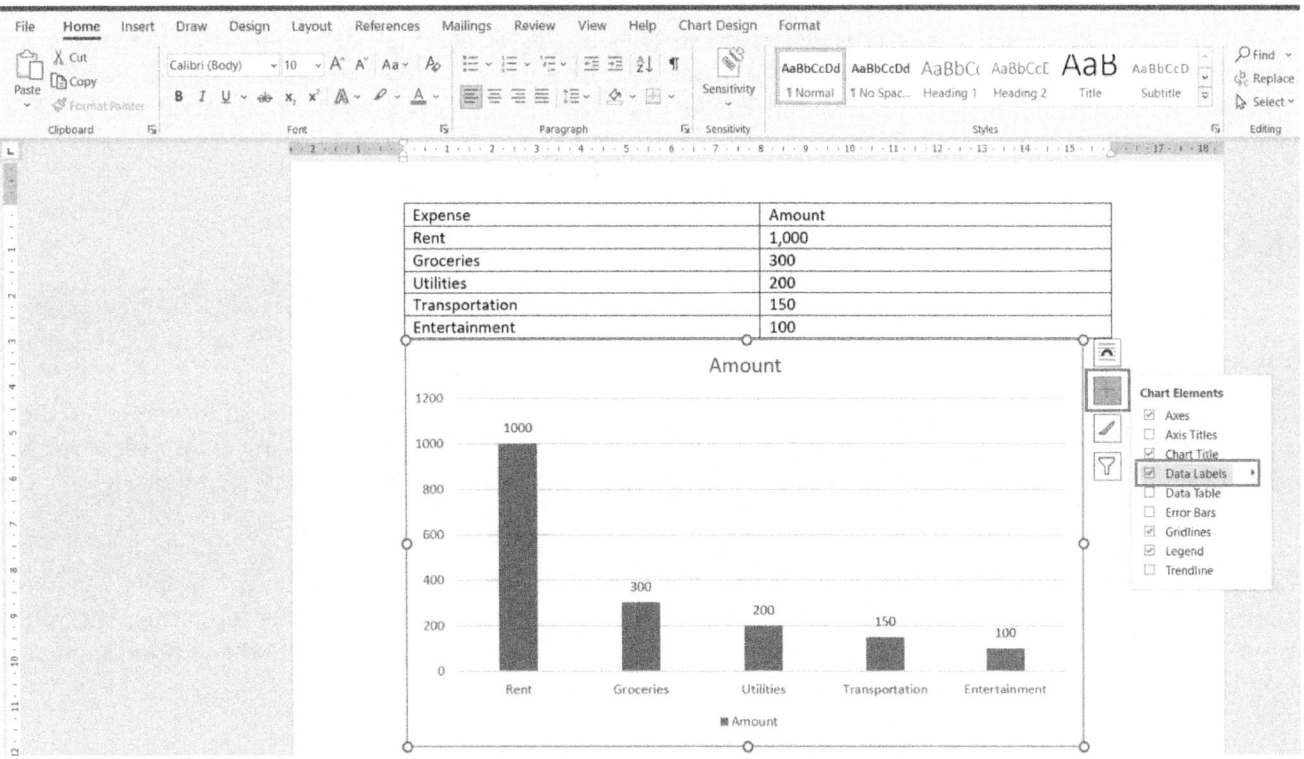

Step 7: Change Chart Title

- To change the chart title, click on the chart title area, and type the desired title.

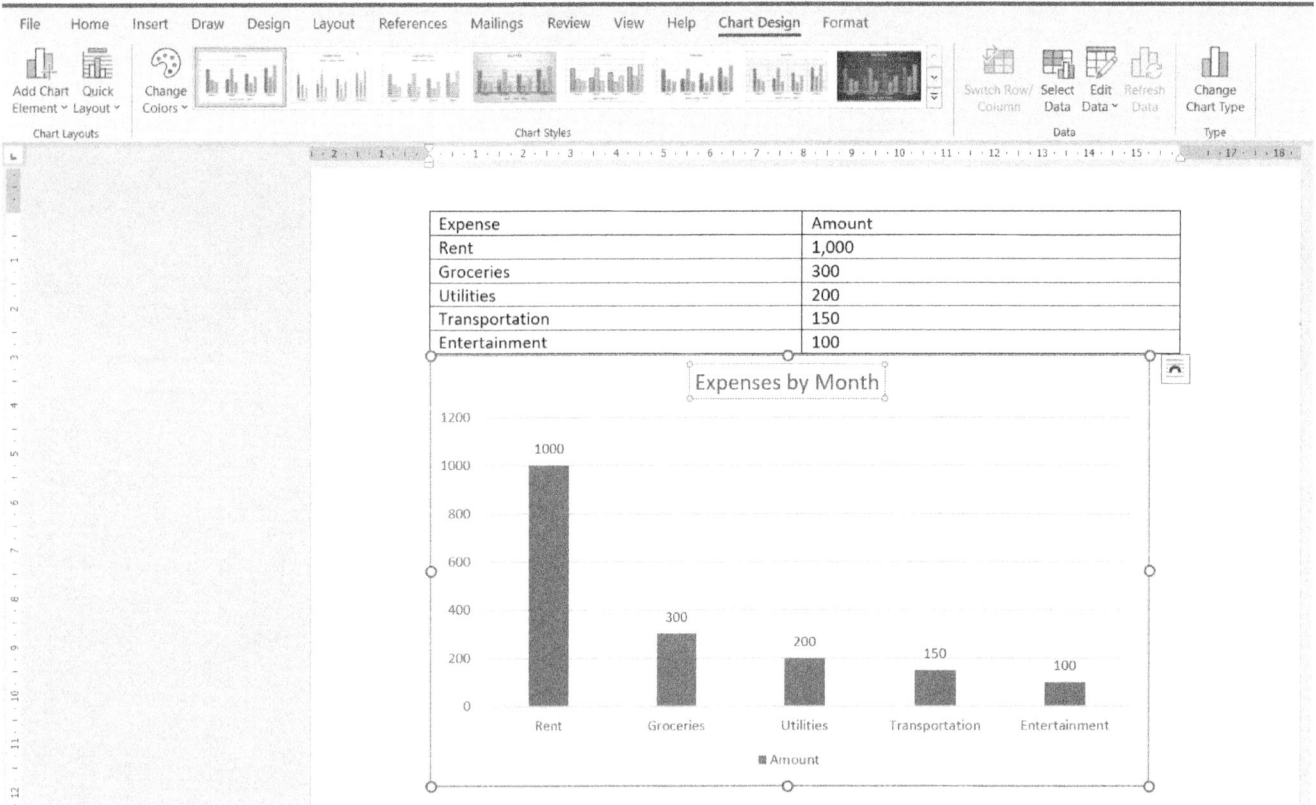

Creating tables and charts in Microsoft Word is a simple process that allows beginners to organise and visualise data effectively. With the step-by-step instructions provided in this section and the use of sample data, you can confidently create tables and charts in your Word documents, enhancing the visual appeal and clarity of your data presentations. Whether it's tracking expenses, organising information, or presenting data for reports, tables, and charts in Microsoft Word offer valuable tools for data representation.

2.7 Styles and Themes in Microsoft Word

2.7.1 What are Styles and Themes in Microsoft Word?

Styles and themes are powerful formatting tools in Microsoft Word that allow users to apply consistent formatting to their documents quickly. Both styles and themes help maintain a cohesive look and feel throughout a document or a set of related documents. Understanding the difference between styles and themes is essential for effective document formatting.

Styles: In Microsoft Word, styles are a collection of formatting settings that can be applied to text, paragraphs, headings, and more. Each style includes specifications for font type, size, colour, alignment, spacing, and other formatting attributes. Styles make it easy to apply consistent formatting across a document and enable users to update the entire document's appearance by changing the properties of a single style.

Themes: Themes, on the other hand, are sets of unified design elements that include colours, fonts, and effects. Themes apply to the entire document and can alter its overall appearance by changing the colours, fonts, and other design aspects. Themes offer a quick way to change the look and feel of a document while maintaining consistent formatting using styles.

2.7.2 Managing Styles and Themes in Microsoft Word - Step-by-Step Instructions for Beginners

Step 1: Open Microsoft Word

- Launch Microsoft Word on your computer by clicking on the Word icon or searching for "Microsoft Word" in your operating system's search bar.

Step 2: Apply Styles to Text

Option A: Use Built-in Styles

- Type or select the text you want to format with a style.

- Go to the "Home" tab in the top menu.

- In the "Styles" group, you will see a list of built-in styles such as "Normal", "Heading 1", "Heading 2", "Title", etc.

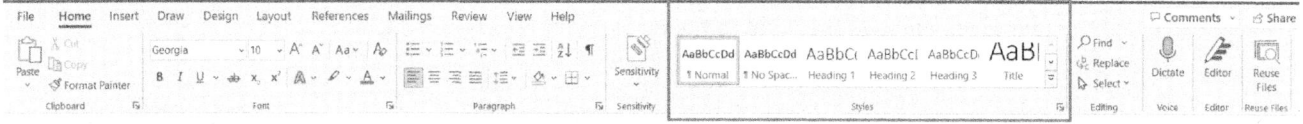

- Highlight the text you want to format, then click on the appropriate style to apply it to the selected text.

Option B: Create a Custom Style

- Format the text the way you want it to appear as a style.

- Select the formatted text.

- Go to the "Home" tab, click on the arrow in the "Styles" group to open the Styles pane.

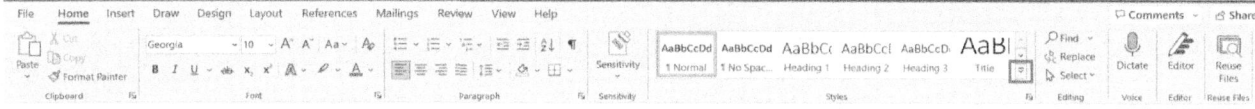

- Click on the "Create a Style" button at the bottom of the Styles pane.

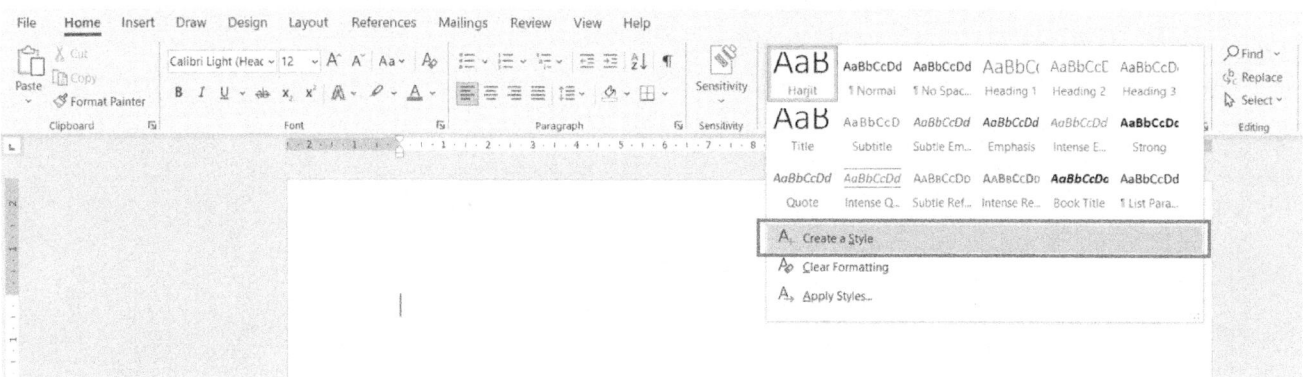

- In the "Create New Style from Formatting" dialog box, give your style a name and modify any additional options if desired. Click "OK" to create the custom style.

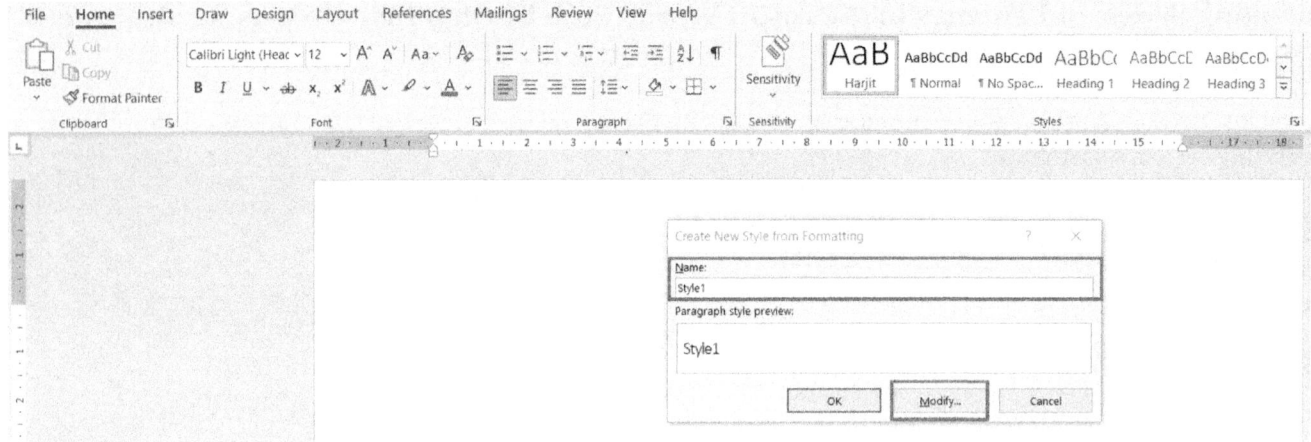

Step 3: Modify or Update Styles

- To modify an existing style, right-click on the style in the Styles pane and select "Modify".

- Make the desired changes to the style's formatting in the "Modify Style" dialog box. Click "OK" to save the changes.

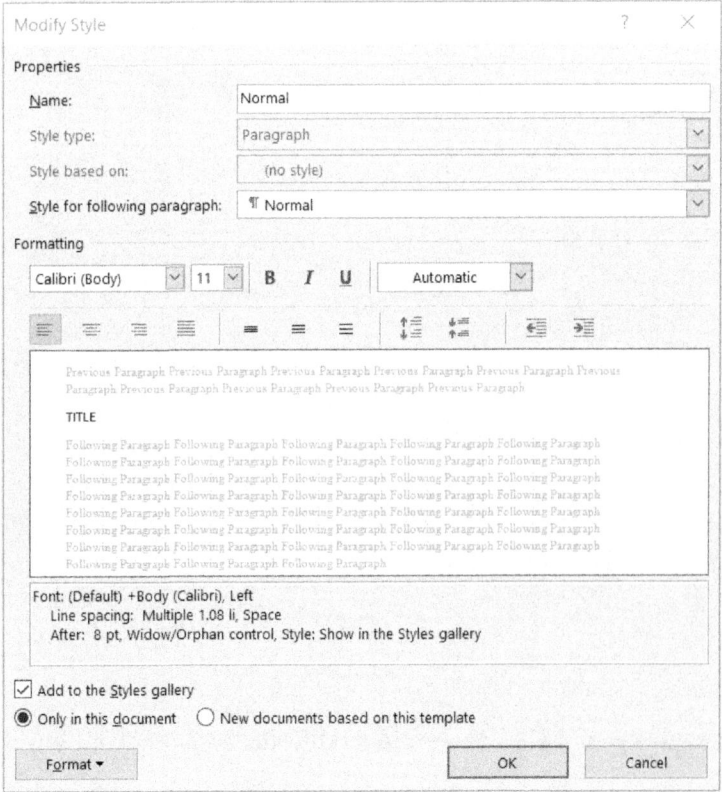

Step 4: Apply Themes to the Document

- Go to the "Design" tab in the top menu.
- In the "Themes" group, you will see a gallery of pre-defined themes.

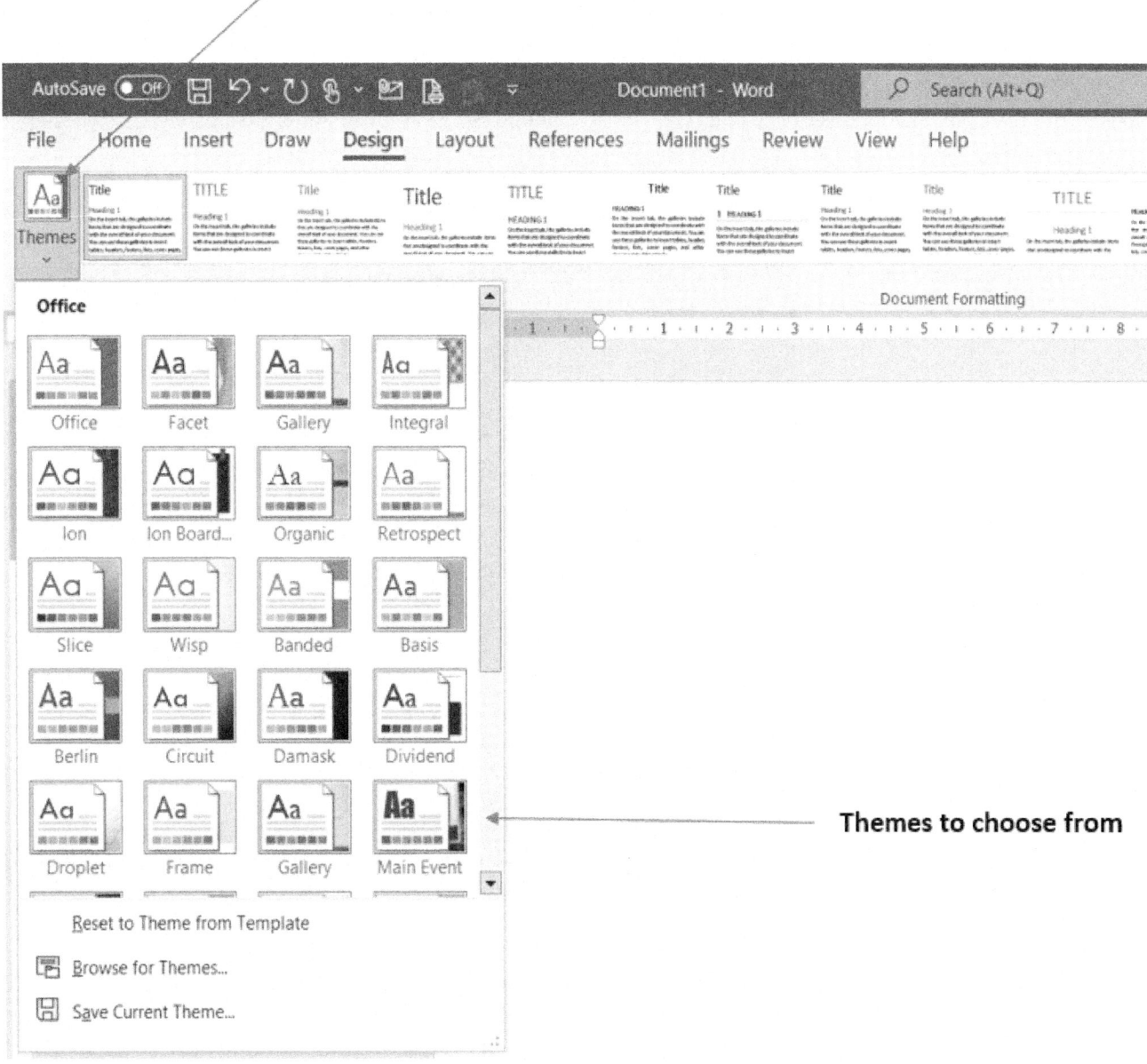

- Hover your mouse over each theme to preview how it will look in your document.

- Click on the desired theme to apply it to your entire document.

Step 5: Customise a Theme

- After applying a theme, go to the "Design" tab.

- Click on the "Theme Colours" or "Theme Fonts" buttons in the Themes group to customise the colours and fonts of the current theme.

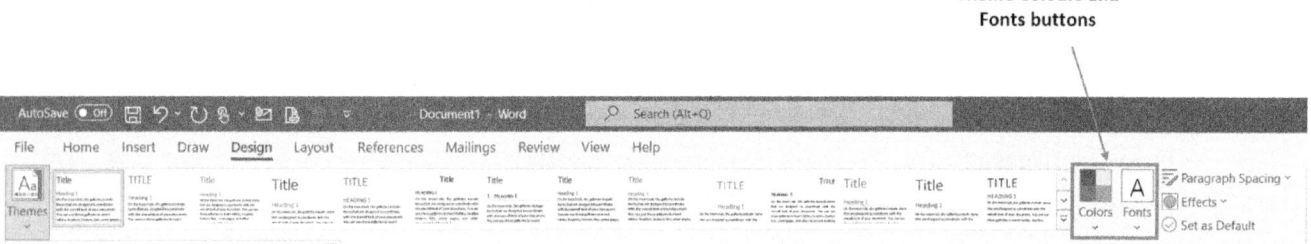

- Choose from the available options or click on "Customise Colours" or "Customise Fonts" to create your own theme.

Styles and themes in Microsoft Word are essential tools for maintaining consistent formatting and design in documents. By following the step-by-step instructions provided in this section, beginners can easily apply and manage styles to format text and paragraphs efficiently, as well as apply themes to change the overall appearance of their documents. Understanding and using styles and themes in Word will greatly enhance the professional look and feel of your documents while ensuring consistency in formatting and design.

2.8 Collaboration and Sharing in Microsoft Word

Microsoft Word offers robust collaboration and sharing features that allow users to work together on documents in real-time and easily share their work with others. Whether you are collaborating with colleagues on a project or sharing a document with friends or clients, Word's collaboration and sharing capabilities streamline the process and enhance productivity. In this chapter, we will explore the collaboration and sharing features in Microsoft Word and provide step-by-step instructions on how to use them effectively.

2.8.1 Collaboration Features in Microsoft Word

Real-time Co-authoring: Multiple users can work on the same document simultaneously, and changes made by one collaborator are instantly visible to others.

Comments and Markup: Users can leave comments, suggestions, and markup on the document to provide feedback or make revisions.

Track Changes: Word allows you to track changes made to the document, making it easy to review and accept or reject modifications.

Version History: You can access the version history of the document to view previous revisions and restore an earlier version if needed.

2.8.2 Sharing Options in Microsoft Word

Sharing Links: You can generate sharing links to the document and control whether others can edit or view only.

Email Sharing: Word allows you to send the document directly via email, either as an attachment or a sharing link.

Cloud Storage Integration: You can save and share documents using cloud storage services like OneDrive or SharePoint.

2.8.3 Step-by-Step Instructions for Collaboration and Sharing

Step 1: Open the Document

- Launch Microsoft Word on your computer and open the document you want to collaborate on or share.

Step 2: Collaboration - Real-time Co-authoring

- Click on the "Share" button in the top right corner of the Word window.

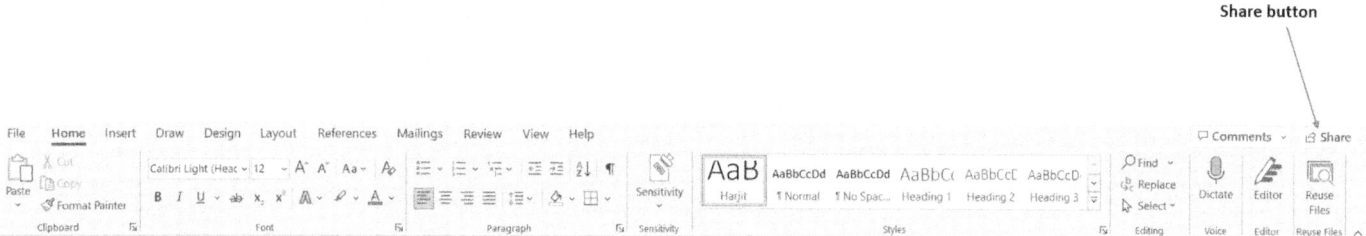

- Enter the email addresses of the collaborators you want to invite. Optionally, you can add a message to the invitation.

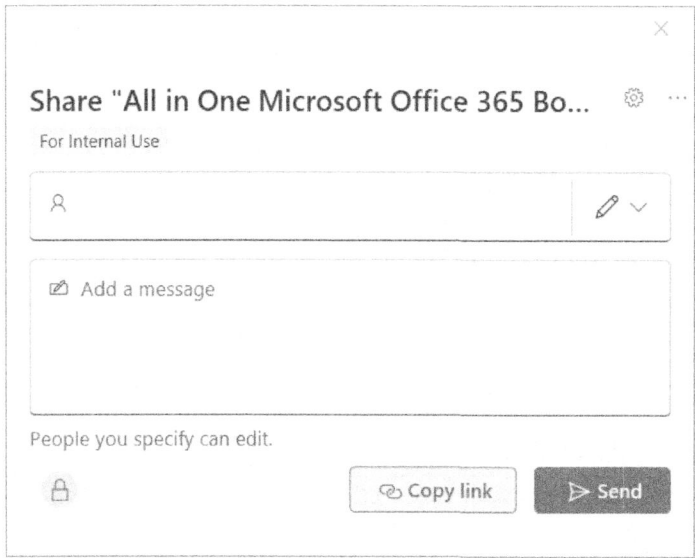

- Choose the permission level for each collaborator (Can Edit or Can View).

- Click on the "Send" button to send the invitations.

- Collaborators will receive an email with a sharing link. When they click the link, the document will open in their Word application, and they can start collaborating in real-time.

Step 3: Collaboration - Comments and Markup

- To add a comment or markup, select the text you want to comment on or mark up.

- Go to the "Review" tab in the top menu and click on "New Comment".

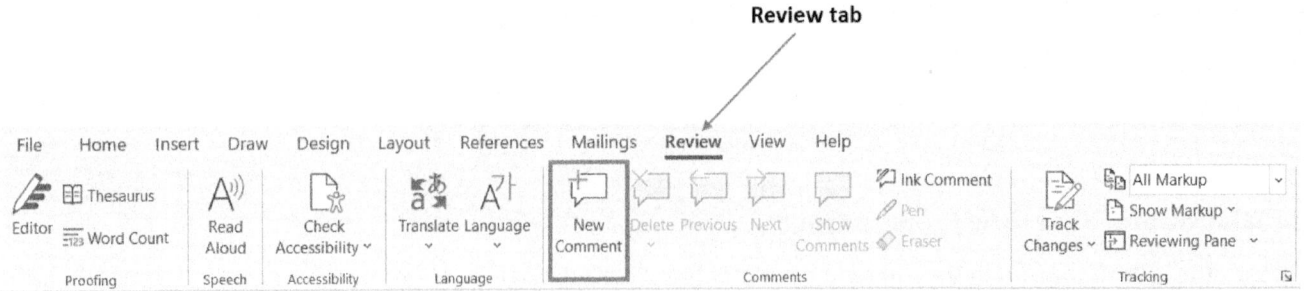

- Type your comment or markup in the comment pane on the right side of the document.

Type your
comments here

Step 4: Collaboration - Track Changes

- Go to the "Review" tab in the top menu and click on "Track Changes" to enable tracking.

- Make changes to the document, and Word will mark the modifications with coloured highlights and strikethroughs.

- Collaborators will be able to see the tracked changes and accept or reject them.

Step 5: Sharing - Sharing Links

- Click on the "Share" button in the top right corner of the Word window.

- Click on "Copy Link" to copy the sharing link to the clipboard.

- You can paste the link into an email, chat, or any other communication method to share the document with others.

Step 6: Sharing - Email Sharing

- Click on the "Share" button in the top right corner of the Word window.

- Choose "Email" from the sharing options.
- Select the permission level (Can Edit or Can View) for the recipients.

- An email window will open with the document attached. Add recipients' email addresses and a message if needed, then send the email.

Step 7: Sharing - Cloud Storage Integration

- Click on the "File" tab in the top left corner of the Word window.

- Choose "Save As" and select your preferred cloud storage service (e.g., OneDrive or SharePoint).

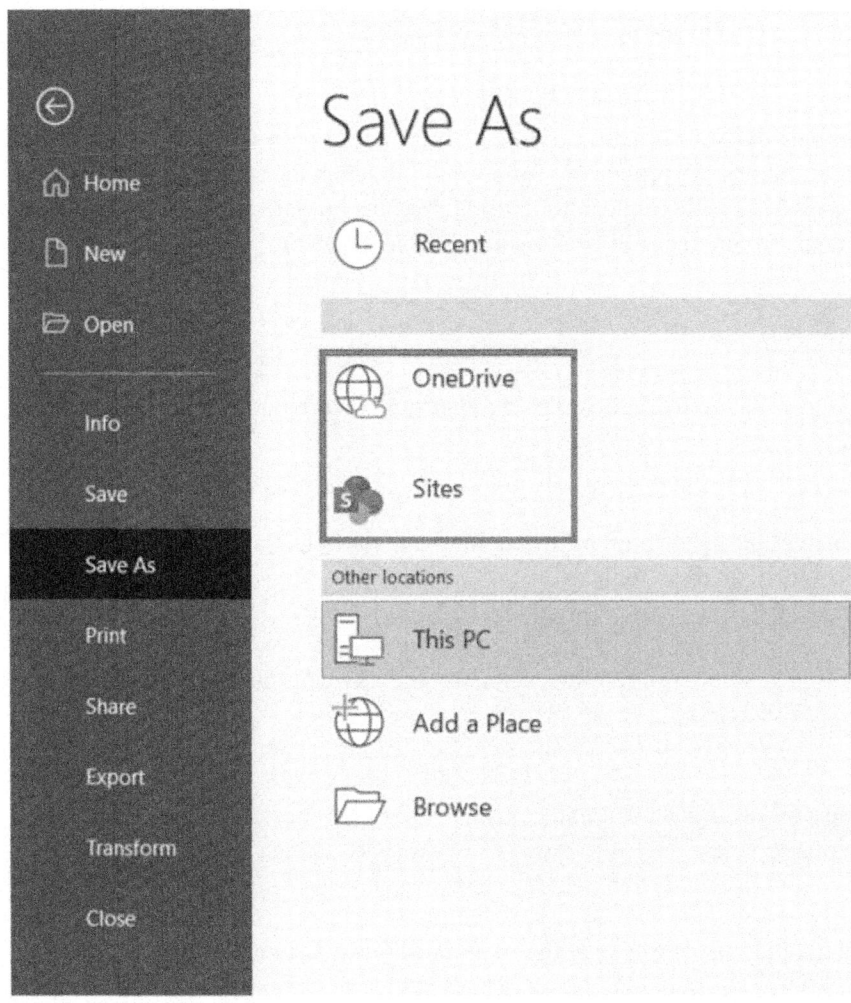

- Choose the destination folder and click "Save".

Collaboration and sharing in Microsoft Word are essential features that promote teamwork, streamline document reviews, and simplify the sharing process. By following the step-by-step instructions in this section, users can effectively collaborate with others in real-time, provide feedback and revisions using comments and markup, and share their documents with colleagues, clients, or friends efficiently. Microsoft Word's collaboration and sharing capabilities enhance productivity, facilitate seamless teamwork, and make document collaboration a breeze for users across various scenarios.

Chapter 3: Microsoft Excel

Microsoft Excel is a powerful and widely used spreadsheet application developed by Microsoft. It is part of the Microsoft Office suite and has been an essential tool for businesses, individuals, and organisations since its release in 1985. Excel is designed to handle complex numerical data, perform calculations, and organise information in a structured and easily understandable format. In this chapter, we will explore what Microsoft Excel is, its key features, and the diverse range of applications for which it is used.

3.1 What is Microsoft Excel?

Microsoft Excel is a spreadsheet software that enables users to create, organise, and analyse data in a grid of rows and columns. Each cell in the grid can contain text, numbers, formulas, or functions, allowing users to perform various calculations and manipulate data efficiently. Excel provides a wide range of tools and functions for data analysis, visualisation, and reporting, making it an indispensable tool for data-driven decision-making and problem-solving.

3.2 Key Features of Microsoft Excel

Data Organisation: Excel's grid-based structure allows users to organise and manage data in a structured manner, making it easy to track, update, and reference information.

Formulas and Functions: Excel offers an extensive library of built-in mathematical, statistical, and logical functions, enabling users to perform complex calculations and automate data analysis.

Data Analysis: Excel provides tools for sorting, filtering, and summarising data, as well as pivot tables and charts for in-depth data analysis and visualisation.

Data Visualisation: Excel's charting capabilities allow users to create various types of charts, graphs, and visual representations of data to convey information effectively.

What-If Analysis: Excel's scenario manager and data tables enable users to explore different scenarios and examine the impact of changes on data and calculations.

Data Sharing and Collaboration: Excel supports real-time collaboration, enabling multiple users to work on the same workbook simultaneously and share data with ease.

3.3 Applications of Microsoft Excel

Microsoft Excel finds applications across various industries and domains due to its versatility and functionality. Some of the common applications of Excel include:

Financial Analysis: Businesses use Excel for budgeting, financial planning, forecasting, and analysing financial data.

Data Management: Excel is used to organise and manage large datasets, perform data cleansing, and prepare data for analysis.

Reporting and Dashboards: Excel is employed to create interactive reports and dashboards that provide a visual representation of data for better decision-making.

Project Management: Excel is utilised for project tracking, resource allocation, and scheduling.

Sales and Inventory Management: Excel helps in tracking sales data, inventory levels, and managing customer records.

Educational and Academic Use: Students and educators use Excel for data analysis, mathematical modelling, and statistical calculations.

3.4 Excel Worksheets and Cells

3.4.1 Understanding Worksheets and Cells in Excel

In Microsoft Excel, a workbook consists of one or more worksheets, and each worksheet is a grid of cells organised into rows and columns. Cells are individual rectangular boxes within the grid, and each cell can contain data such as text, numbers, formulas, or functions. Worksheets are used to organise and analyse data, making Excel an efficient tool for managing various types of information.

3.4.2 Working with Worksheets and Cells

Step 1: Open Microsoft Excel

- Launch Microsoft Excel on your computer by clicking on the Excel icon or searching for "Microsoft Excel" in your operating system's search bar.

Step 2: Create a New Workbook

- When Excel opens, you'll see a new blank workbook with one worksheet (Sheet1) already created. To add more worksheets, click on the plus sign (+) at the bottom left of the workbook. This action will create a new worksheet (Sheet2).

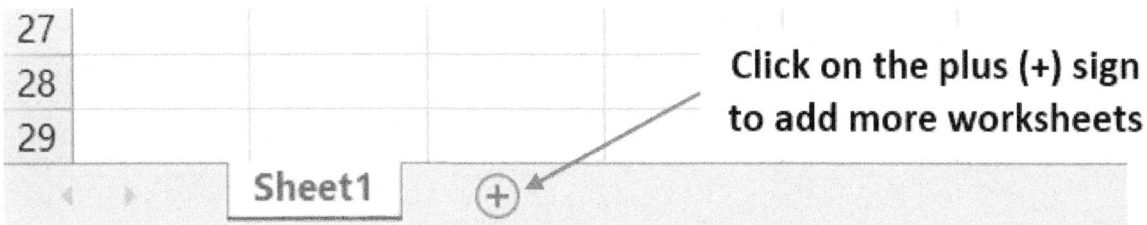

- Sample Data: For our example, let's consider a small dataset of students and their respective test scores.

	A	B	C
1	Student Name	Test Score	
2	John	85	
3	Lisa	92	
4	Mike	78	
5	Sarah	89	
6	Emily	95	
7			

Step 3: Rename Worksheets

- To rename a worksheet, right-click on the sheet tab (e.g., Sheet1) at the bottom of the workbook.

- Choose "Rename" from the context menu and enter a new name, such as "Test Scores".

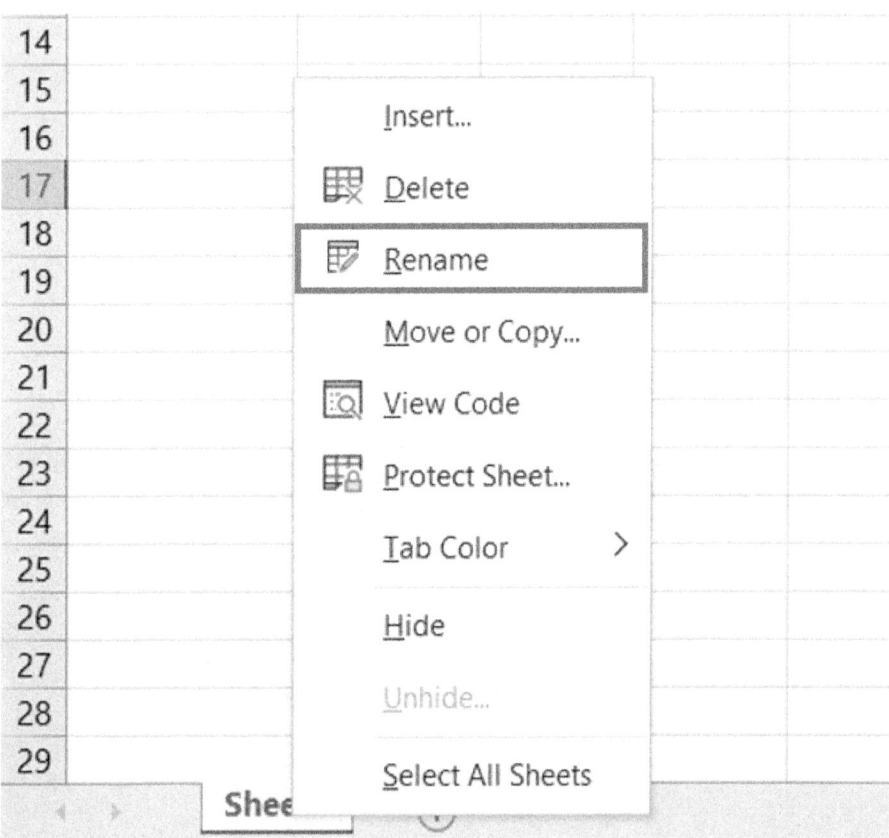

Step 4: Enter Data into Cells

- In the "Test Scores" worksheet click on cell A1 and type "Student Name".

- Click on cell B1 and type "Test Score".

- Enter the sample data provided in the table into cells A2:B6.

Step 5: Formatting Cells

- To format cells, such as changing font size, bolding text, or applying number formatting, select the cells you want to format (e.g., A2:B6).

- Use the Home tab in the top menu to access formatting options. For instance, you can change font size, make text bold, apply currency or percentage formatting to numbers, and more.

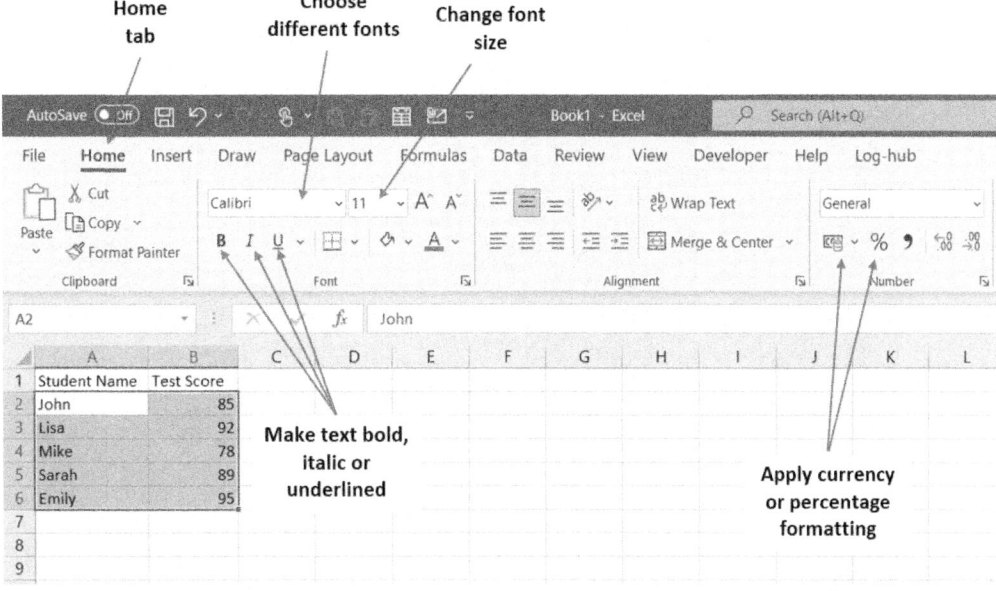

Step 6: AutoSum Function

- To calculate the total test score using the AutoSum function, click on cell B7 (the cell below the "Test Score" column).

- Go to the Formulas tab in the top menu.

- Click on the "AutoSum" button (sigma symbol) in the Function Library group.

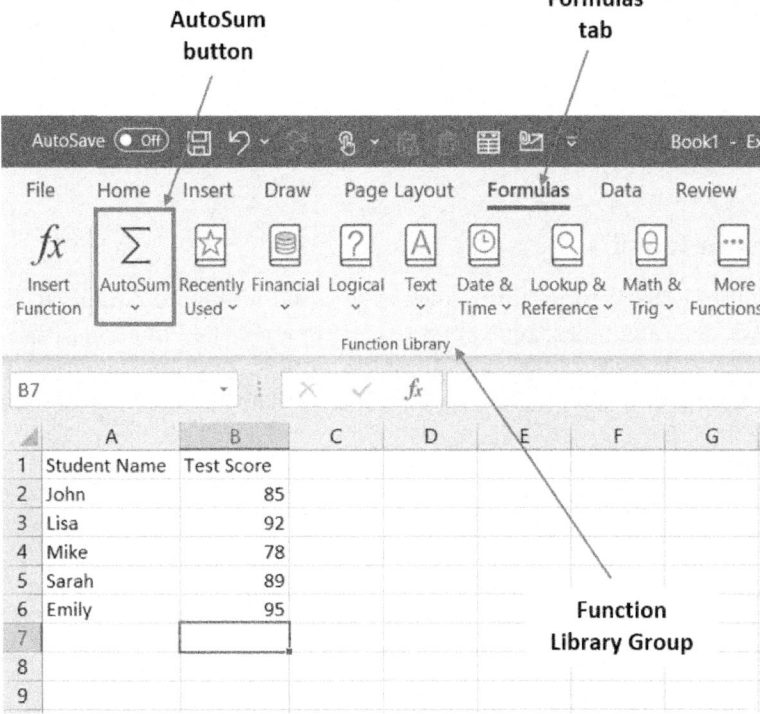

- Excel will automatically detect the range of data to sum (B2:B6). Press "Enter" to apply the formula, and the average test score will appear in cell B7.

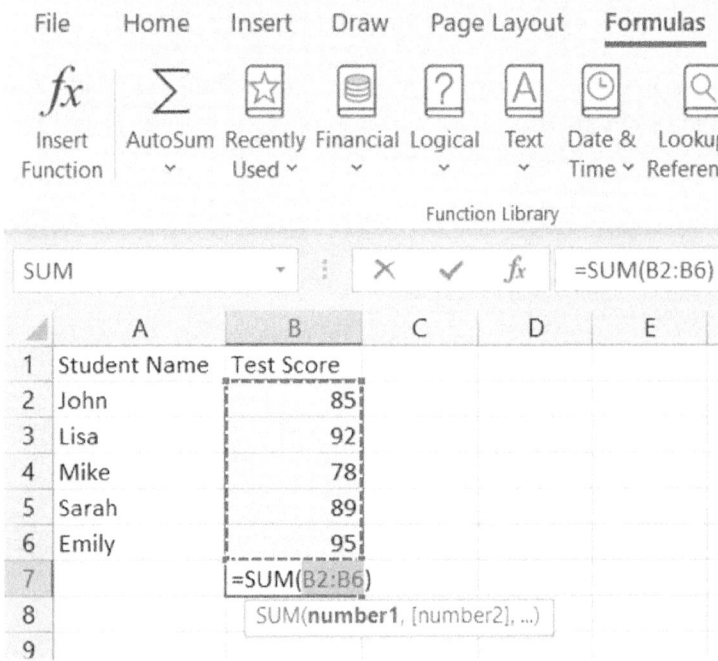

Step 7: Copying and Pasting Data

- To copy the total test score (cell B7) to another location, select the cell, press "Ctrl + C" (or right-click and choose "Copy").

- Go to the desired location, and press "Ctrl + V" (or right-click and choose "Paste") to paste the value.

Microsoft Excel's worksheets and cells provide a structured way to organise and analyse data effectively. By following the step-by-step instructions provided in this section and using the sample data, beginners can easily create, manage, and format worksheets and cells in Excel. Excel's versatility and array of functions make it a powerful tool for data management, analysis, and reporting, suitable for various tasks ranging from simple data entry to complex calculations and financial modelling.

3.5 Formulas and Functions in Excel

3.5.1 Understanding Formulas and Functions in Excel

In Microsoft Excel, formulas and functions are essential tools used to perform calculations and automate data analysis. Formulas are expressions that use mathematical operators, cell references, and values to calculate results. Functions, on the other hand, are pre-built formulas designed to perform specific tasks, such as summing numbers, finding averages, and performing statistical analyses. Understanding formulas and functions is crucial for manipulating data and deriving valuable insights from the information stored in Excel worksheets.

3.5.2 Most Common Functions Used in Excel

Excel offers a wide range of functions catering to various needs. Some of the most common functions used in Excel are:

- **SUM**: Calculates the sum of a range of numbers.

- **AVERAGE**: Calculates the average of a range of numbers.

- **MAX**: Returns the largest value in a range of numbers.

- **MIN**: Returns the smallest value in a range of numbers.

- **COUNT**: Counts the number of cells that contain numerical values in a range.

- **IF**: Performs a logical test and returns one value if the condition is met and another if it's not.

- **VLOOKUP**: Searches for a value in the first column of a table array and returns a corresponding value in another column.

- **COUNTIF**: Counts the number of cells that meet a specific criterion in a range.

3.5.3 Step-by-Step Instructions for Writing Formulas and Functions

Step 1: Open Microsoft Excel

- Launch Microsoft Excel on your computer by clicking on the Excel icon or searching for "Microsoft Excel" in your operating system's search bar.

Step 2: Enter Data into Cells

- In a new or existing worksheet, enter data into the cells that you want to use in your formulas and functions.

- Sample Data: Let's consider a simple dataset of students and their test scores.

	A	B	C
1	Student Name	Test Score	
2	John	85	
3	Lisa	92	
4	Mike	78	
5	Sarah	89	
6	Emily	95	
7			

Step 3: Writing Formulas

- To write a formula, click on the cell where you want the result to appear (e.g., C2).

- Type the equal sign (=) to begin the formula.

- Use mathematical operators (+, -, *, /) to perform calculations. For example, to calculate the total test score for John and Lisa, type "=B2+B3" in cell C2 and press "Enter".

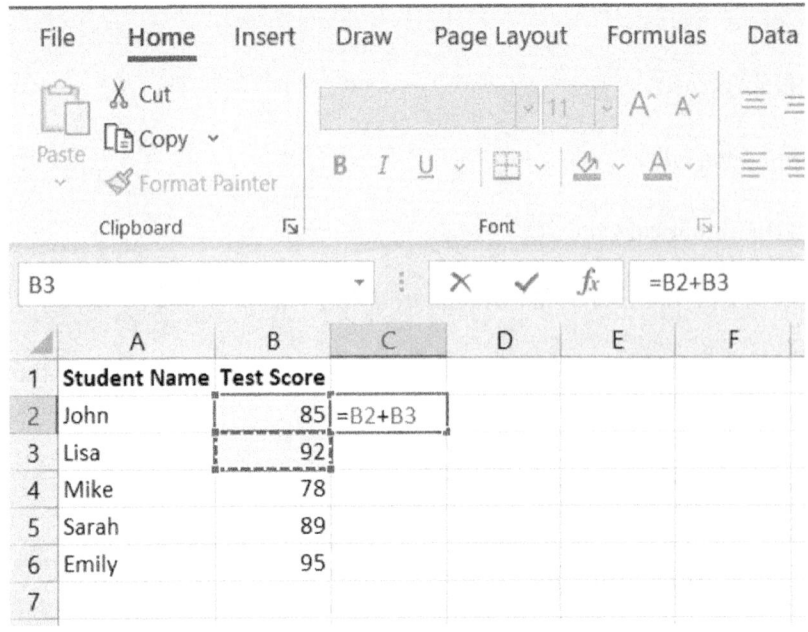

- Excel will display the result (177) in cell C2.

Step 4: Using Functions

- To use a function, click on the cell where you want the result to appear (e.g., B7).

- Type the equal sign (=) to begin the function.

- Start typing the function name. For example, type "SUM(".

- Select the range of cells you want to include in the function (e.g., B2:B6).

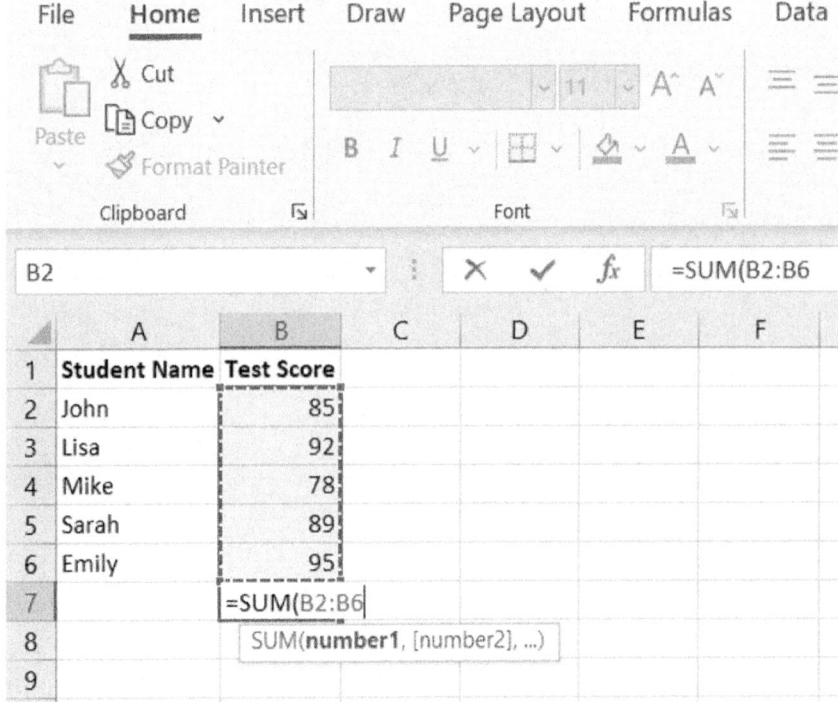

- Close the function with a closing parenthesis ")".
- Press "Enter," and Excel will display the sum of test scores (439) in cell B7.

| B7 | | | | ✕ | ✓ | *fx* | =SUM(B2:B6) |

	A	B	C	D	E	F	G
1	Student Name	Test Score					
2	John	85					
3	Lisa	92					
4	Mike	78					
5	Sarah	89					
6	Emily	95					
7		439					
8							

Step 5: Applying More Functions

- To find the average test score, click on cell B8.

- Type the equal sign (=) to begin the function.

- Start typing "AVERAGE(".

- Select the range of cells (B2:B6) and close the function with a closing parenthesis ")".

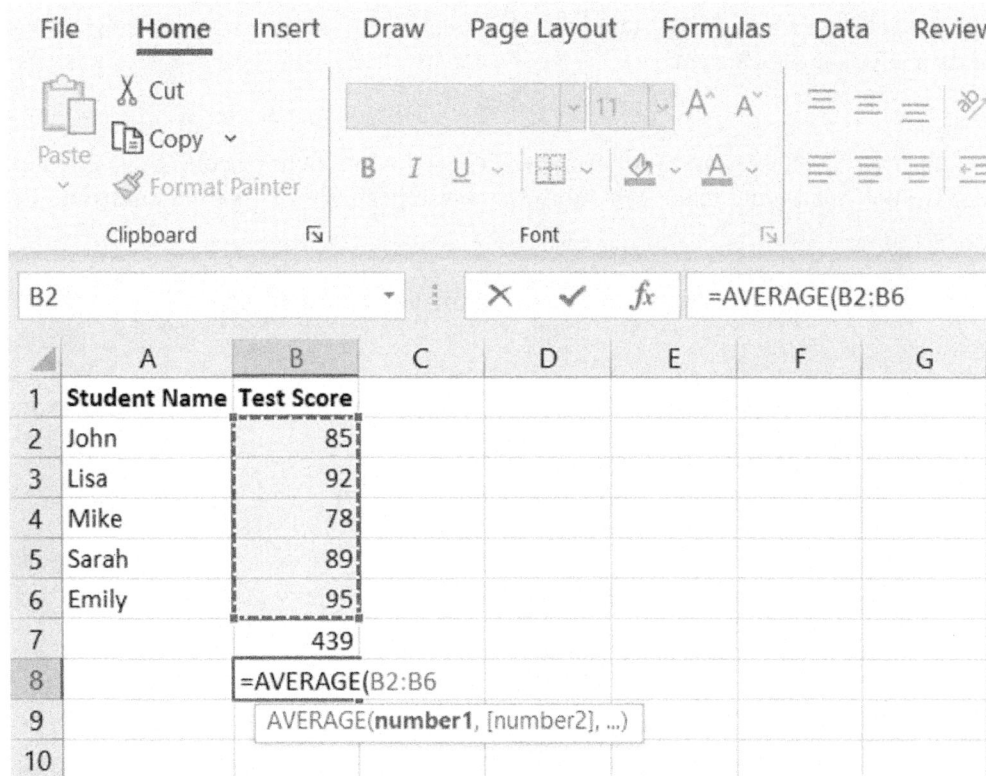

- Press "Enter," and Excel will display the average test score (87.8) in cell B8.

Formulas and functions in Microsoft Excel are powerful tools that enable users to perform calculations and analyse data efficiently. By following the step-by-step instructions provided in this section and using the sample data, beginners can confidently write formulas and use common functions to manipulate data and gain insights from their Excel worksheets. Excel's extensive library of functions provides users with the flexibility to perform various calculations and analyses, making it an indispensable tool for data-driven decision-making and problem-solving.

I have written some comprehensive books on Excel formulas and functions to help you to become a master on this subject. To find out more about the books and to buy them from Amazon then please type the link below to your web browser.

www.amazon.co.uk/dp/B0868RV3D5

3.6 Sorting, Filtering, and Conditional Formatting

3.6.1 Understanding Sorting, Filtering, and Conditional Formatting in Excel

Sorting, filtering, and conditional formatting are powerful features in Microsoft Excel that help users manage, analyse, and visualise data effectively.

Sorting: Sorting allows users to arrange data in ascending or descending order based on a specific column or criteria. This helps in organising data and identifying trends or patterns easily.

Filtering: Filtering allows users to display specific data based on certain criteria. It helps in focusing on relevant information and hiding unnecessary data, making data analysis more efficient.

Conditional Formatting: Conditional formatting enables users to format cells based on predefined conditions or rules. This feature helps highlight important data, spot trends, and make data more visually appealing and easier to interpret.

3.6.2 Step-by-Step Instructions for Sorting, Filtering, and Conditional Formatting

Step 1: Open Microsoft Excel

- Launch Microsoft Excel on your computer by clicking on the Excel icon or searching for "Microsoft Excel" in your operating system's search bar.

Step 2: Enter Data into Cells

- In a new or existing worksheet, enter data into the cells that you want to sort, filter, and apply conditional formatting.

- Sample Data: Let's consider a dataset of students and their test scores.

	A	B	C
1	Student Name	Test Score	
2	John	85	
3	Lisa	92	
4	Mike	78	
5	Sarah	89	
6	Emily	95	
7			

Step 3: Sorting Data

- To sort data, click on any cell within the data range (e.g., cell A2).

- Go to the "Data" tab in the top menu.

- In the "Sort & Filter" group, click on the "Sort A to Z" or "Sort Z to A" button to sort the data in ascending or descending order, respectively.

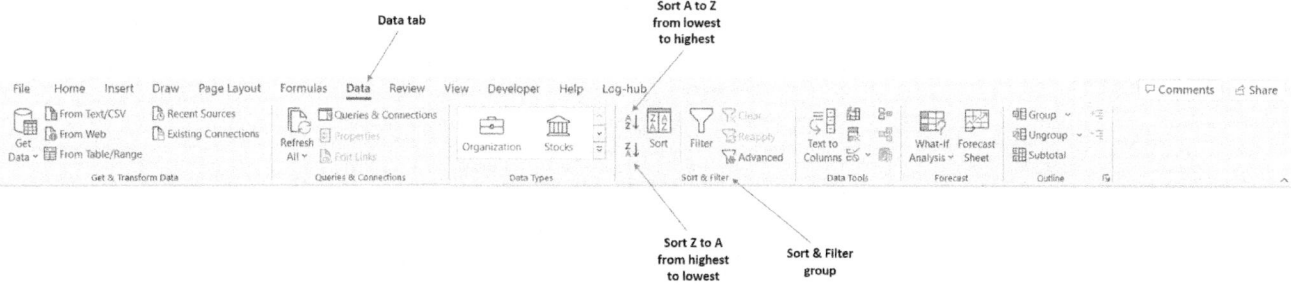

Step 4: Filtering Data

- To apply a filter, click on any cell within the data range (e.g., cell A2).

- Go to the "Data" tab in the top menu.

- In the "Sort & Filter" group, click on the "Filter" button. Small drop-down arrows will appear next to each column header.

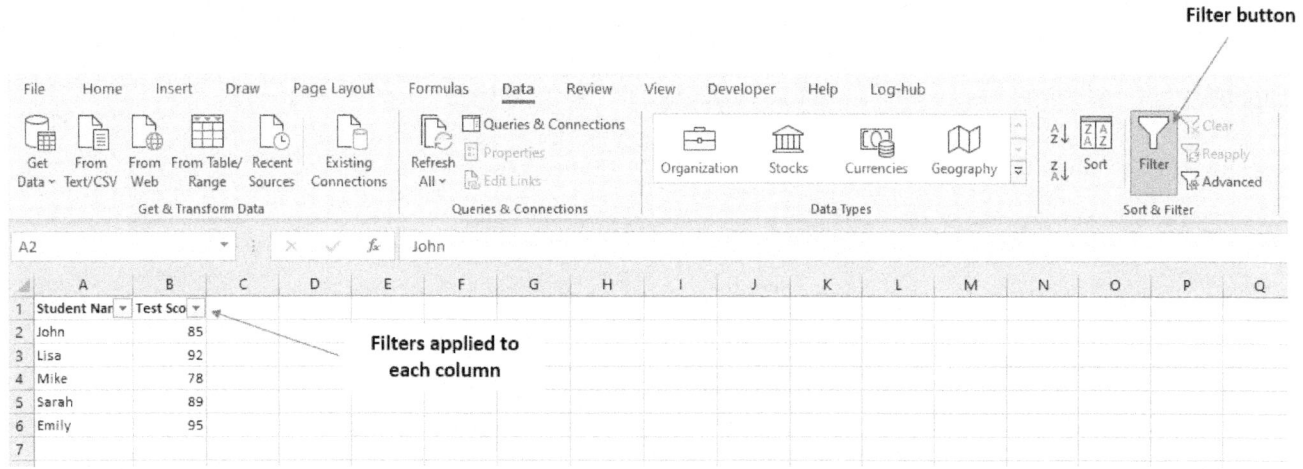

- Click on the drop-down arrow in the column header (e.g., "Test Score").

- Uncheck the "Select All" box to clear all selections, then check the box corresponding to the value or condition you want to filter (e.g., select scores greater than 85).

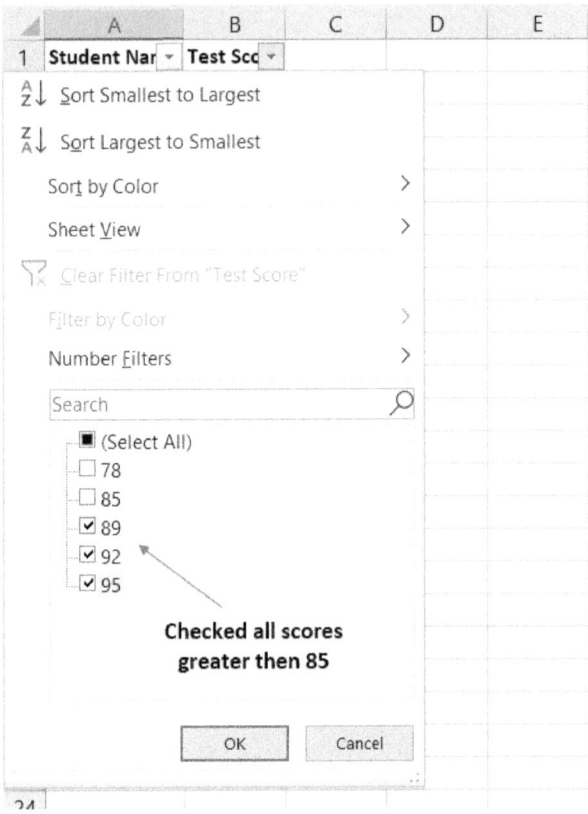

- Click "OK," and Excel will display only the rows that meet the filtering criteria.

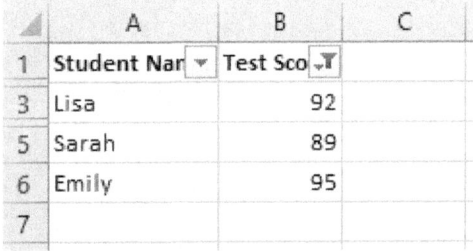

Step 5: Conditional Formatting

- To apply conditional formatting, select the data range (e.g., B2:B6, which contains test scores).

- Go to the "Home" tab in the top menu.

- In the "Styles" group, click on the "Conditional Formatting" button.

- Choose the type of conditional formatting you want to apply (e.g., "Highlight Cells Rules" -> "Greater Than").

- Enter the threshold value (e.g., 90) and choose the formatting style (e.g., "Light Red Fill with Dark Red Text").

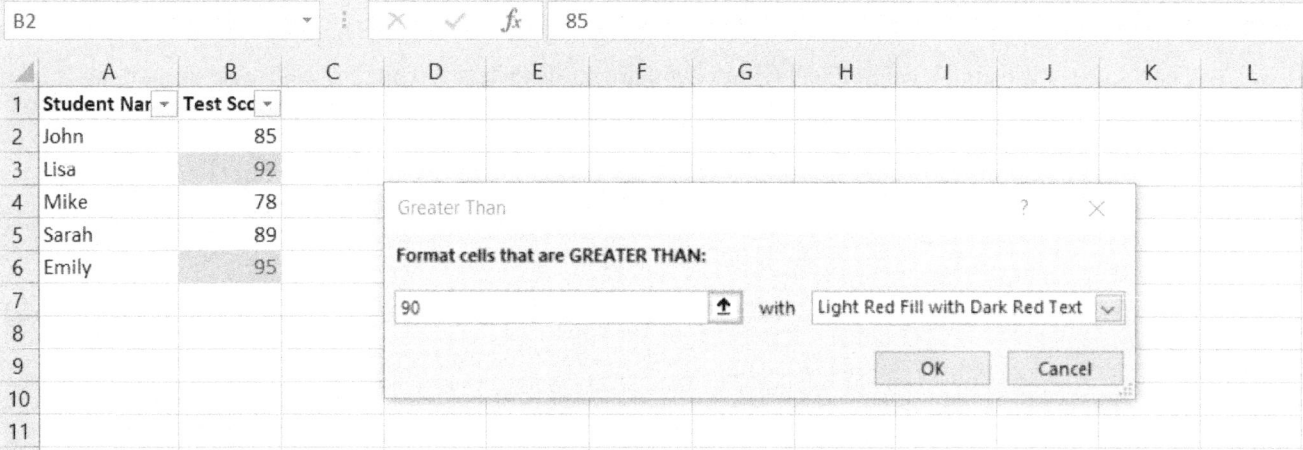

- Click "OK," and Excel will apply conditional formatting to the cells with test scores greater than 90.

	A	B	C
1	Student Nar ▾	Test Scc ▾	
2	John	85	
3	Lisa	92	
4	Mike	78	
5	Sarah	89	
6	Emily	95	
7			

Sorting, filtering, and conditional formatting are valuable features in Microsoft Excel that allow users to manage and analyse data efficiently. By following the step-by-step instructions provided in this section and using the sample data, beginners can effectively sort, filter, and apply conditional formatting to their Excel worksheets. These features enhance data organisation, analysis, and presentation, making Excel a versatile tool for data manipulation and visualisation.

3.7 Collaboration and Sharing in Excel

Excel offers powerful collaboration and sharing features that allow users to work together on the same workbook and share their data with others. Whether you need to collaborate with colleagues or share data with clients, Excel's collaboration and sharing capabilities streamline the process and enhance productivity. In this chapter, we will explore how to collaborate and share data in Microsoft Excel with step-by-step instructions.

3.7.1 Collaboration Features in Excel

Real-time Co-authoring: Multiple users can edit the same Excel workbook simultaneously, and changes made by one collaborator are instantly visible to others.

Comments and Notes: Users can leave comments and notes on cells to provide feedback, clarification, or additional information.

Track Changes: Excel allows you to track changes made by collaborators, making it easy to review and accept or reject modifications.

3.7.2 Sharing Options in Excel

Excel Online: You can share a workbook using Excel Online, which enables users to collaborate in real-time using a web browser.

Email Attachment: Excel allows you to send a copy of the workbook as an email attachment to others.

Cloud Storage Integration: You can save the Excel workbook to a cloud storage service like OneDrive or SharePoint and share a link to the file with others.

3.7.3 Step-by-Step Instructions for Collaboration and Sharing

Step 1: Open Microsoft Excel

- Launch Microsoft Excel on your computer by clicking on the Excel icon or searching for "Microsoft Excel" in your operating system's search bar.

Step 2: Create or Open a Workbook

- Create a new workbook or open an existing workbook that you want to collaborate on or share.

Step 3: Collaborate with Real-time Co-authoring

- Save the workbook to a cloud storage service like OneDrive or SharePoint.

- Click on the "Share" button in the top right corner of the Excel window.

Share button

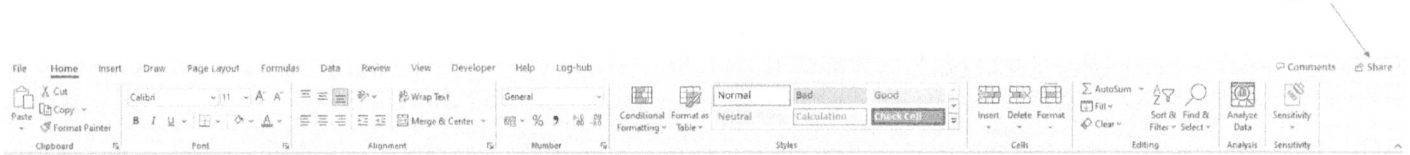

- In the "Share with People" pane, enter the email addresses of the collaborators you want to invite.

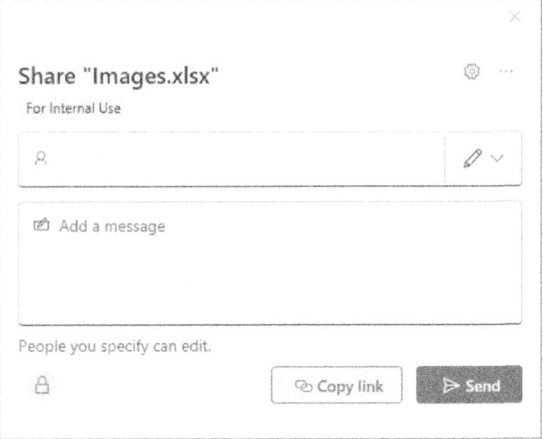

- Choose the permission level for each collaborator (Can Edit or Can View).

- Optionally, you can include a message to the recipients.

- Click on the "Send" button to send the invitations.

- Collaborators will receive an email with a link to the shared workbook. They can click on the link to open the workbook in Excel Online and start collaborating in real-time.

Step 4: Add Comments and Notes

- To add a comment, select the cell you want to comment on.

- Go to the "Review" tab in the top menu.

- Click on the "New Comment" button in the "Comments" group.

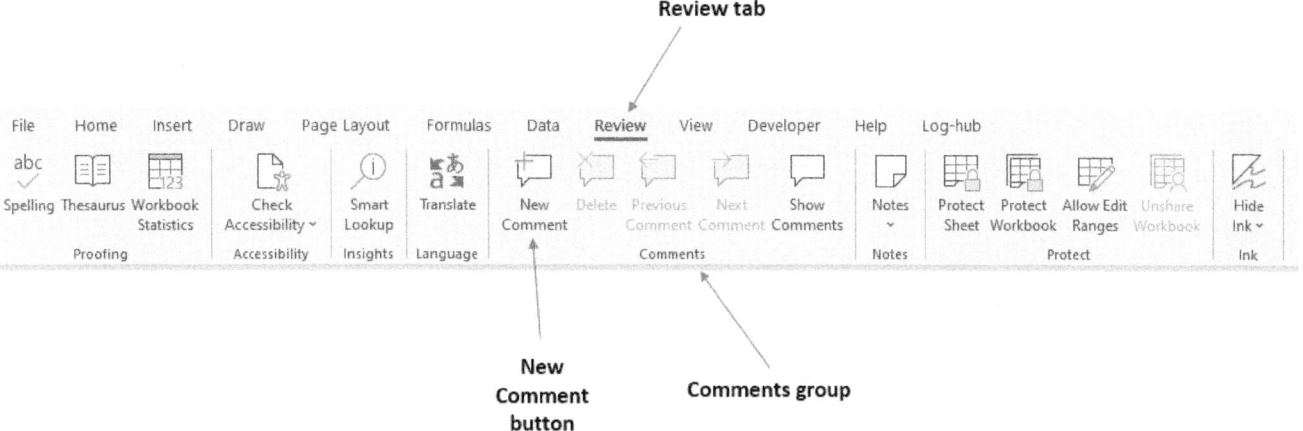

- Type your comment in the comment box that appears on the right side of the worksheet.

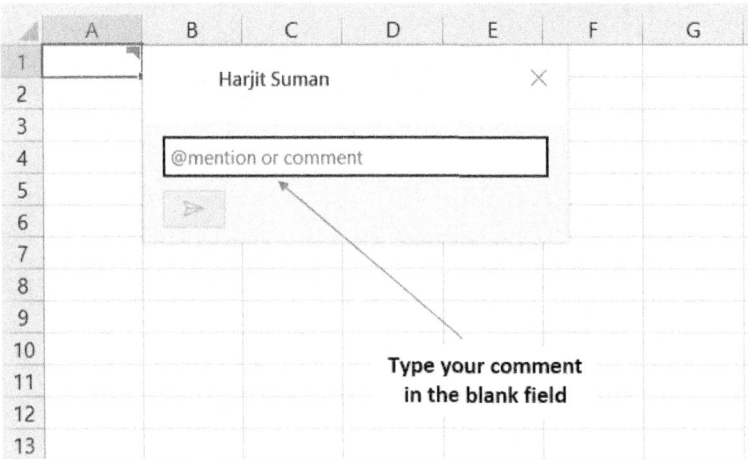

Step 5: Track Changes

- Go to the "Review" tab in the top menu.

- Click on the "Track Changes" button in the "Changes" group to enable tracking.

- Make changes to the workbook, and Excel will mark the modifications with coloured highlights and notes.

- To review changes, go to the "Review" tab and click on the "Track Changes" button again. Choose "Accept/Reject Changes" to manage modifications.

Step 6: Share via Email or Cloud Storage

- Save the workbook to your local drive or cloud storage.

- Go to the "File" tab in the top left corner.

- Choose "Share" from the menu.

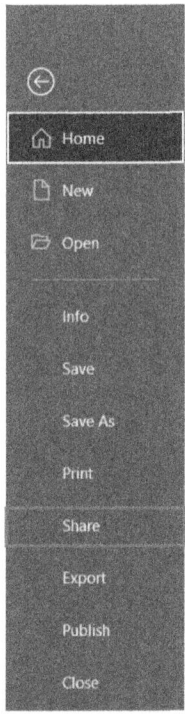

- Click on the 3 dots on the top right of the dialog box and then "Send a copy" and choose whether you want to send the attachment as an Excel workbook or a PDF.

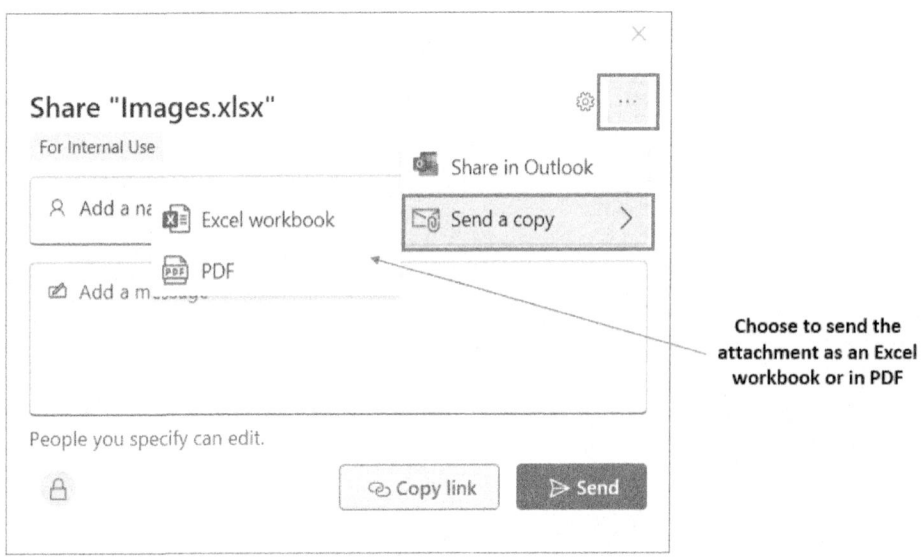

- Enter the recipients' email addresses and a message if desired, then send the email.

Collaboration and sharing in Microsoft Excel are powerful features that promote teamwork and streamline the data sharing process. By following the step-by-step instructions provided in this section, users can effectively collaborate in real-time, add comments and track changes, and share Excel workbooks with colleagues, clients, or stakeholders efficiently. Excel's collaboration and sharing capabilities enhance productivity and facilitate seamless teamwork, making it an essential tool for collaborative data analysis and reporting.

Chapter 4: Microsoft PowerPoint

4.1 What is Microsoft PowerPoint?

Microsoft PowerPoint is a powerful presentation software developed by Microsoft as part of the Microsoft Office suite. It is designed to create dynamic and visually engaging slideshows, also known as presentations, that help users effectively communicate ideas, information, and data to an audience. PowerPoint provides a user-friendly interface with a wide range of tools and features, making it a popular choice for professionals, educators, students, and anyone seeking to create compelling visual presentations.

4.2 What is PowerPoint Used For?

PowerPoint is primarily used for creating presentations for various purposes, including:

Business Presentations: Professionals use PowerPoint to deliver sales pitches, project updates, financial reports, and business proposals to clients, colleagues, and stakeholders.

Educational Presentations: Educators and students use PowerPoint to create engaging lectures, class presentations, and educational materials.

Marketing and Advertising: Marketing professionals use PowerPoint to design eye-catching advertisements, marketing campaigns, and product presentations.

Training and Workshops: Trainers and workshop facilitators use PowerPoint to deliver interactive and informative training sessions.

Personal Projects: Individuals can use PowerPoint for personal projects, such as creating photo albums, event invitations, or travel diaries.

4.3 Benefits of Using Microsoft PowerPoint

Using Microsoft PowerPoint offers numerous advantages that enhance the presentation creation process and improve the overall impact of the delivered content:

Visual Appeal: PowerPoint enables users to incorporate images, graphics, charts, and multimedia elements, making presentations visually engaging and memorable.

Organisation: PowerPoint's slide-based structure allows users to organise information into concise and structured segments, facilitating better comprehension and retention of content.

Customisation: PowerPoint provides extensive customisation options, allowing users to tailor presentations to their specific needs and branding requirements.

Interactivity: PowerPoint supports animations, transitions, and hyperlinks, enabling presenters to create interactive and dynamic slideshows.

Presenter Tools: PowerPoint includes presenter view, which offers notes, timers, and slide previews to assist presenters during the presentation.

Collaboration: PowerPoint allows multiple users to collaborate on the same presentation simultaneously, fostering teamwork and creativity.

Audience Engagement: With its multimedia features and design capabilities, PowerPoint can captivate audiences and hold their attention throughout the presentation.

Portability: PowerPoint presentations can be saved in various formats, making them easily shareable through email, cloud storage, or portable devices.

4.4 Creating a Presentation in PowerPoint

Step 1: Open Microsoft PowerPoint

- Launch Microsoft PowerPoint on your computer by clicking on the PowerPoint icon or searching for "Microsoft PowerPoint" in your operating system's search bar.

Step 2: Choose a Presentation Template

- PowerPoint offers a variety of pre-designed presentation templates to choose from. Select a template that suits your presentation's theme and purpose.

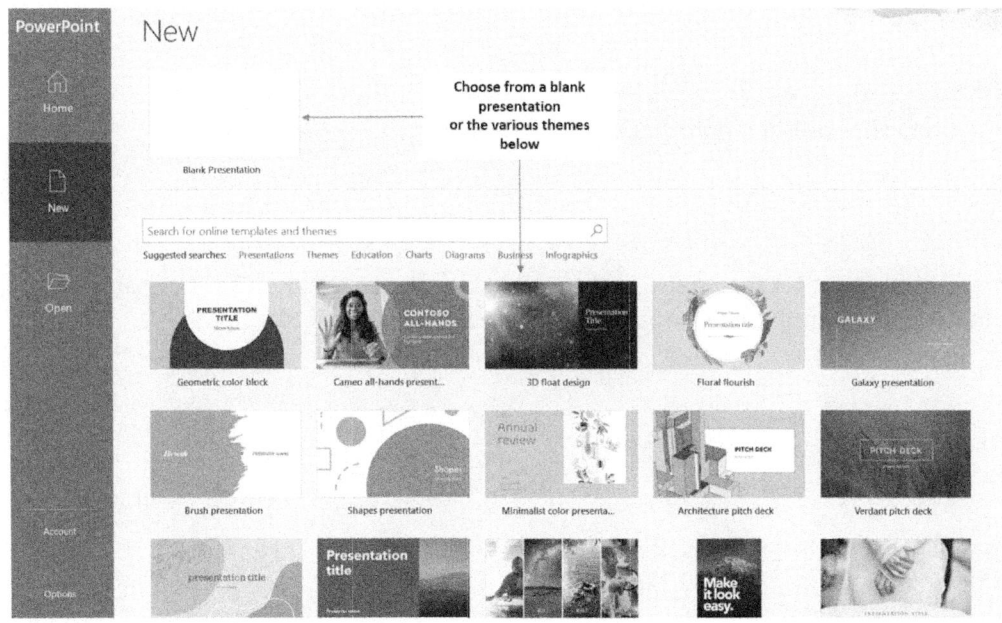

Step 3: Add Slides

- In the "Home" tab under the "Slides" group, click on the "New Slide" button to add a new slide.

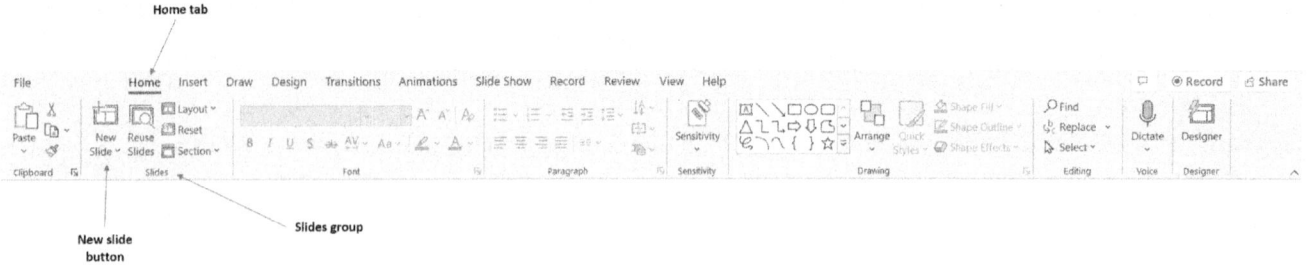

- Choose a slide layout from the available options (e.g., Title Slide, Title and Content, Picture with Caption, etc.) by clicking the down arrow in the "New Slide" button.

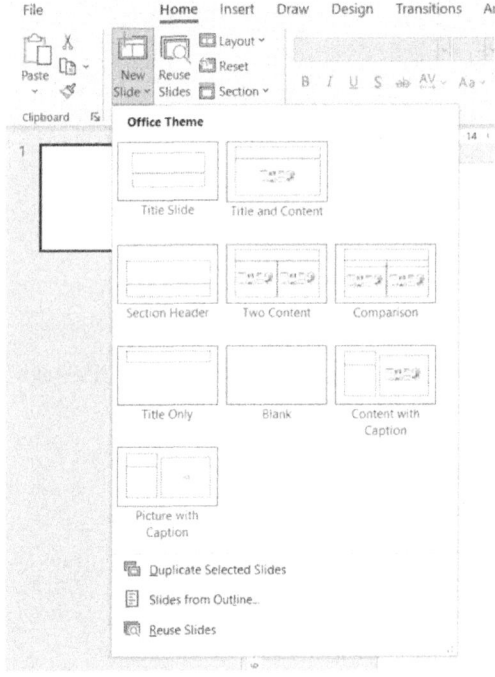

- Repeat this step to add more slides to your presentation.

Step 4: Enter Text and Content

- Click on the placeholders on each slide to enter text and content relevant to your presentation. For example, add titles, bullet points, images, charts, and multimedia elements to convey your message effectively.

Step 5: Customise Slide Design

- Go to the "Design" tab in the top menu.

- Browse through different design themes and colour schemes.

- Select the theme and colour scheme that best matches your presentation's style.

Step 6: Save Your Presentation

- Click on the "File" tab in the top left corner, then select "Save As".

- Choose a location on your computer to save the presentation, give it a name, and click "Save".

4.5 Editing a Presentation in PowerPoint

Step 1: Open an Existing Presentation

- Launch Microsoft PowerPoint and open the presentation you want to edit by clicking on "Open" in the "File" tab or selecting it from the list of recent files.

Step 2: Rearrange Slides

- To rearrange slides, click and drag the slide thumbnails in the left-hand navigation pane to the desired position.

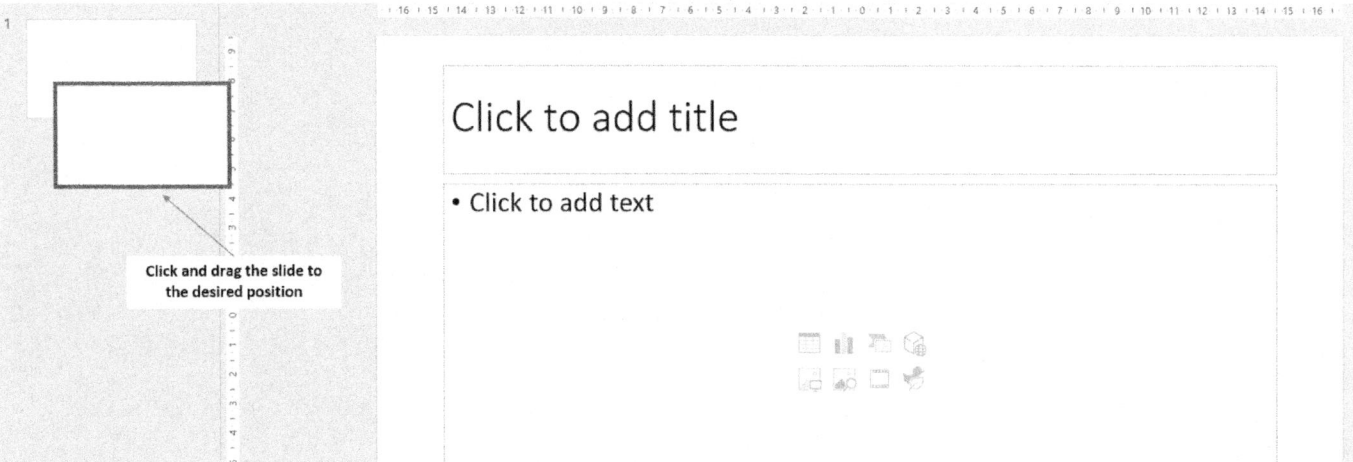

Step 3: Edit Text and Content

- Click on the text or content you want to edit within a slide.

- Make the necessary changes, such as adding or removing text, modifying bullet points, or updating images.

Step 4: Add or Remove Slides

- As mentioned in the previous section, to add a new slide, click on the "New Slide" button in the left-hand navigation pane.

- To delete a slide, right-click on the slide thumbnail and choose "Delete Slide".

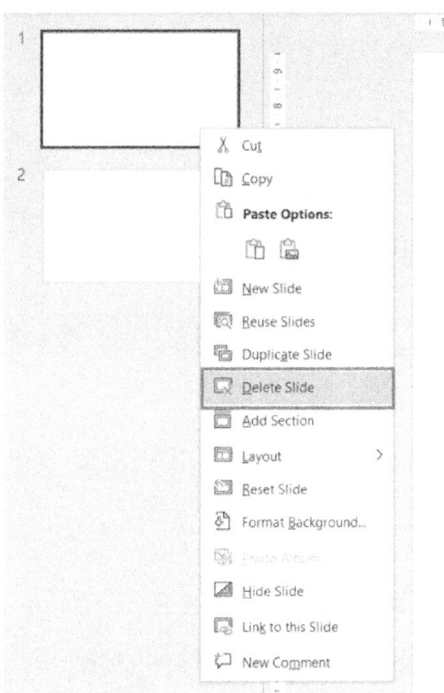

Step 5: Apply Slide Transitions

- Go to the "Transitions" tab in the top menu.

- Choose a transition effect from the available options.

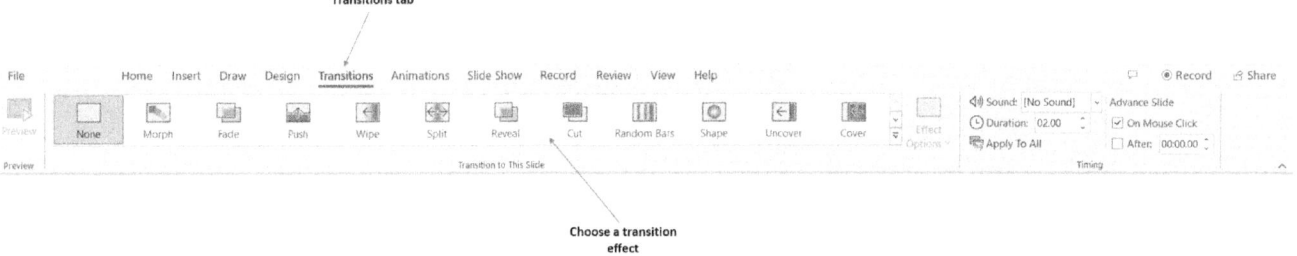

- Click on the slide where you want to apply the transition or select multiple slides and apply the same transition to all of them.

Step 6: Review and Proofread

- Review your presentation for any errors or inconsistencies. Use the "Spelling" feature in the "Review" tab to check spelling and grammar.

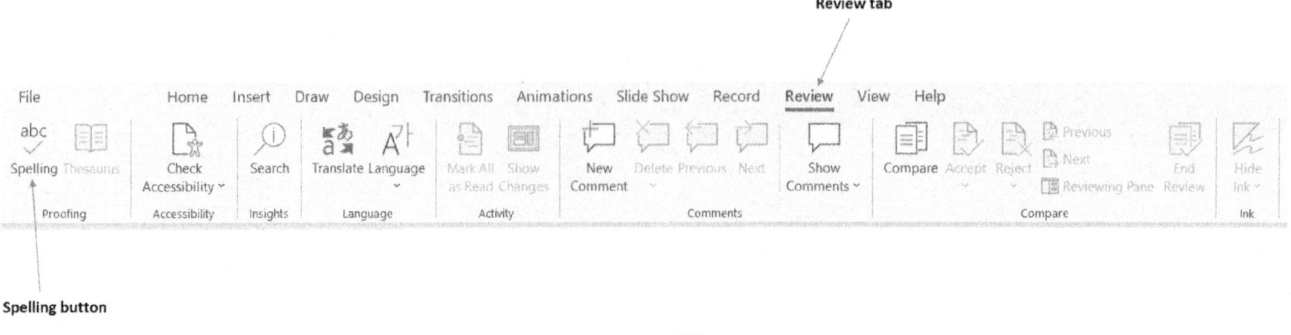

Step 7: Save Your Edited Presentation

- Click on the "File" tab in the top left corner, then select "Save" or "Save As" to save your edited presentation with the changes.

4.6 Adding Images and Multimedia in PowerPoint

PowerPoint offers various multimedia features that allow users to create visually engaging presentations. In this section, we will explore step-by-step instructions on how to add images, and multimedia elements to your PowerPoint presentation.

4.6.1 Adding Images to Your Presentation

Step 1: Open PowerPoint and Your Presentation

- Launch Microsoft PowerPoint and open the presentation you want to edit.

Step 2: Go to the Slide Where You Want to Add an Image

- Navigate to the slide where you want to insert an image.

Step 3: Insert an Image

- Go to the "Insert" tab in the top menu.

- Click on the "Picture" button in the "Images" group.

- Choose whether you want to insert a picture from your computer by selecting "This Device", a stock image or an online picture.

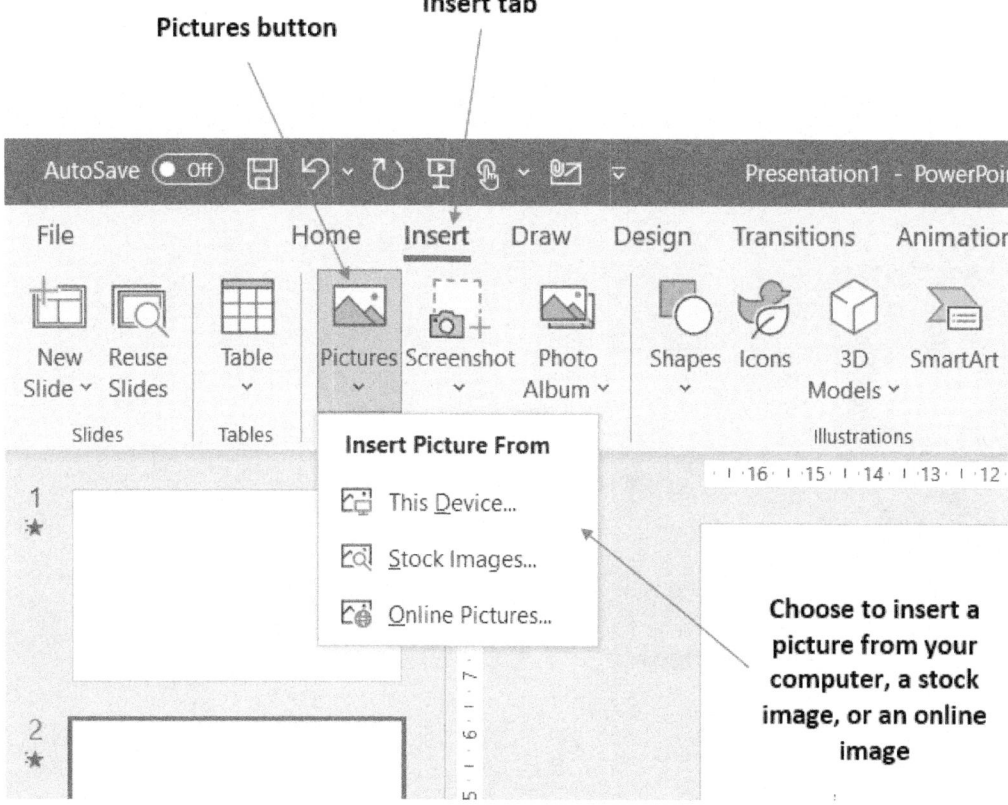

- Find the image you want to insert, select it, and click "Insert".

Step 4: Resize and Position the Image (Optional)

- After inserting the image, you can click and drag the image to reposition it on the slide or use the corner handles to resize the image as needed.

Step 5: Add Alt Text to the Image (Optional)

- For accessibility purposes and to help search engines understand your content, you can add alt text to the image.

- Right-click on the image and select "Edit Alt Text".

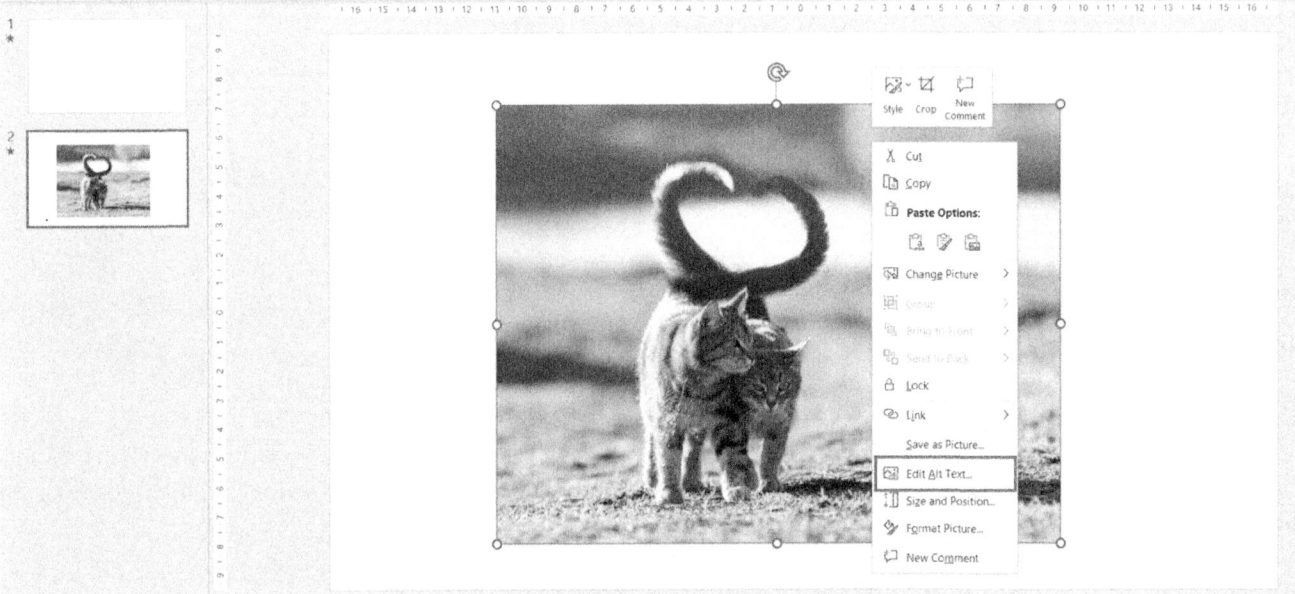

- Enter a brief and descriptive alt text for the image.

Step 6: Save Your Edited Presentation

- Click on the "File" tab in the top left corner, then select "Save" or "Save As" to save your presentation with the added image.

4.6.2 Adding Multimedia Elements to Your Presentation

Step 1: Open PowerPoint and Your Presentation

- Launch Microsoft PowerPoint and open the presentation you want to edit.

Step 2: Go to the Slide Where You Want to Add Multimedia

- Navigate to the slide where you want to insert multimedia elements.

Step 3: Insert a Video or Audio Clip

- Go to the "Insert" tab in the top menu.

- Click on the "Video" or "Audio" button in the "Media" group.

- To insert a video, choose whether you want to insert a video from your computer by selecting "This Device", a stock video or an online video.

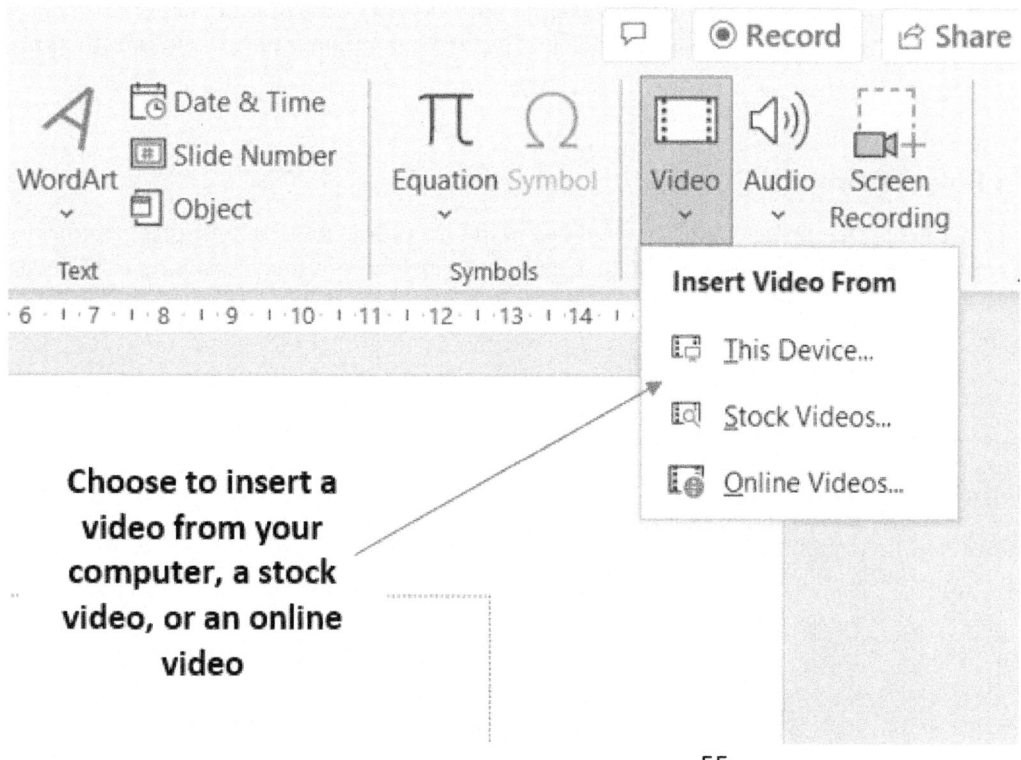

Choose to insert a video from your computer, a stock video, or an online video

- Find the video or audio file you want to insert, select it, and click "Insert".

Step 4: Resize and Position the Multimedia (Optional)

- After inserting the multimedia element, you can click and drag the element to reposition it on the slide or use the corner handles to resize the element as needed.

Step 5: Set Playback Options (Optional)

- For videos, you can click on the video to access the "Playback" tab in the top menu.

- Use the options in the "Video Options" group to adjust settings, such as starting the video automatically or looping it.

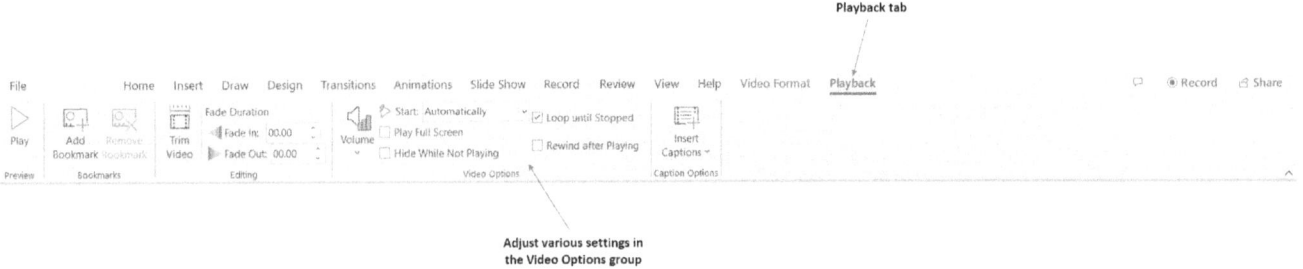

Step 6: Save Your Edited Presentation

- Click on the "File" tab in the top left corner, then select "Save" or "Save As" to save your presentation with the added multimedia elements.

4.7 Understanding Animations in PowerPoint

Animations in Microsoft PowerPoint add movement and visual effects to slides, making presentations more engaging and dynamic. Animations can be applied to text, images, charts, and other elements on slides, allowing presenters to reveal content gradually or emphasise key points effectively. In this section, we will explore what animations are and how to apply them to slides in PowerPoint.

4.7.1 What are Animations in PowerPoint?

Animations in PowerPoint refer to visual effects that bring elements on slides to life by adding motion, entrance, emphasis, or exit effects. These effects can be controlled to occur automatically or triggered by user actions, such as mouse clicks or keystrokes. Animations enhance presentations by creating a sense of flow, guiding the audience's attention, and making content more memorable and engaging.

4.7.2 Step-by-Step Instructions to Apply Animation to Slides in PowerPoint

Step 1: Open Microsoft PowerPoint

- Launch Microsoft PowerPoint on your computer by clicking on the PowerPoint icon or searching for "Microsoft PowerPoint" in your operating system's search bar.

Step 2: Open Your Presentation

- Open the presentation to which you want to add animations by clicking on "Open" in the "File" tab or selecting it from the list of recent files.

Step 3: Go to the Slide You Want to Animate

- Navigate to the slide you want to apply animation to by clicking on the slide thumbnail in the left-hand navigation pane.

Step 4: Select the Element to Animate

- Click on the element (e.g., text box, image, shape) you want to animate. A border or selection handles will appear around the element when it's selected.

Step 5: Access Animation Options

- Go to the "Animations" tab in the top menu.

- In the "Advanced Animation" group, click on the "Add Animation" button to reveal the animation options. Alternatively, select an animation from the "Animation" group.

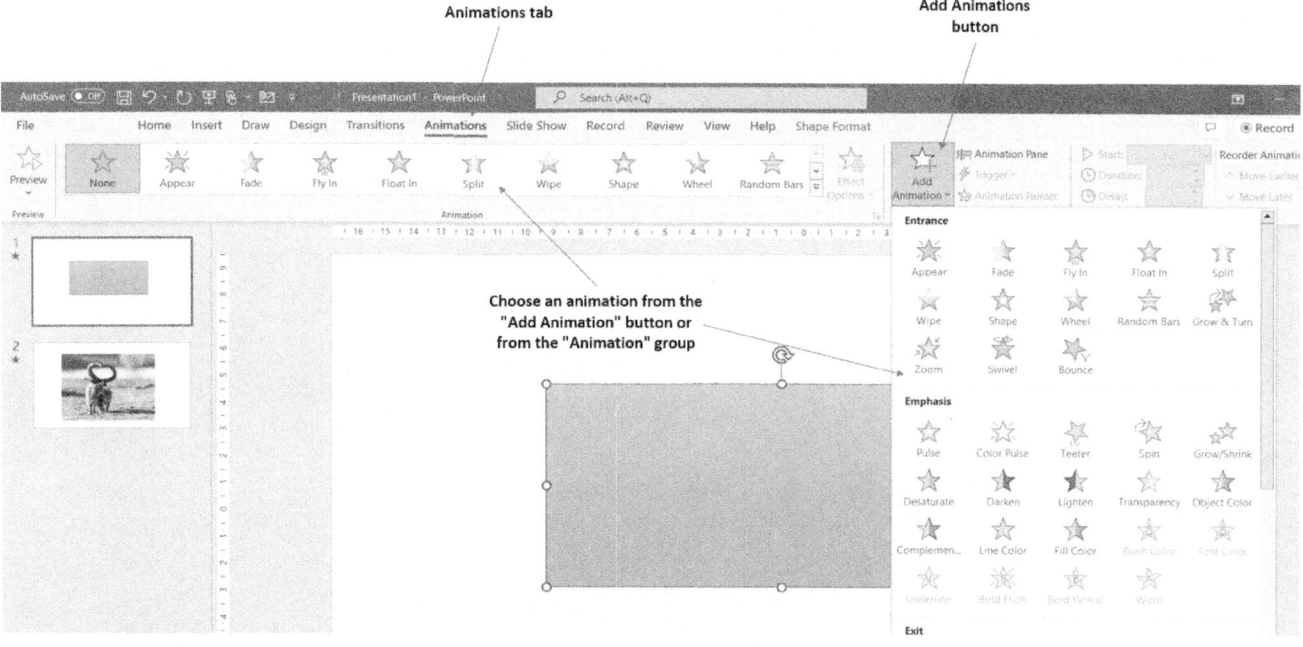

Step 6: Choose an Animation Effect

- Browse through the available animation effects (e.g., Fade, Fly In, Zoom) and click on the desired effect. A preview of the animation will be displayed on the slide.

Step 7: Customise Animation Settings (Optional)

- After applying the animation, you can customise its settings.

- To change the order of animations, click on the "Animation Pane" button in the "Advanced Animation" group.

- In the Animation Pane, drag and drop animations to reorder them.

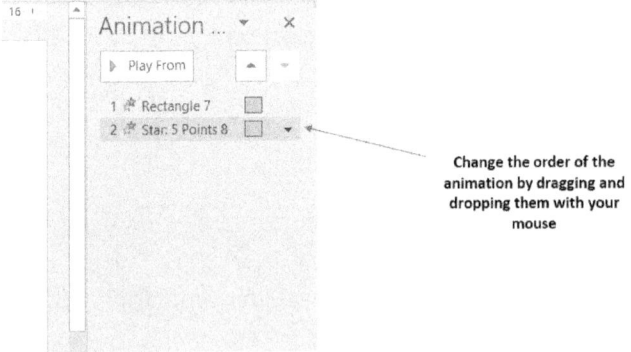

Change the order of the animation by dragging and dropping them with your mouse

- To set the animation's start time or duration, select the animation in the Animation Pane and click on "Start" or "Duration" buttons in the "Timing" group.

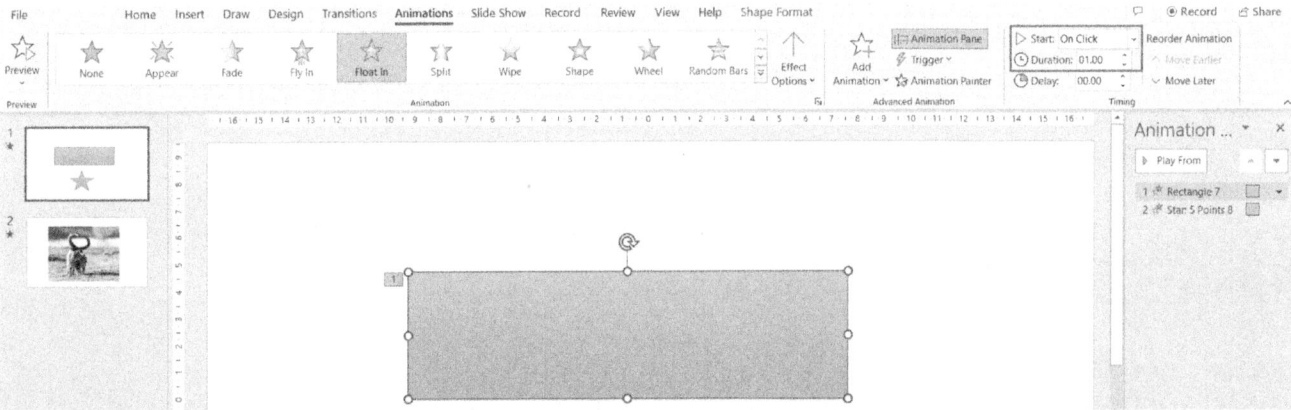

- Choose the desired start option (e.g., On Click, With Previous) and adjust the delay and duration settings.

Step 8: Preview Animations

- To preview animations, go to the "Slide Show" tab in the top menu.

- Click on the "From Current Slide" button to start the slide show from the selected slide.

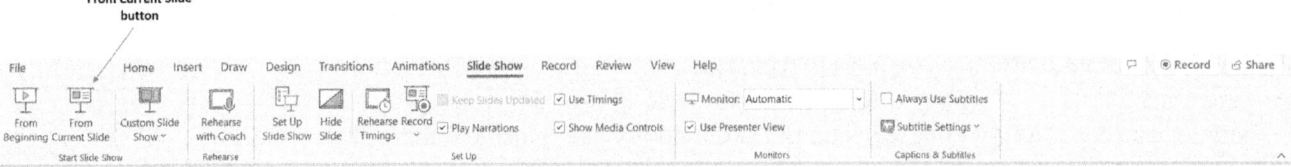

- Observe the animations as they play through the slide show.

Step 9: Save Your Presentation

- Click on the "File" tab in the top left corner, then select "Save" or "Save As" to save your presentation with the applied animations.

Animations in PowerPoint add visual appeal and interactivity to presentations, making them more engaging and memorable for the audience. By following the step-by-step instructions provided in this section, users can confidently apply animation effects to elements on slides, control their timing and settings, and preview their animations in PowerPoint. Animations are a valuable tool for presenters to emphasise key points, maintain audience interest, and deliver dynamic and impactful presentations.

4.8 Delivering a Presentation in PowerPoint

Delivering a presentation in PowerPoint is the culmination of your hard work in creating and preparing your slides. A successful presentation involves effective communication, engaging with your audience, and maintaining their interest throughout. In this section, we will explain how to deliver a presentation and provide step-by-step instructions to guide you through the process in Microsoft PowerPoint.

4.8.1 How to Deliver a Presentation in PowerPoint

Be Prepared: Familiarise yourself with the content, flow, and key points of your presentation. Practice speaking aloud, and time yourself to ensure that your presentation fits within the allotted time.

Dress Appropriately: Dress in a professional manner that aligns with the audience and the setting of your presentation.

Check Equipment and Setup: Arrive early to the presentation venue and test the equipment (projector, microphone, etc.) to ensure everything works correctly.

Establish Eye Contact: Make eye contact with different members of the audience to create a connection and keep them engaged.

Speak Clearly and Confidently: Speak clearly and confidently, projecting your voice to reach all parts of the room. Avoid speaking too fast or too slow.

Engage the Audience: Use a variety of engagement techniques, such as asking questions, sharing anecdotes, or using visual aids, to involve the audience actively.

Manage Nervousness: If you feel nervous, take deep breaths, and remind yourself that it's normal to have some nervousness before a presentation. Focus on delivering your message, and the nerves will likely subside as you get into your flow.

Handle Q&A: Be prepared to answer questions from the audience after your presentation. Listen carefully and provide clear and concise answers.

4.8.2 Step-by-Step Instructions for Delivering a Presentation in PowerPoint

Step 1: Open Microsoft PowerPoint

- Launch Microsoft PowerPoint on your computer by clicking on the PowerPoint icon or searching for "Microsoft PowerPoint" in your operating system's search bar.

Step 2: Open Your Presentation

- Open the presentation you want to deliver by clicking on "Open" in the "File" tab or selecting it from the list of recent files.

Step 3: Go to Slide Show Mode

- In the bottom right corner of the PowerPoint window, click on the "Slide Show" button to enter Slide Show mode.

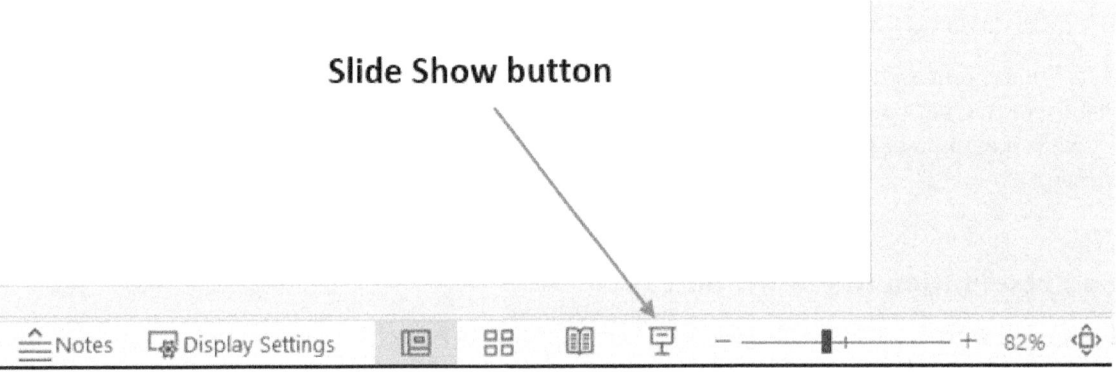

- Alternatively, press "F5" on your keyboard to start the presentation from the beginning.

Step 4: Navigate Through Slides

- Use the arrow keys on your keyboard or click the left mouse button to advance to the next slide.

- Press "Backspace" to go back to the previous slide.

Step 5: Utilise Slide Navigation Tools (Optional)

- During the presentation, you can use additional navigation tools, such as:

    o Press "Spacebar" to advance to the next slide.

    o Press a number + "Enter" to go to a specific slide. For example, if you want to see slide 5, press "5" + "Enter".

    o Press "B" or "." to blank the screen (useful for focusing audience attention on yourself).

Step 6: Interact with the Audience

- Engage the audience during your presentation by:

    o Maintaining eye contact and smiling.

- ○ Encouraging questions or comments.

- ○ Using gestures and body language to emphasise points.

Step 7: End the Presentation

- Conclude your presentation with a summary of key points and a call to action if relevant.

Step 8: Exit Slide Show Mode

- Press "Esc" on your keyboard to exit Slide Show mode and return to the normal PowerPoint view.

Step 9: Save Your Presentation

- Click on the "File" tab in the top left corner, then select "Save" to save any changes you made during or after the presentation.

Delivering a presentation in Microsoft PowerPoint requires preparation, confidence, and engaging with your audience effectively. By following the step-by-step instructions provided in this section and using the tips for delivering a successful presentation, you can confidently present your content, keep the audience engaged, and deliver a compelling and memorable PowerPoint presentation. Remember to practice, manage your nerves, and use the tools available in PowerPoint to enhance your delivery and connect with your audience.

4.9 Collaboration and Sharing in PowerPoint

Collaboration and sharing in Microsoft PowerPoint enable multiple users to work together on a presentation, making it a valuable tool for team projects, feedback collection, and seamless content creation. In this section, we will explore how to collaborate and share PowerPoint presentations with step-by-step instructions.

4.9.1 Collaboration Features in PowerPoint

Real-time Co-authoring: Multiple users can simultaneously edit the same PowerPoint presentation, and changes are reflected in real-time.

Comments and Review: Users can leave comments on specific slides or elements, providing feedback and suggestions for improvements.

Version History: PowerPoint keeps track of changes made to the presentation, allowing users to review and restore previous versions.

4.9.2 Sharing Options in PowerPoint

Share via Email: You can send a copy of the presentation as an email attachment to collaborators.

OneDrive or SharePoint: Save the PowerPoint presentation to OneDrive or SharePoint and share the link with collaborators to enable real-time co-authoring.

4.9.3 Step-by-Step Instructions for Collaboration and Sharing in PowerPoint

Step 1: Open Microsoft PowerPoint

- Launch Microsoft PowerPoint on your computer by clicking on the PowerPoint icon or searching for "Microsoft PowerPoint" in your operating system's search bar.

Step 2: Create or Open a Presentation

- Create a new presentation or open an existing one that you want to collaborate on or share.

Step 3: Collaboration and Real-time Co-authoring

- Save the presentation to OneDrive or SharePoint by clicking on the "File" tab in the top left corner.

- Select "Save As" from the menu.

- Choose "OneDrive" or "SharePoint" as the location to save the presentation.

- Select the desired folder and click "Save".

- To share the presentation, click on the "Share" button in the top right corner of the PowerPoint window.

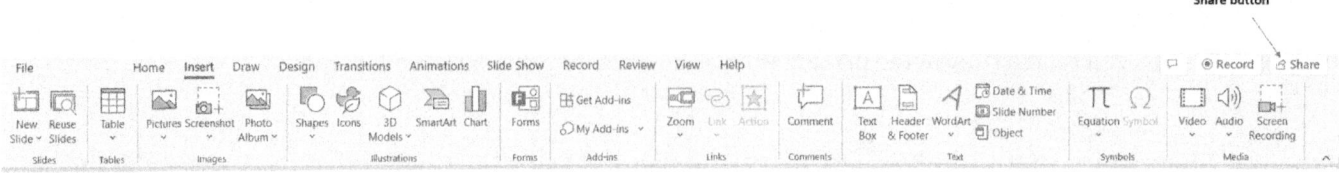

- In the "Share with People" pane, enter the email addresses of the collaborators you want to invite and optionally, include a message to the recipients.

Enter the email addresses of the people you want to share the presentation with

Enter a message

- Choose the permission level for each collaborator (Can Edit or Can View).

- Click on the "Send" button to send the invitations.

Step 4: Collaborate and Review

- Collaborators will receive an email invitation with a link to the shared presentation.

- Click on the link to open the presentation in PowerPoint.

- All collaborators can now simultaneously edit the presentation in real-time.

- Each collaborator's changes are reflected instantly, and the cursor shows their name or initials.

Step 5: Add Comments and Review

- To add comments and review, select the element or slide you want to comment on.

- Go to the "Review" tab in the top menu.

- Click on the "New Comment" button in the "Comments" group.

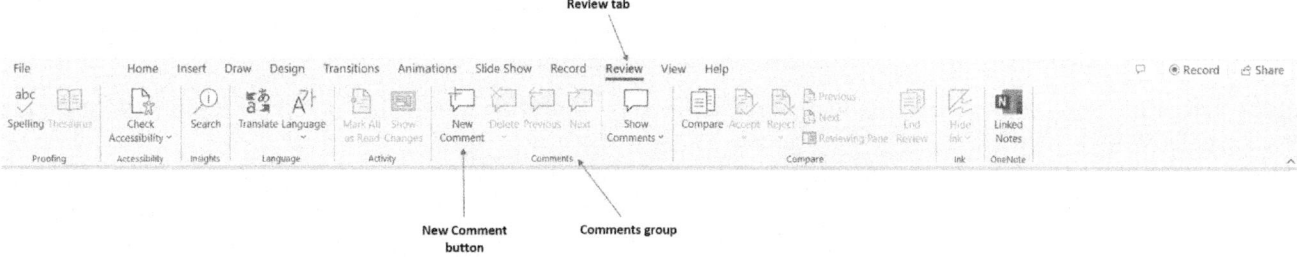

- Type your comment in the comment box that appears on the right side of the slide.

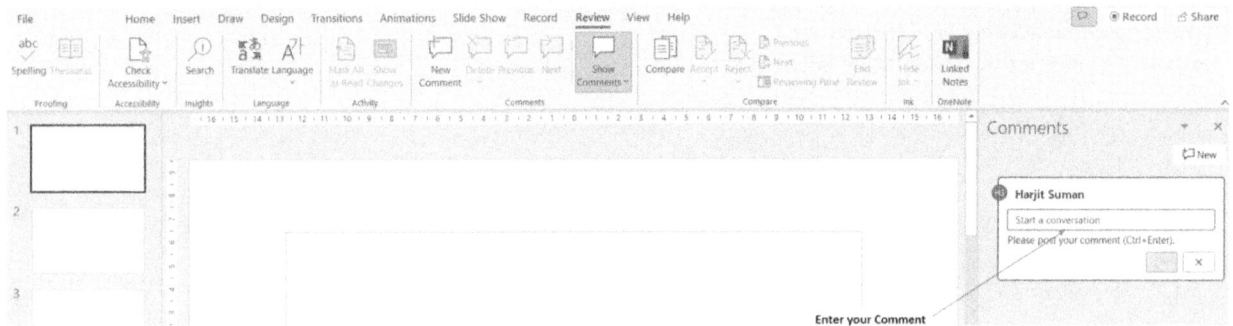

Step 6: Save and Review Version History

- As collaborators work on the presentation, PowerPoint automatically saves the changes.

- To access version history, go to the "File" tab in the top left corner.

- Select "Info" from the menu.

- Click on the "Version History" button on the right side.

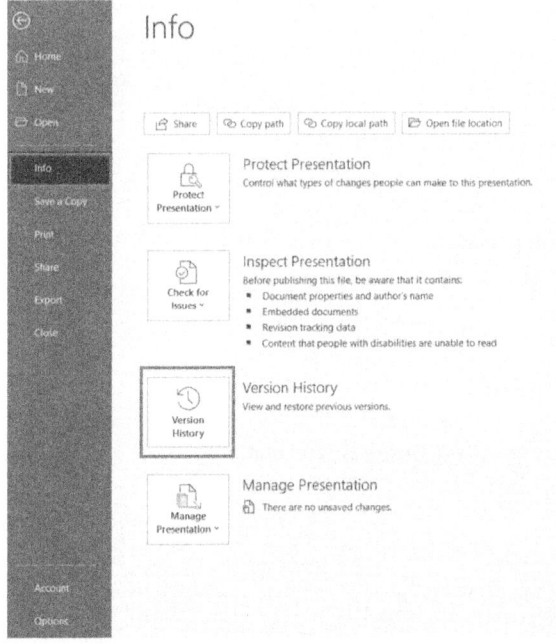

- Choose the desired version to review or revert to a previous version.

Step 7: Save the Final Presentation

- After collaboration and review, save the final version of the presentation by clicking on the "File" tab and selecting "Save" or "Save As".

Collaboration and sharing in Microsoft PowerPoint streamlines the process of creating and editing presentations in a team setting. By following the step-by-step instructions provided in this section, users can effectively collaborate in real-time, share PowerPoint presentations, leave comments, and review version history. These features enhance teamwork, facilitate efficient content creation, and make PowerPoint a powerful tool for seamless collaboration on presentations.

Chapter 5: Microsoft Outlook

5.1 What is Microsoft Outlook?

Microsoft Outlook is a popular personal information manager and email client developed by Microsoft. It is part of the Microsoft Office suite and is widely used for managing emails, calendars, contacts, tasks, and other personal and professional information. Outlook is available as a desktop application for Windows and macOS, as well as web and mobile versions for cross-platform accessibility.

5.2 How Microsoft Outlook is Used?

Email Management: Outlook allows users to send, receive, and organise emails efficiently. It supports various email protocols such as POP3, IMAP, and Exchange, enabling seamless integration with different email services.

Calendar and Schedule Management: Outlook's calendar feature helps users schedule appointments, events, and meetings. Users can set reminders, invite attendees, and view their schedules in daily, weekly, or monthly formats.

Contacts Management: Outlook's contact management features enable users to store and organise contact information, including names, email addresses, phone numbers, and more.

Task Management: Outlook offers a built-in task management system, allowing users to create to-do lists, set deadlines, and track the progress of their tasks.

Notes and Journal: Users can create notes to jot down ideas or important information. The journal feature allows users to record activities and events for future reference.

Integration with Other Microsoft Applications: Outlook seamlessly integrates with other Microsoft Office applications, such as Word, Excel, and PowerPoint, allowing users to attach files and access additional functionalities.

5.3 Benefits of Using Microsoft Outlook

Efficient Email Management: Outlook streamlines email communication, categorising, and organising emails to improve productivity.

Unified Interface: With its unified interface, Outlook provides a one-stop platform to manage emails, calendars, contacts, and tasks, saving time and effort.

Calendar and Scheduling: Outlook's calendar feature helps users stay organised by scheduling events, meetings, and appointments effectively.

Collaboration: Outlook's integration with Microsoft Exchange and Microsoft 365 enables seamless collaboration and sharing of calendars, emails, and files with colleagues and teams.

Task Management: The task feature in Outlook assists users in prioritising and tracking tasks, ensuring that deadlines are met.

Contacts Management: Outlook's contact management system simplifies the process of storing and accessing contact information.

Offline Access: Outlook offers offline access to emails and calendar events, allowing users to work even when an internet connection is not available.

Security: Outlook employs robust security features, including spam filtering and encryption, to protect users from phishing attacks and data breaches.

Mobile Compatibility: Outlook's mobile app allows users to access their emails, calendars, and contacts on the go, enhancing productivity and responsiveness.

Integration with Office Applications: Outlook's integration with other Microsoft Office applications enhances workflow efficiency and simplifies file sharing.

5.4 Managing Email in Microsoft Outlook

Managing email efficiently is crucial for maintaining productivity and staying organised. Microsoft Outlook offers a range of tools and features to help users effectively manage their email inbox, handle incoming messages, and stay on top of their communication. In this section, we will provide step-by-step instructions on how to manage email in Outlook, along with relevant data to illustrate the process.

5.4.1 Step-by-Step Instructions for Managing Email in Outlook

Step 1: Open Microsoft Outlook

- Launch Microsoft Outlook on your computer by clicking on the Outlook icon or searching for "Microsoft Outlook" in your operating system's search bar.

Step 2: Access Your Email Inbox

- Upon opening Outlook, you will be directed to your email inbox, which displays your incoming emails.

Step 3: Read and Organise New Emails

- To review new emails, click on individual emails in the inbox to read their content and view any attachments.

- To flag an email as important, right-click on the email in the inbox and choose "Follow Up". Another sub menu will appear. Select the option when the email needs to be actioned by.

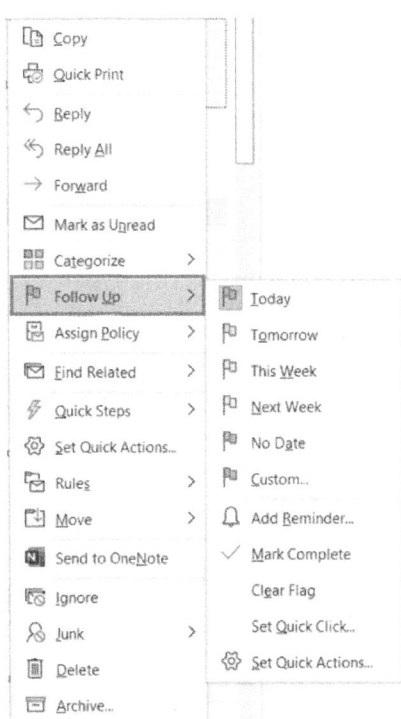

- To mark emails as unread, right-click on an email and select "Mark as Unread" to indicate that you haven't read it yet.

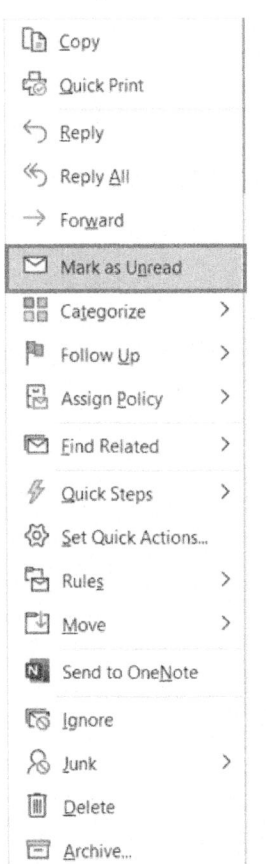

Step 4: Organise Emails Using Folders

- To create folders, right-click on your email account's inbox and choose "New Folder".

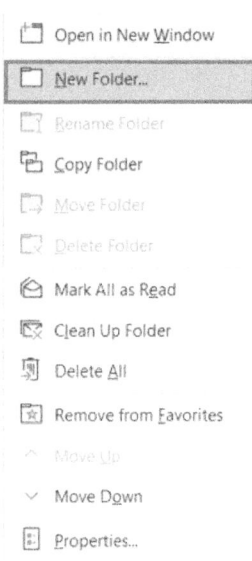

- Name the folder (e.g., "Work," "Personal," "Project A") and click "OK".

- To move emails to folders, select the email you want to move, and then drag and drop it into the appropriate folder.

Step 5: Use Rules to Manage Incoming Emails

- To create a rule, go to the "Home" tab in the top menu.

- Click on "Rules" in the "Move" group and select "Manage Rules & Alerts".

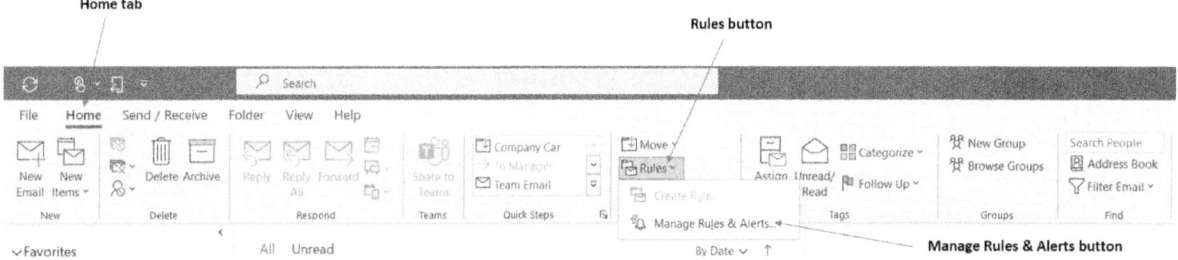

- Click on "New Rule".

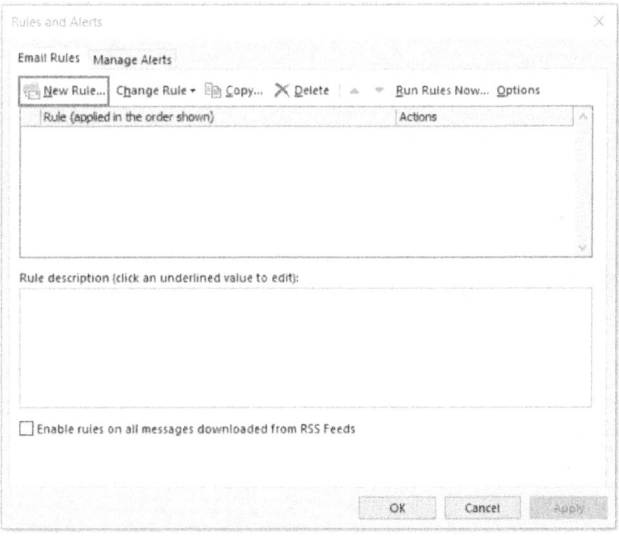

- Select a rule template (e.g., "Move messages from someone to a folder") and click "Next".

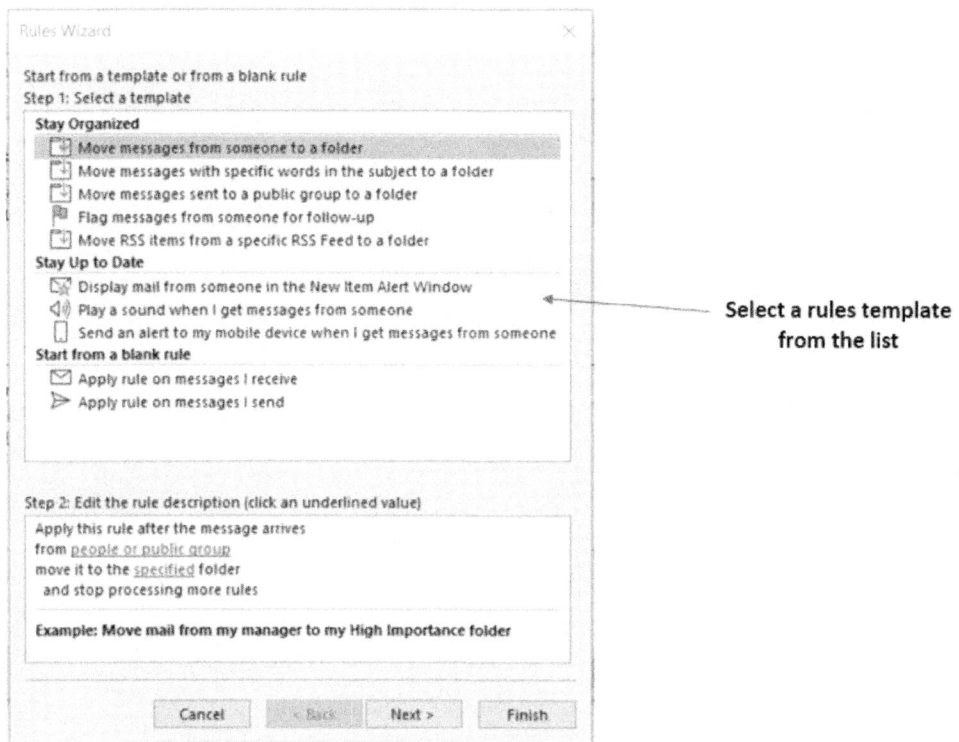

- Follow the on-screen instructions to set up conditions for the rule (e.g., sender's name or email address).

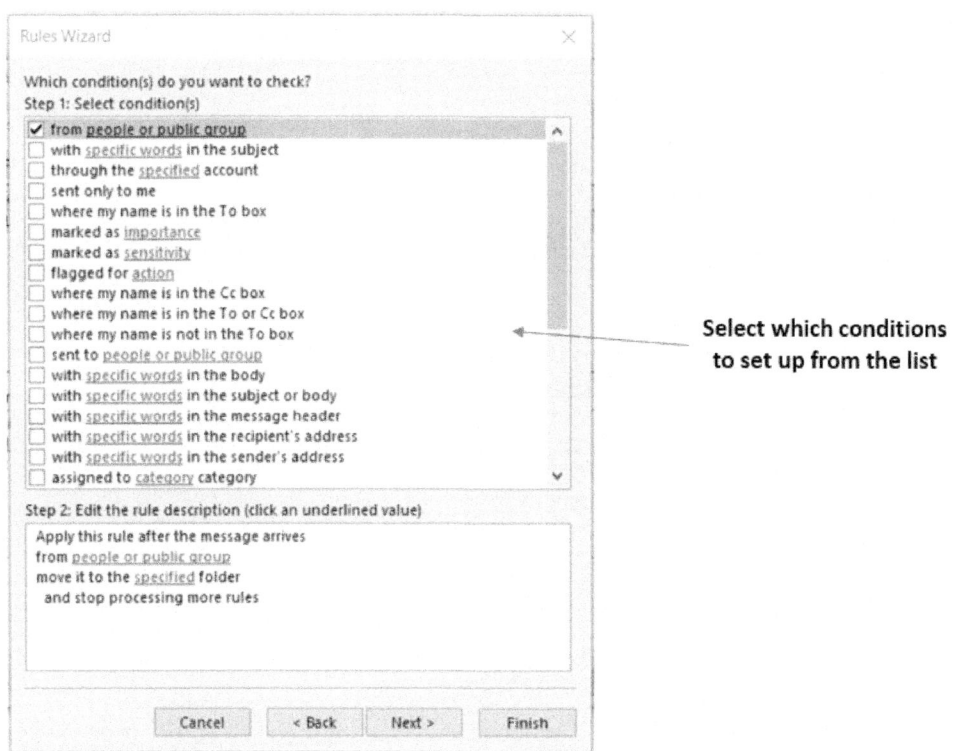

- Click "Next".

- Select the action you want the rule to take (e.g., move the email to a specific folder).

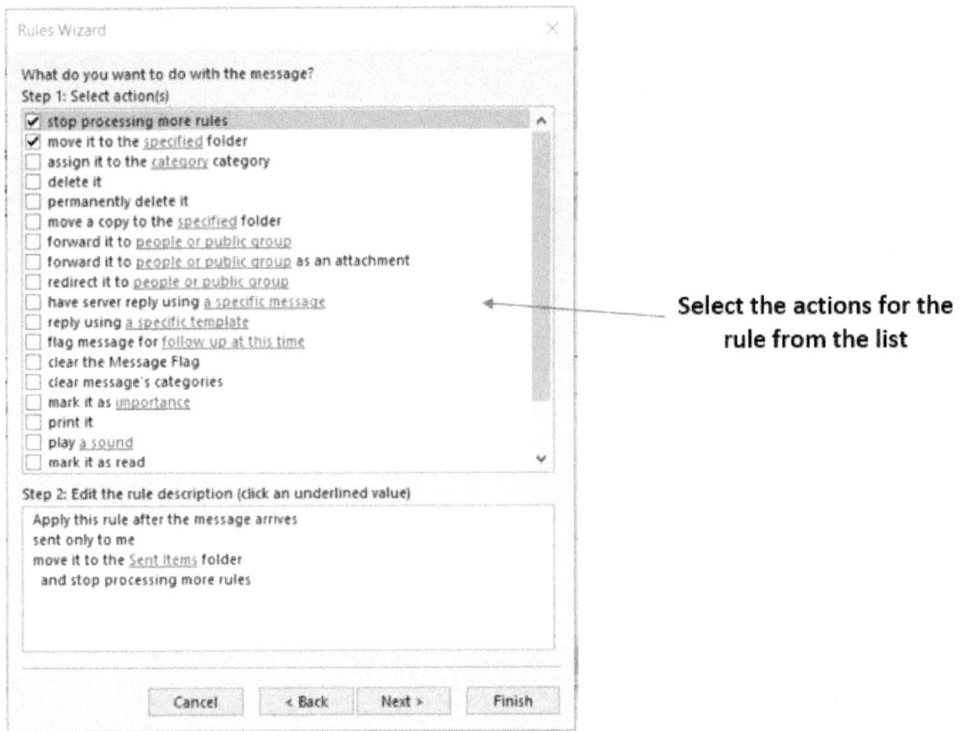

Select the actions for the rule from the list

- Click "Next".

- If needed, set up exceptions to the rule.

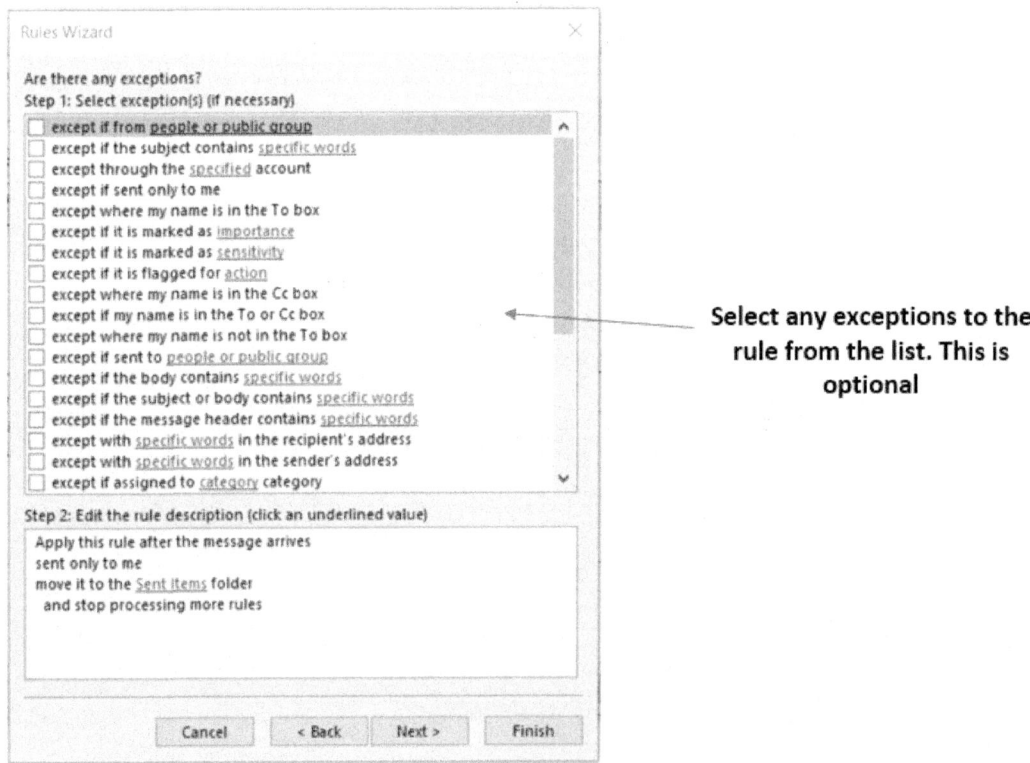

Select any exceptions to the rule from the list. This is optional

- Click "Next" to proceed.

- Enter a name for the rule (e.g., "Move Work Emails to Work Folder").

70

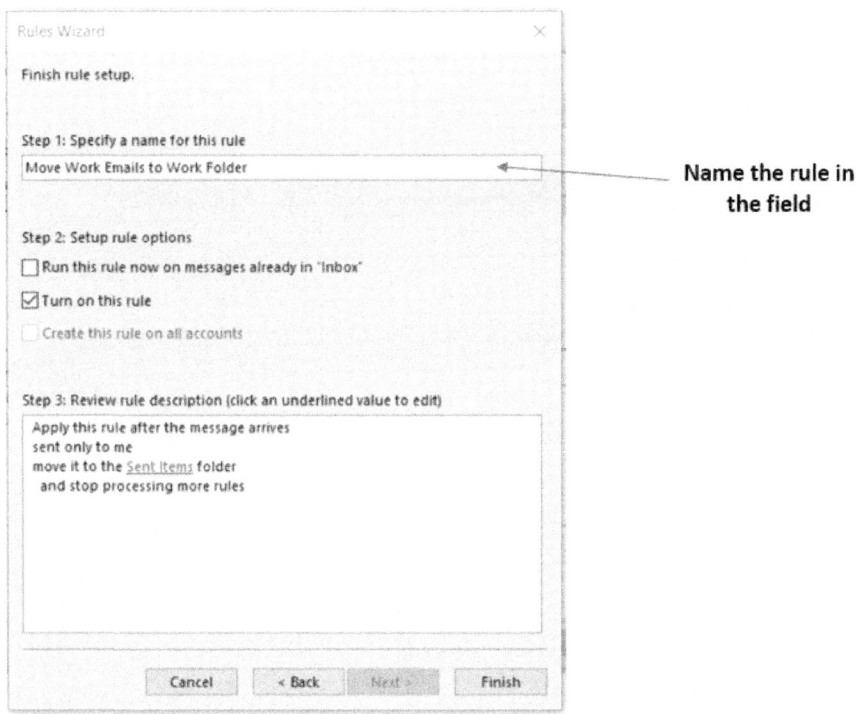

* Click "Finish".

Step 6: Use Search and Filters

* To search for specific emails, use the search bar at the top of the Outlook window and then type the keywords related to the email you are looking for.

Search bar

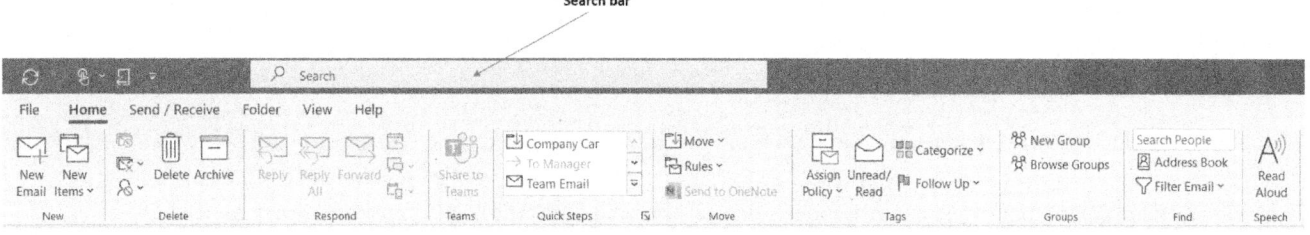

* To use filters, in the search bar, click on the "Filter Email" button to filter emails based on criteria such as unread status, date, sender, and more.

Step 7: Archive or Delete Emails

* Select the email(s) you want to archive and click on the "Archive" button in the top menu in the "Home" tab.

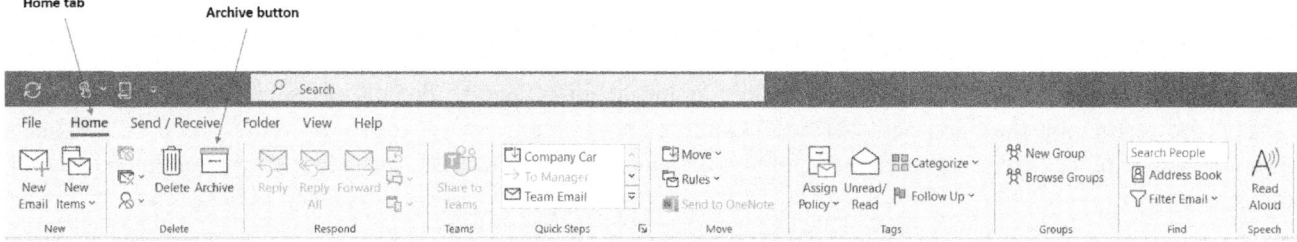

- To delete emails, select the email(s) you want to delete and click on the "Delete" button in the top menu in the "Home" tab.

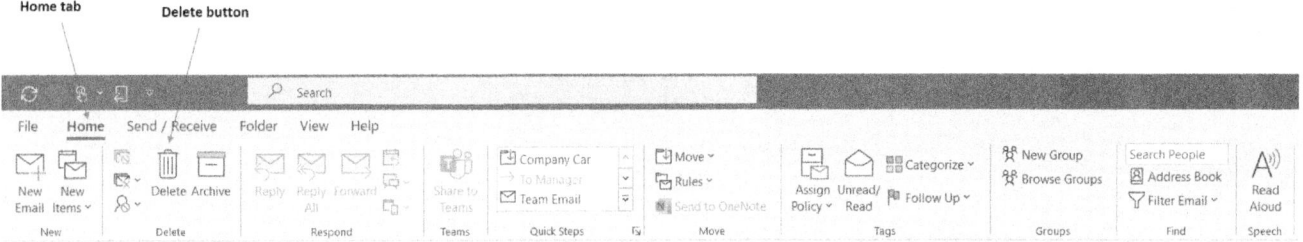

Step 8: Create Quick Steps (Optional)

- Go to the "Home" tab in the top menu.

- Click on "Create New" in the "Quick Steps" group.

Create New button   Quick Steps group

- Follow the on-screen instructions to set up a Quick Step to perform common actions with one click (e.g., reply and move to a folder).

Step 9: Mark Emails as Read (Optional)

- By default, emails are marked as read when you click on them.

- To mark multiple selected emails as read, right-click on the selected emails and choose "Mark as Read".

Microsoft Outlook provides a range of tools and features to help users manage their email effectively, maintain organisation, and boost productivity. By following the step-by-step instructions provided in this section and utilising Outlook's capabilities to organise emails into folders, create rules and filters, and use quick steps, users can manage their email inbox efficiently. With Outlook's search and filtering options, users can quickly locate specific emails, and the archive and delete functions help keep the inbox clutter-free. Outlook's email management features make it a valuable tool for handling emails, enabling users to stay organised and focused on essential tasks and communications.

5.5 Organising with Folders and Categories in Outlook

Organising emails and other items in Microsoft Outlook is essential for efficient information management. Folders and categories are two powerful tools that help users sort, group, and prioritise their emails, calendar events, contacts, and tasks. In this section, we will explore how to organise with folders and categories in Outlook, providing step-by-step instructions for effective organisation.

5.5.1 Organising with Folders in Outlook

Step 1: Create subfolders

- Right-click on an existing folder.

- Select "New Folder" from the context menu.

- Name the subfolder and click "OK".

- To move emails to subfolders, select the email(s) you want to move to the subfolder.

- Drag and drop the selected email(s) onto the subfolder in the left-hand navigation pane.

Step 2: Rename and Organise Folders (Optional)

- Right-click on a folder or subfolder.

- Choose "Rename Folder" from the context menu.

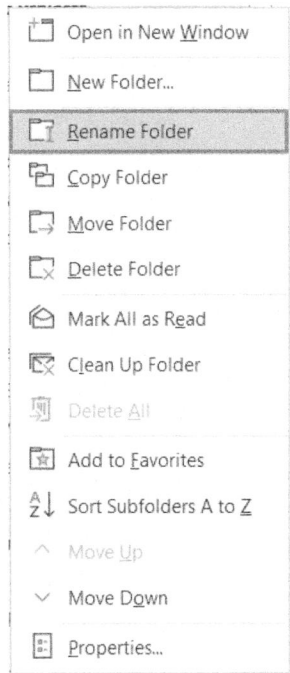

- Enter the new name for the folder and press "Enter".

5.5.2 Organising with Categories in Outlook

Step 1: Assign Categories to Items

- Select the item you want to assign a category to (e.g., email, calendar event, contact, task).

- Go to the "Tags" group on the Outlook Ribbon in the "Home" tab.

Step 2: Create a New Category

- Click on the "Categorize" button in the "Tags" group.

- Select "All Categories" from the drop-down menu.

Categorize button

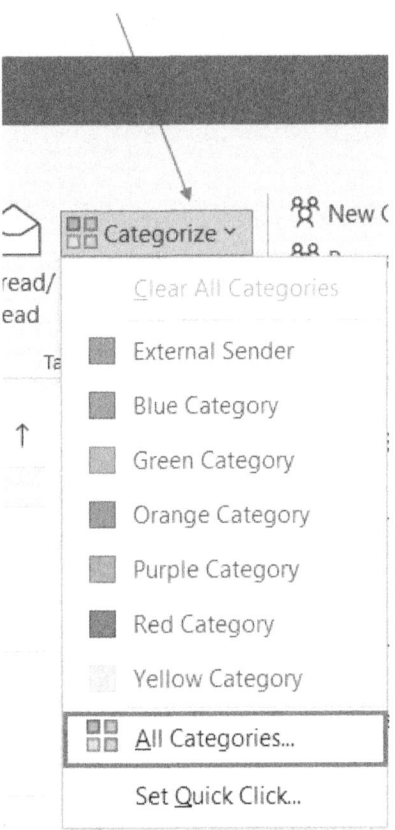

- Click on "New" to create a new category.

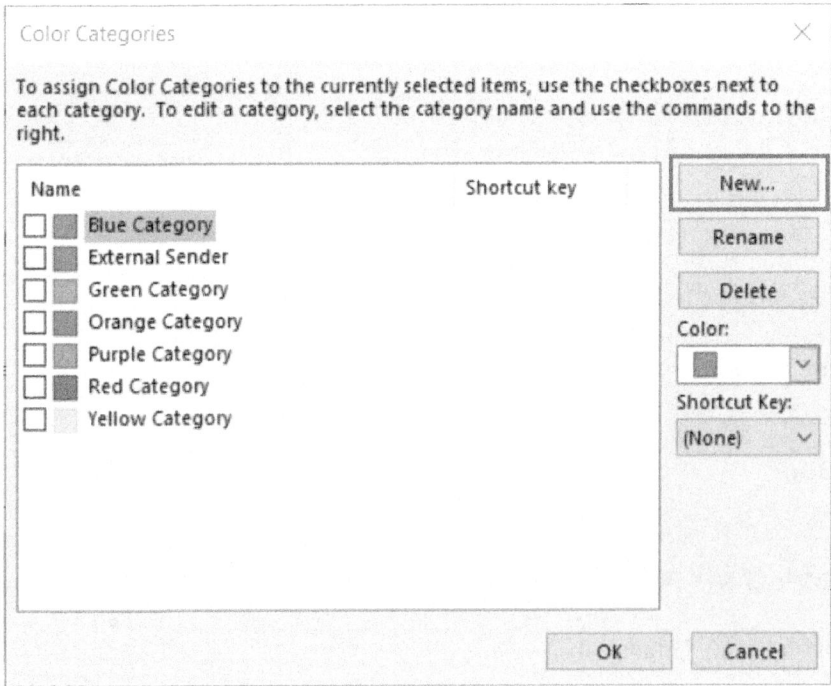

- Enter a name for the category and choose a colour.

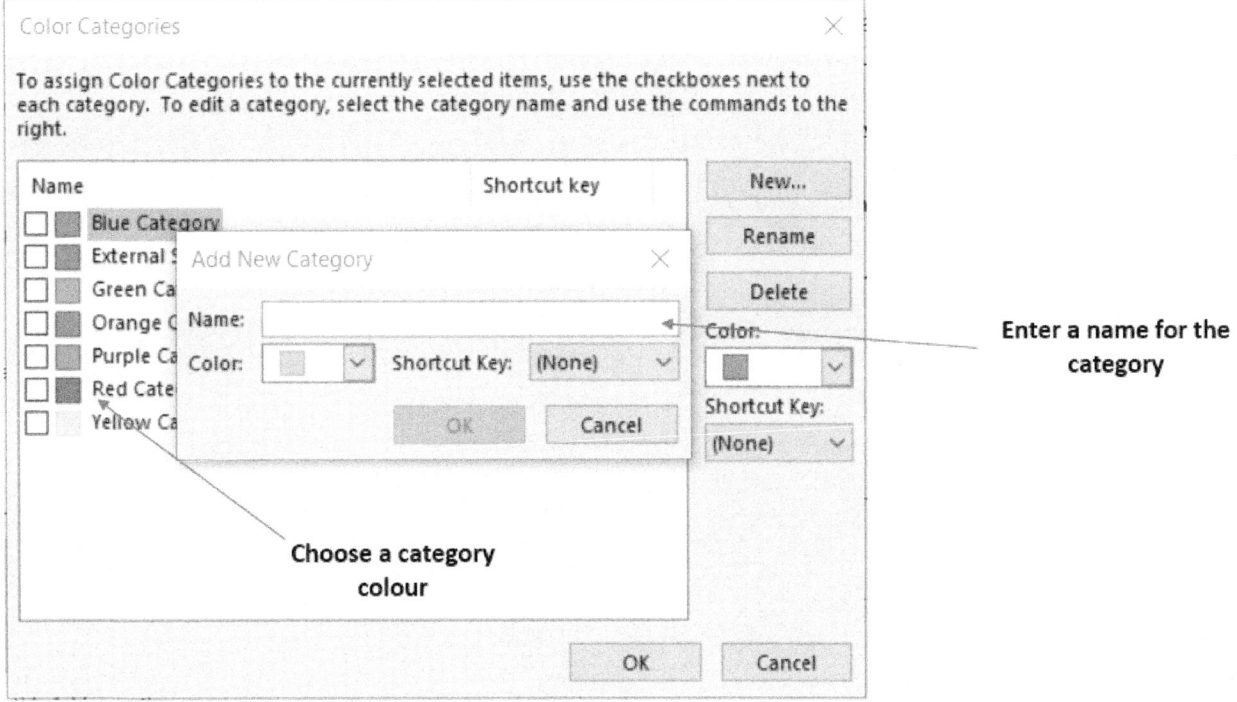

- Click "OK" to save the new category.

Step 3: Assign Categories to Multiple Items

- To assign the same category to multiple items, select all the items you want to categorise (use Ctrl or Shift for multiple selections).

- Click on the "Categorize" button in the "Tags" group.

- Choose the desired category from the list.

Step 4: Filter and Group Items by Categories (Optional)

- Go to the "View" tab on the Outlook Ribbon.

- In the "Arrangement" group, select the category or categories you want to filter or group by.

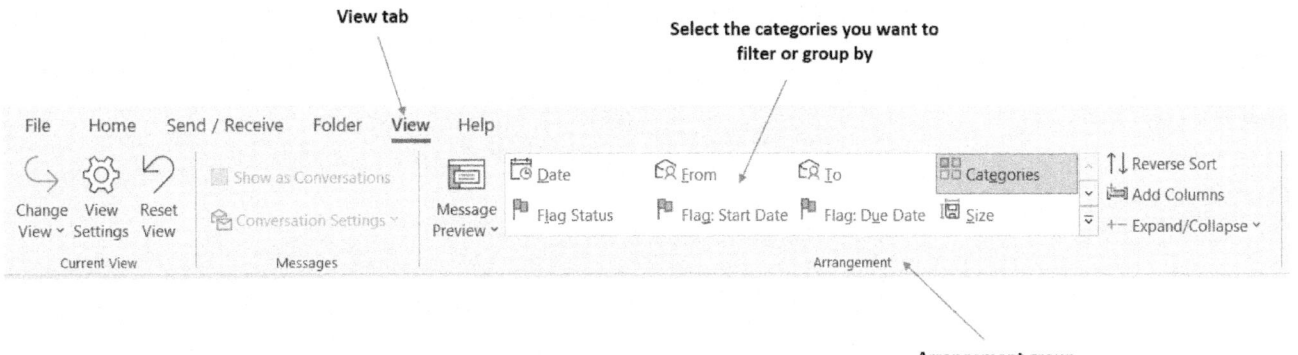

Step 5: Manage Categories (Optional)

- To manage categories, go to the "Categorize" button in the "Tags" group.

- Select "All Categories" from the drop-down menu.

- To rename categories, select a category and then click the "Rename" button and enter the new name.

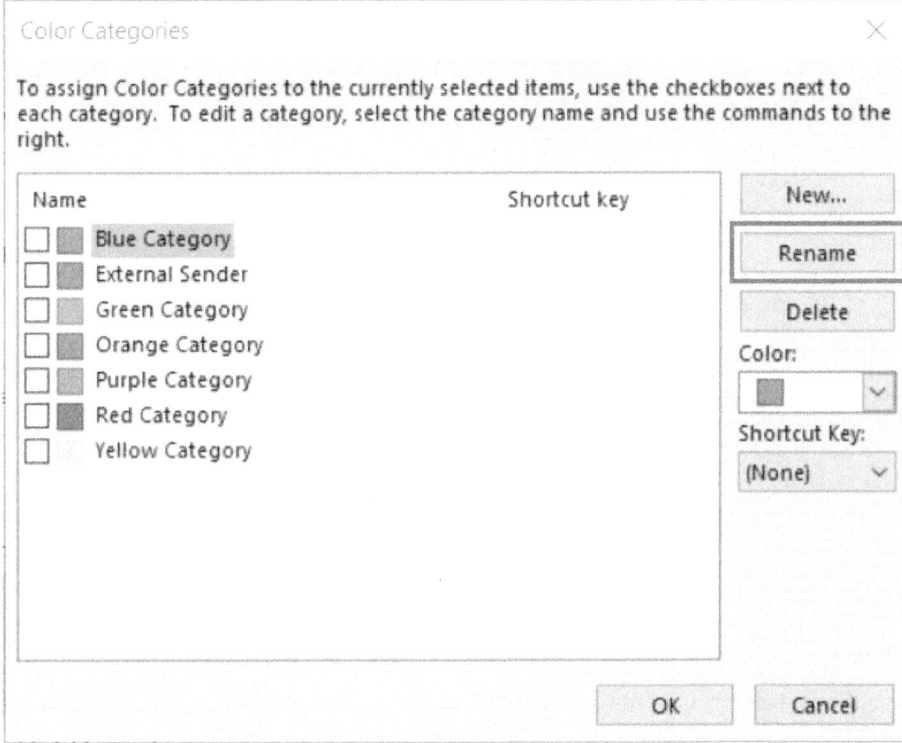

- To change category colours, select a category, click on the "Color" drop-down box, and choose a new colour.

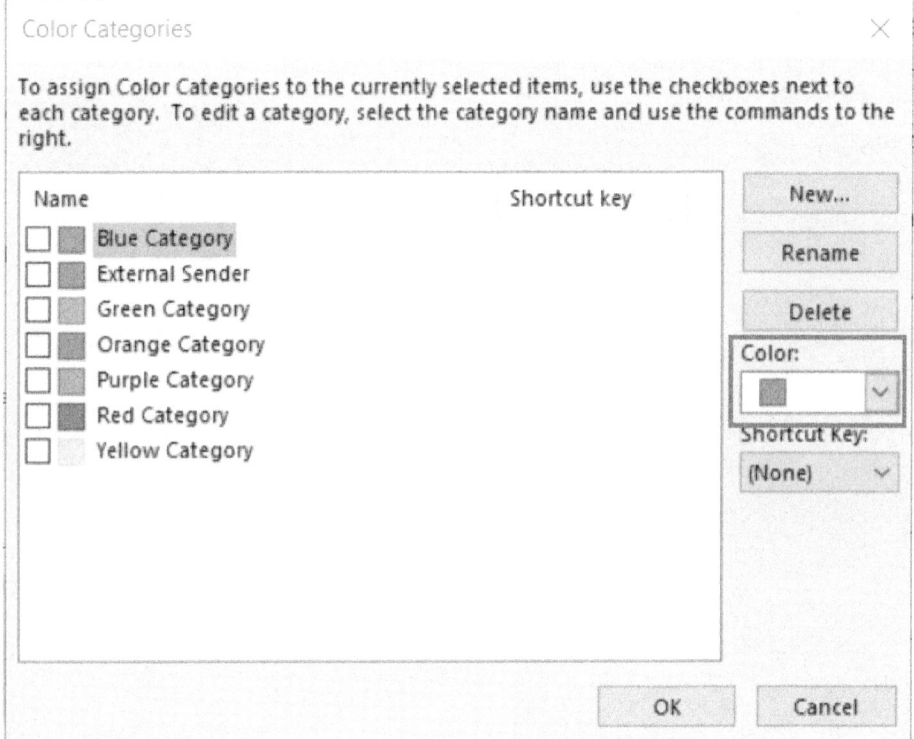

- To delete categories, select a category and then click the "Delete" button.

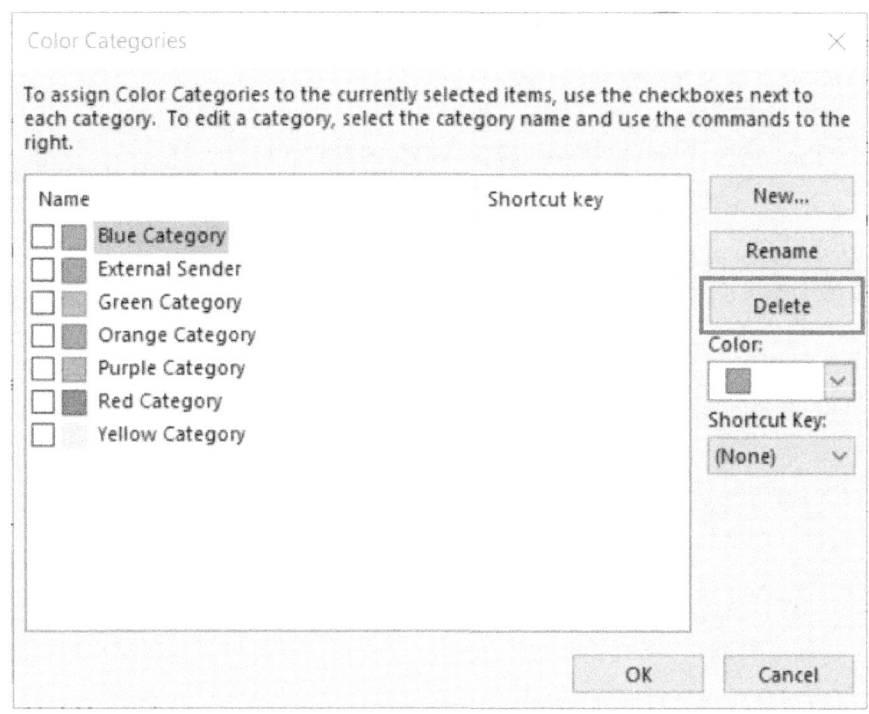

Folders and categories in Microsoft Outlook are powerful tools that enable users to effectively organise and manage their emails, calendar events, contacts, and tasks. By following the step-by-step instructions provided in this section, users can create folders, move items, and organise their information based on their preferences and needs. Additionally, by using categories, users can assign colours to items, group, and filter information, and streamline their organisation process. Outlook's folder and category features contribute to enhanced productivity, easy access to information, and a well-organised and clutter-free email inbox and other data.

5.6 Calendars and Scheduling in Microsoft Outlook

Calendars and scheduling are essential features in Microsoft Outlook that help users manage their time, appointments, meetings, and events effectively. Outlook's calendar feature allows users to organise their schedules, set reminders, and stay on top of their commitments. In this section, we will explore how to use calendars and schedule events in Outlook, providing step-by-step instructions for efficient time management.

5.6.1 Accessing the Calendar in Outlook

Step 1: Open Microsoft Outlook

- Launch Microsoft Outlook on your computer by clicking on the Outlook icon or searching for "Microsoft Outlook" in your operating system's search bar.

Step 2: Navigate to the Calendar

- In the bottom left corner of the Outlook window, click on the "Calendar" icon.

5.6.2 Creating and Scheduling Events

Step 1: Create a New Event

- In the calendar view, go to the date when you want to schedule an event.

- In the "Home" tab click on "New Appointment" in the "New" group to open the Appointment window.

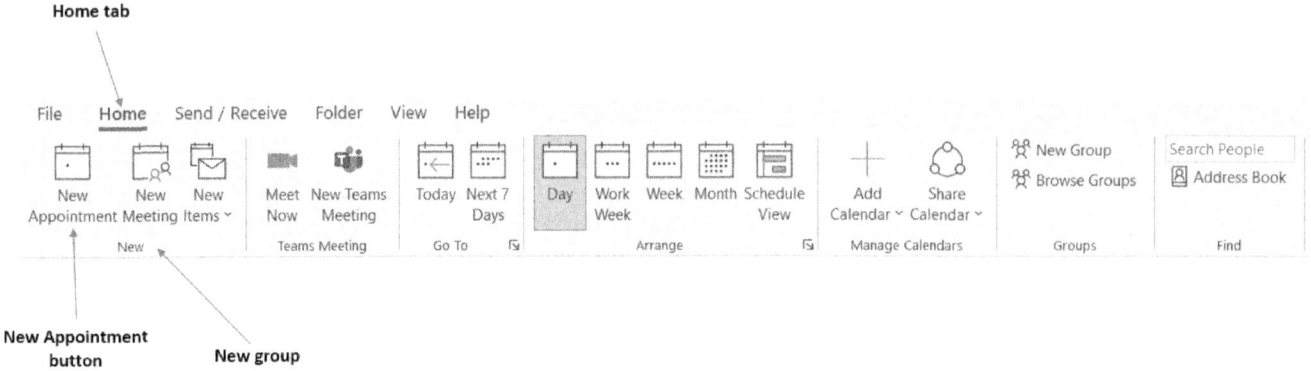

Step 2: Add Event Details

- Enter the event's subject (e.g., Meeting with Team, Doctor's Appointment).

- Specify the start date and time.

- Set the end date and time (if the event has a specific duration).

- Choose the appropriate time zone (if necessary).

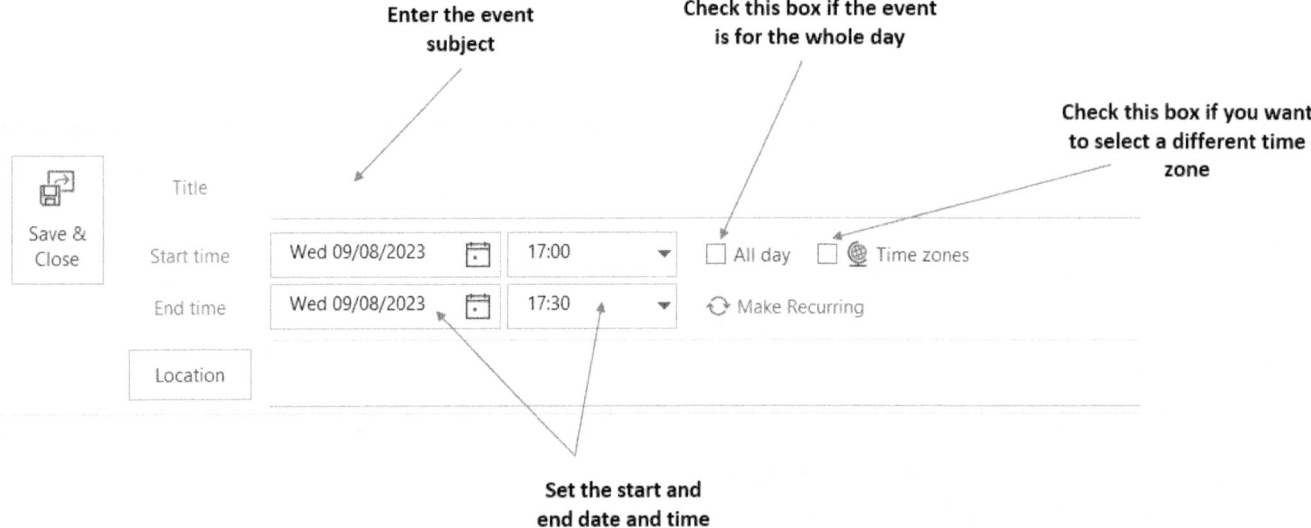

Step 3: Set a Reminder (Optional)

- To set a reminder for the event, click on the "Reminder" drop-down menu in the top menu.

- Choose the desired time before the event when you want to be reminded (e.g., 15 minutes, 1 hour).

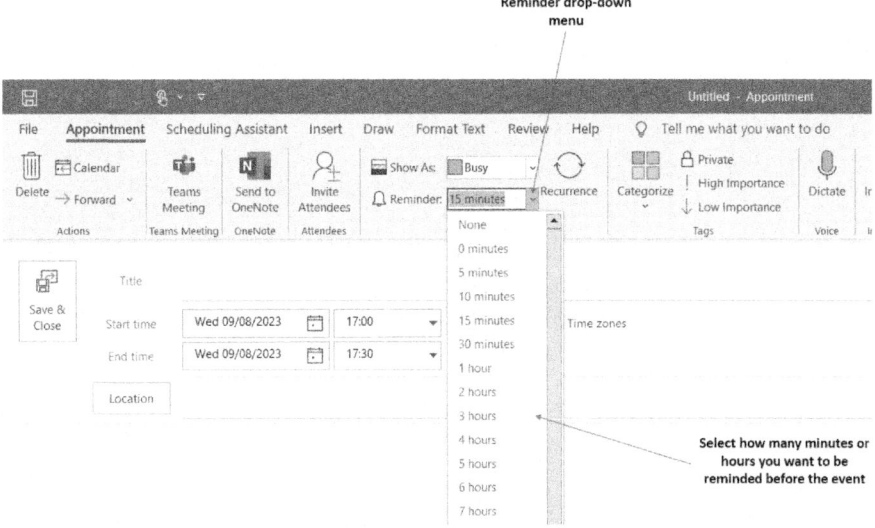

Step 4: Add a Location (Optional)

- If the event has a physical location, enter the address in the "Location" field.

Step 5: Categorise the Event (Optional)

- Click on the "Categorize" button in the "Appointment" tab.

- Choose a colour category to categorise the event.

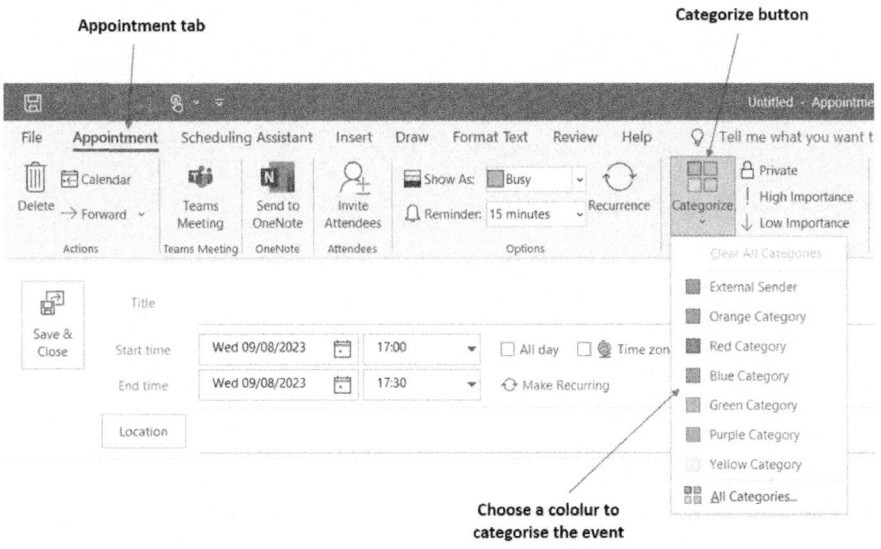

Step 6: Save the Event

- Click on the "Save & Close" button to save the event to your calendar.

5.6.3 Editing and Deleting Events

Step 1: Edit an Event

- Double-click on the event you want to edit in the calendar view.

- Make the necessary changes in the "Appointment" window (e.g., update the subject, date, time, location).

- Click on the "Save & Close" button to save the changes.

Step 2: Delete an Event

- Right-click on the event in the calendar view.

- Select "Delete" from the context menu to remove the event from your calendar.

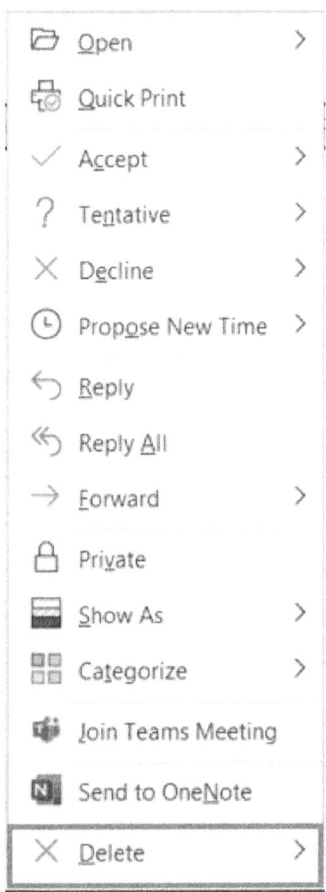

5.6.4 View and Manage Multiple Calendars

Step 1: Overlay Calendars

- Go to the "View" tab in the top menu.

- Click on the "Overlay" button in the "Arrangement" group.

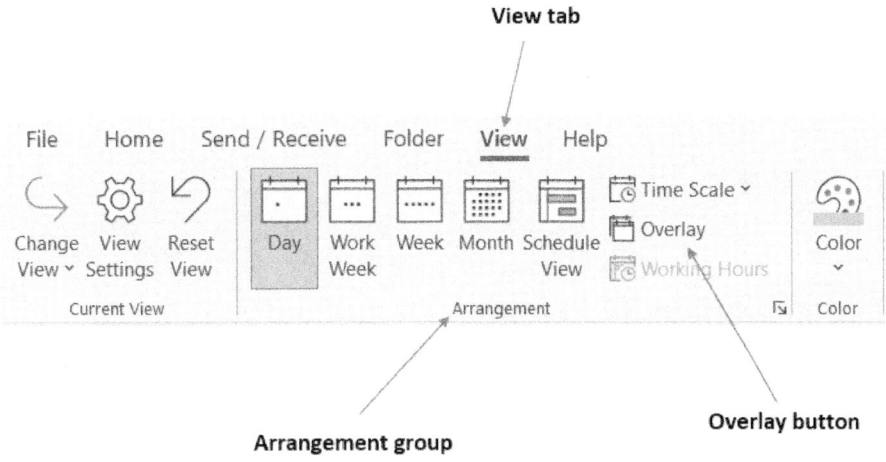

View tab

Arrangement group

Overlay button

- Choose the calendars you want to overlay.

Step 2: Manage Calendar Permissions (Optional)

- Go to the "File" tab in the top left corner.

- Select "Options" from the menu.

- Click on "Calendar" in the Outlook Options window.

- Under the "Calendar options" section, click on "Free/Busy Options".

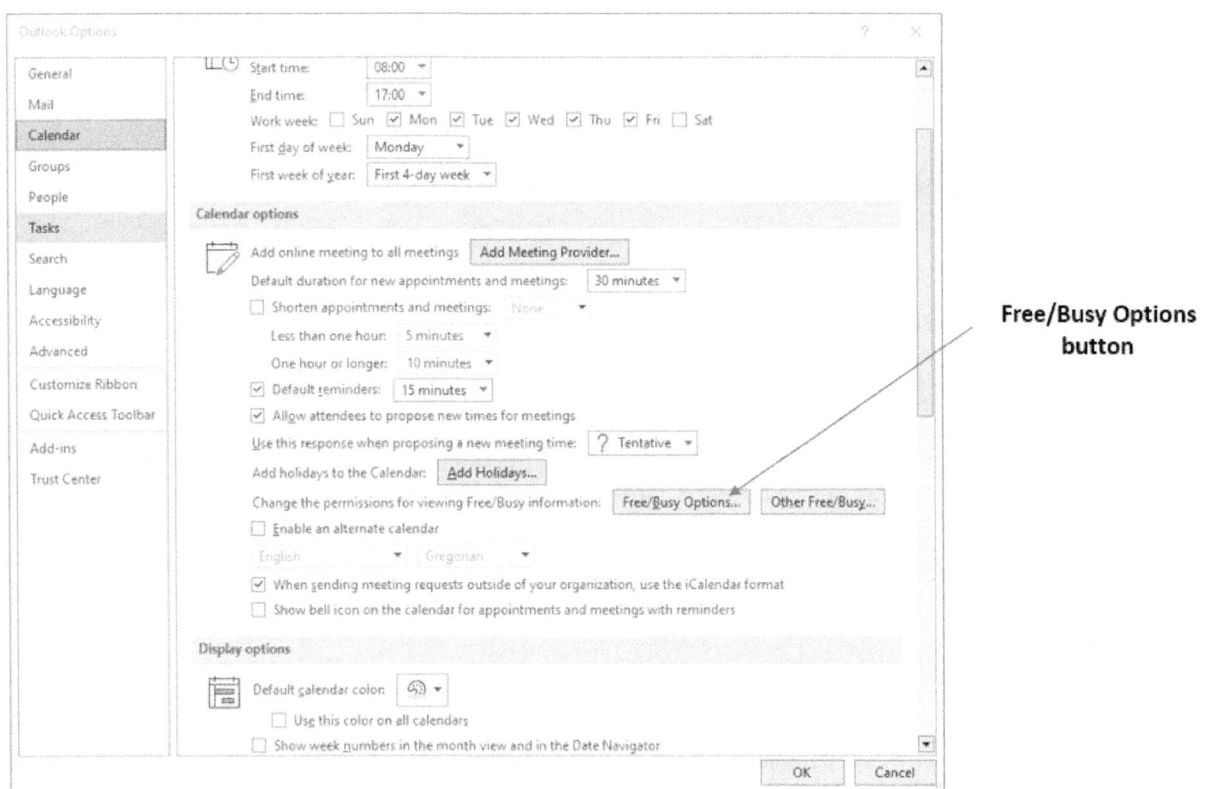

Free/Busy Options button

- Select the appropriate permission you want to give under "Permissions" then press the "OK" button.

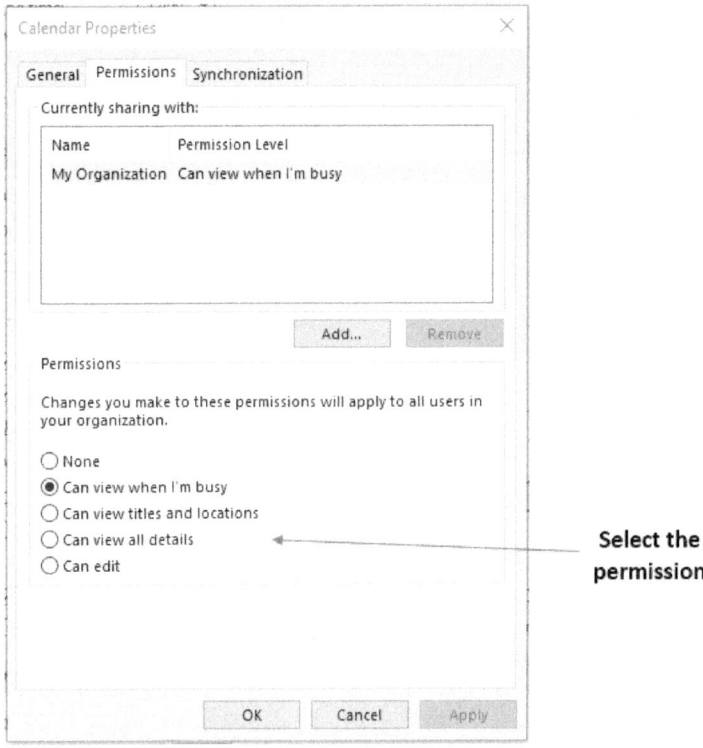

Step 3: Share Your Calendar (Optional)

- In the calendar view, click on the "Share Calendar" button in the "Home" tab.

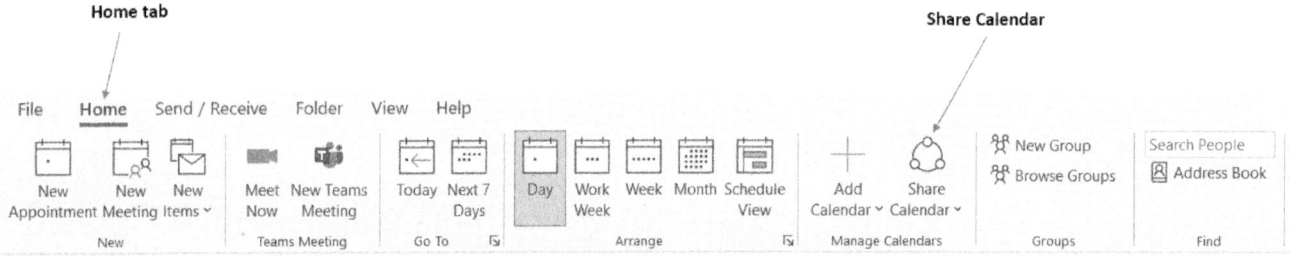

- Choose the desired sharing method (e.g., email, web page) and follow the on-screen instructions.

Calendars and scheduling in Microsoft Outlook provide users with powerful tools for effective time management and organising events. By following the step-by-step instructions provided in this section, users can easily create, schedule, edit, and delete events in their Outlook calendars. The ability to categorise events, set reminders, and manage multiple calendars allows users to stay organised, be on time, and optimise their productivity. With Outlook's calendar and scheduling features, users can streamline their daily activities, appointments, and meetings, ensuring they stay on top of their commitments and never miss an important event.

5.7 Contacts and People in Microsoft Outlook

Contacts and People in Microsoft Outlook provide users with a centralised and organised way to store and manage their contact information. Outlook's Contacts feature allows users to maintain a list of individuals' names, email addresses, phone numbers, and other relevant details. In this section, we will explore how to use Contacts and People in Outlook, providing step-by-step instructions for efficient contact management.

5.7.1 Accessing Contacts and People in Outlook

Step 1: Open Microsoft Outlook

- Launch Microsoft Outlook on your computer by clicking on the Outlook icon or searching for "Microsoft Outlook" in your operating system's search bar.

Step 2: Navigate to Contacts or People

- In the bottom left corner of the Outlook window, click on the "Contacts" icon to access the Contacts view.

5.7.2 Adding a New Contact

Step 1: Create a New Contact

- In the Contacts view, click on the "New Contact" button in the "Home" tab.

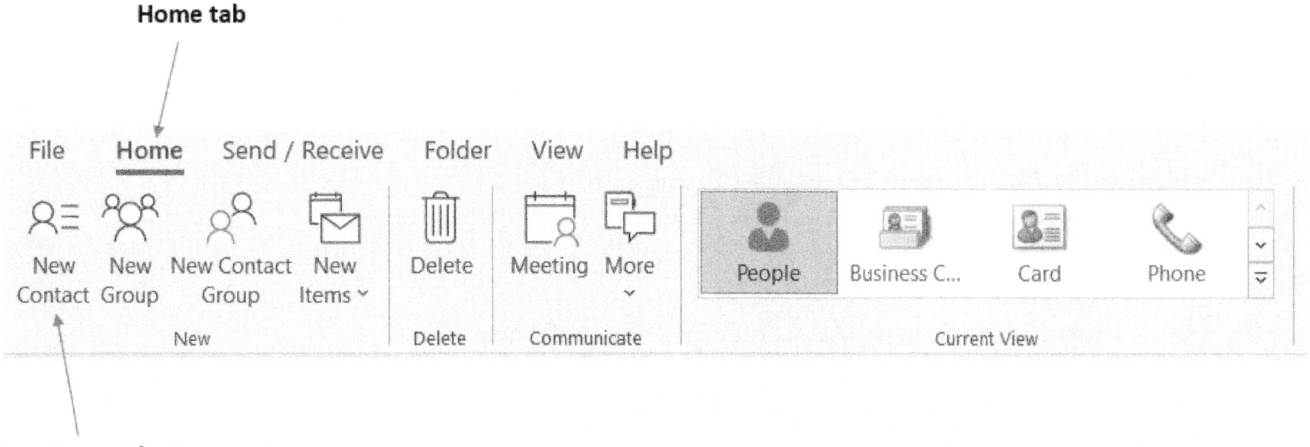

Step 2: Enter Contact Details

- Fill in the contact's name, email address, phone number, and other relevant information in the provided fields.

Step 3: Save the Contact

- Click on the "Save & Close" button to save the new contact in your Outlook Contacts.

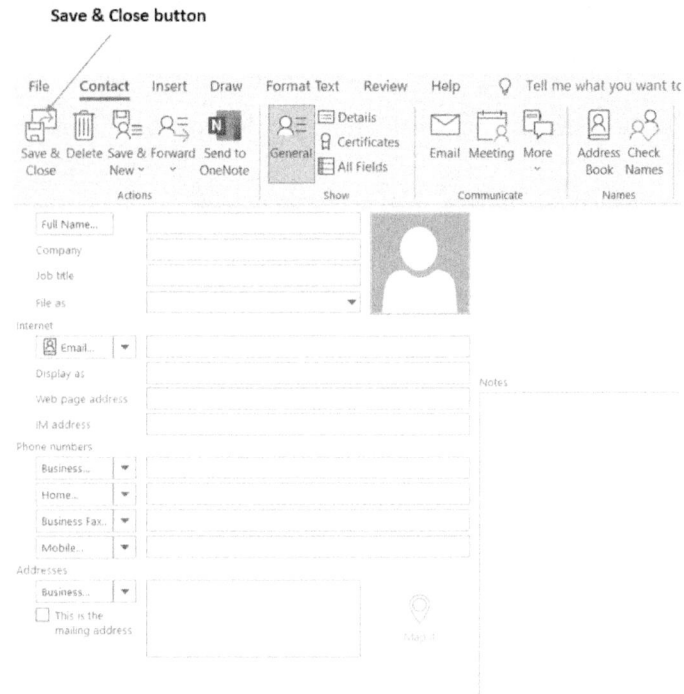

5.7.3 Editing and Deleting Contacts

Step 1: Edit a Contact

- In the Contacts view, locate the contact you want to edit.

- Double-click on the contact's name to open the "Contact Card".

Step 2: Modify Contact Details

- Make the necessary changes to the contact's information in the "Contact Card".

- Click on the "Save & Close" button to save the updated contact.

Step 3: Delete a Contact

- In the Contacts view, find the contact you want to delete.

- Right-click on the contact's name and select "Delete".

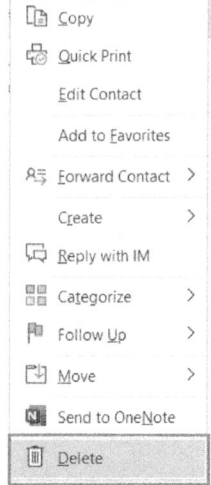

5.7.4 Categorising and Organising Contacts

Step 1: Categorise a Contact (Optional)

- In the Contacts view, select the contact you want to categorise.

- In the "Home" tab, go to the "Categorize" button in the "Tags" group.

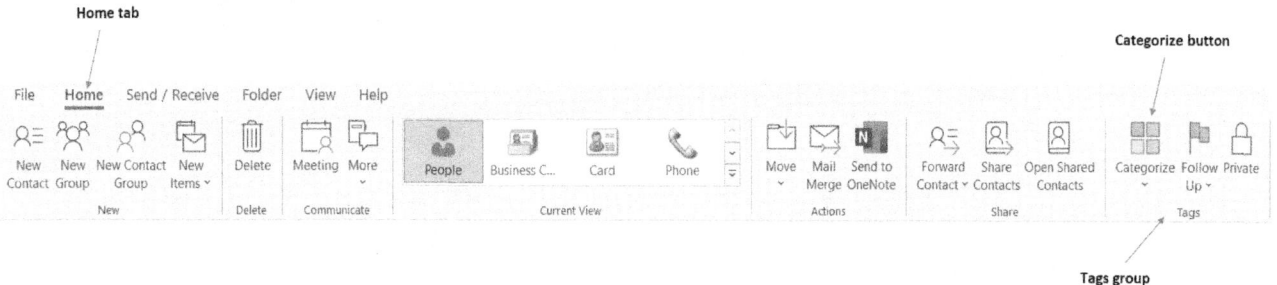

Step 2: Choose a Category

- Click on the "Categorize" button, and a list of available colour categories will appear.

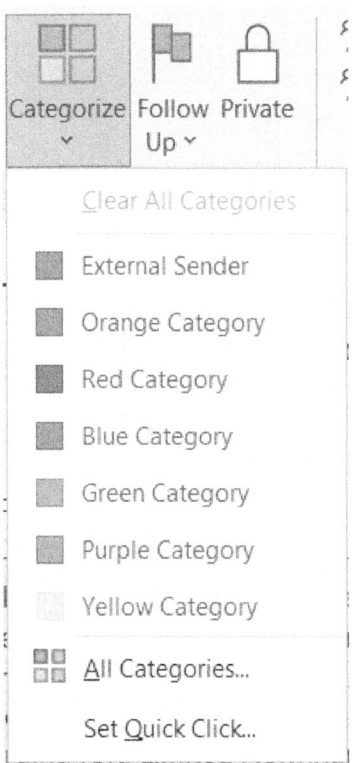

- Select the appropriate category for the contact.

Step 3: Organise Contacts into Folders (Optional)

- In the Contacts view, right-click on a contact.

- Choose "Move" from the context menu and select the desired folder to move the contact to.

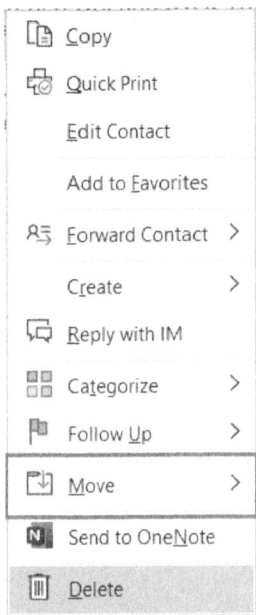

5.7.5 Searching and Filtering Contacts

Step 1: Search for a Contact

- In the Contacts view, use the search bar at the top of the window.

Search bar

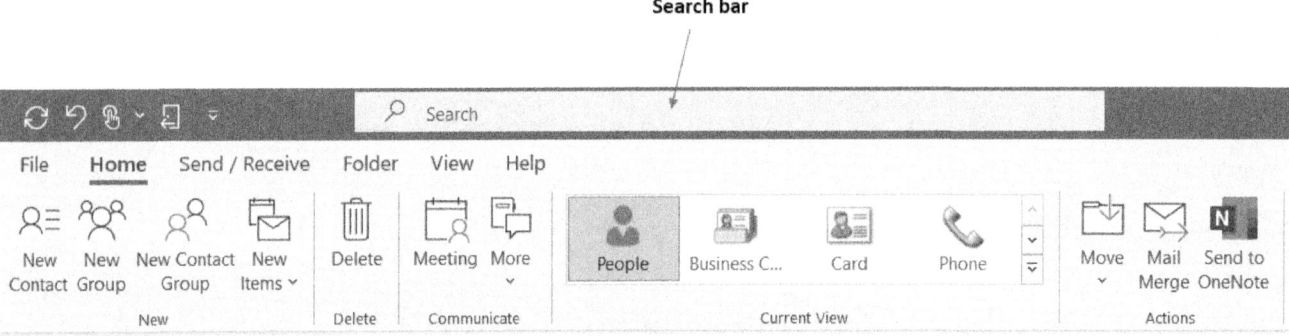

- Type the name or any relevant information about the contact.

Step 2: Filter Contacts (Optional)

- In the "Home" tab, click on the "Filter" button in the "Current View" group.

Home tab

Filter buttons

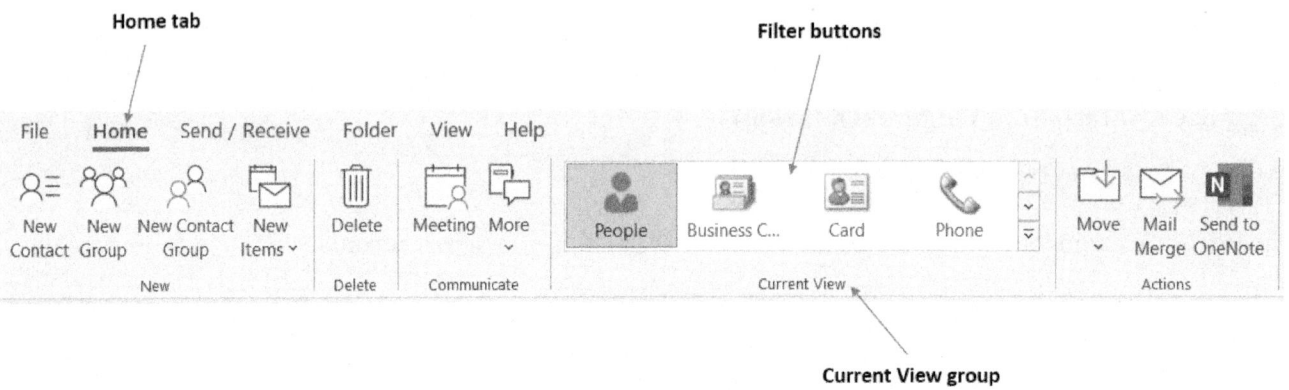

Current View group

- Choose the filtering options to display contacts based on specific criteria.

Contacts and People in Microsoft Outlook offer a convenient and organised way to manage contact information. By following the step-by-step instructions provided in this section, users can easily add, edit, and delete contacts, as well as categorise and organise them. Outlook's Contacts features streamline contact management, ensuring that users have quick access to essential contact information whenever they need it. Whether for personal or professional use, Outlook's contact management capabilities help users maintain an updated and well-organised list of contacts for effective communication and collaboration.

5.8 Using Tasks and Notes in Microsoft Outlook

Tasks and Notes in Microsoft Outlook are valuable features for managing to-do lists, setting reminders, and jotting down important information. Outlook's Tasks feature allows users to create and track tasks, while Notes provide a space for quick notetaking and organising thoughts. In this section, we will explore how to use Tasks and Notes in Outlook, providing step-by-step instructions for effective task management and note-taking.

5.8.1 Accessing Tasks and Notes in Outlook

Step 1: Open Microsoft Outlook

- Launch Microsoft Outlook on your computer by clicking on the Outlook icon or searching for "Microsoft Outlook" in your operating system's search bar.

Step 2: Navigate to Tasks or Notes

- In the bottom left corner of the Outlook window, click on the "Tasks" icon to access the Tasks view.

- Alternatively, click on the ellipsis in the bottom left corner and then on "Notes" in the "Navigation Options" menu to access the Notes view.

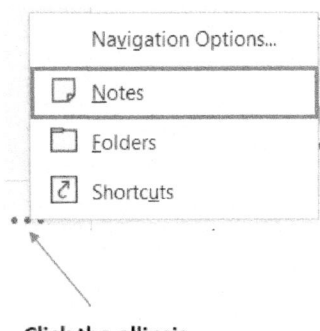

Click the ellipsis

5.8.2 Using Tasks in Outlook

Step 1: Create a New Task

- In the Tasks view, click on the "New Task" button.

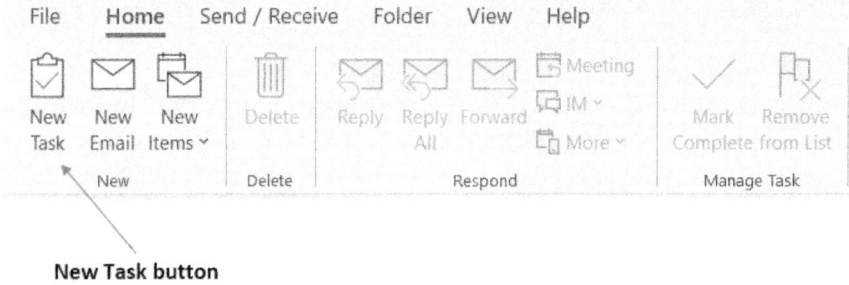

New Task button

Step 2: Enter Task Details

- Enter the task's subject or title in the provided field.

- Set the start and due dates for the task (if applicable).

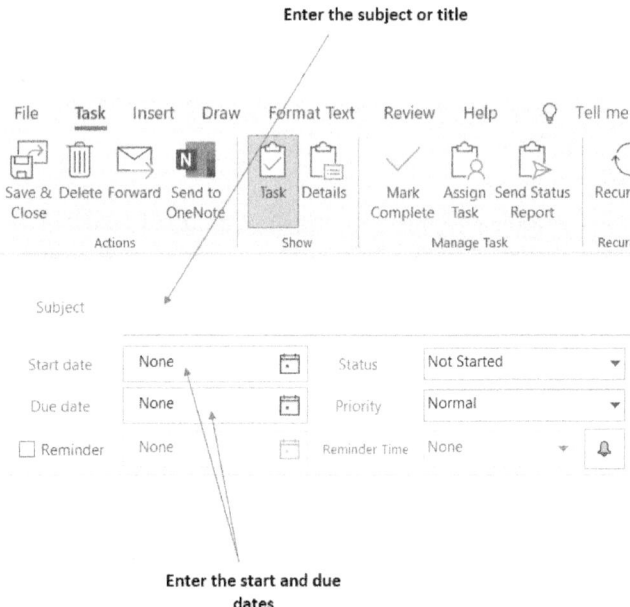

Enter the subject or title

Enter the start and due dates

Step 3: Set Task Priority (Optional)

- Use the "Priority" drop-down menu to select the priority level of the task (e.g., High, Normal, Low).

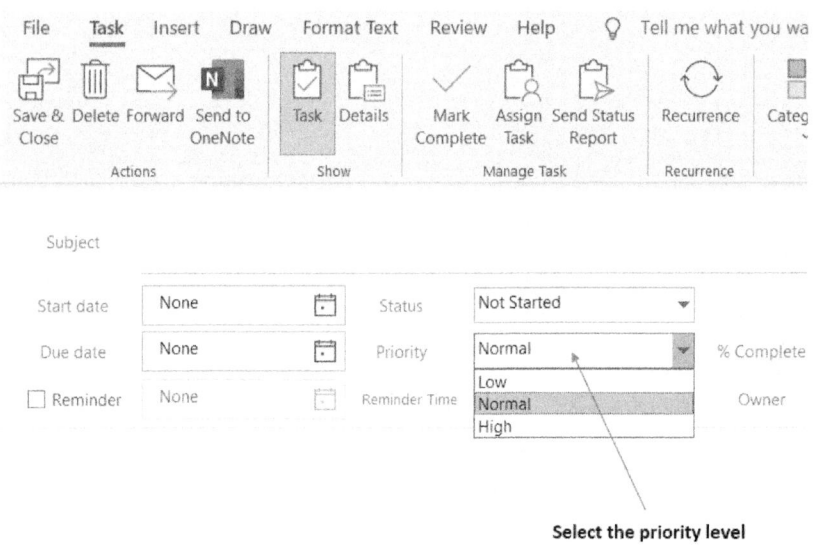

Select the priority level

Step 4: Add Task Notes (Optional)

- Use the "Notes" field to add any additional information or details related to the task.

Step 5: Save the Task

- Click on the "Save & Close" button to save the new task in your Outlook Tasks.

5.8.3 Editing and Deleting Tasks

Step 1: Edit a Task

- In the Tasks view, locate the task you want to edit.

- Double-click on the task to open the "Task" window.

Step 2: Modify Task Details

- Make the necessary changes to the task's information in the "Task" window.

- Click on the "Save & Close" button to save the updated task.

Step 3: Delete a Task

- In the Tasks view, find the task you want to delete.

- Right-click on the task and select "Delete".

5.8.4 Using Notes in Outlook

Step 1: Create a New Note

- In the Notes view, click on the "New Note" button.

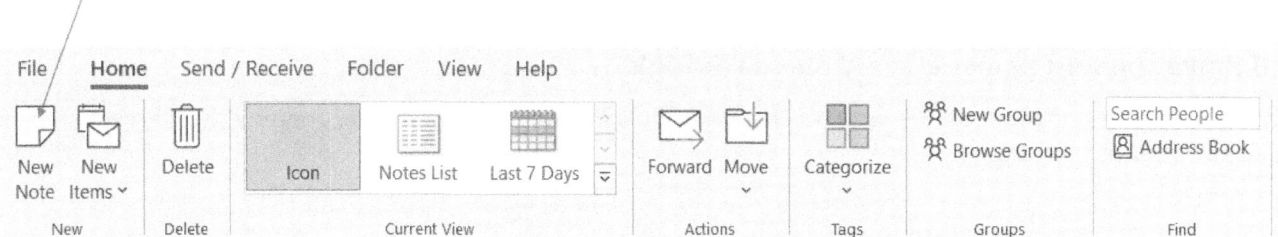

Step 2: Enter Note Content

- Type your notes or information in the provided space.

Step 3: Save the Note

- Click on the "X" on the top right corner of the note to close it. The note will automatically be saved in your Outlook Notes.

5.8.5 Editing and Deleting Notes

Step 1: Edit a Note

- In the Notes view, locate the note you want to edit.

- Double-click on the note to open the "Note" window.

Step 2: Modify Note Content

- Make the necessary changes to the note's content in the "Note" window.

- Click on the "X" on the top right corner of the note to save the updated note.

Step 3: Delete a Note

- In the Notes view, find the note you want to delete.

- Right-click on the note and select "Delete".

Tasks and Notes in Microsoft Outlook offer users' convenient tools for managing to-do lists, setting reminders, and jotting down important information. By following the step-by-step instructions provided in this section, users can easily create, edit, and delete tasks and notes in Outlook. With the Tasks feature, users can efficiently track and prioritise their tasks, ensuring they stay on top of their commitments. On the other hand, Notes provide a quick and accessible space for jotting down thoughts and information. Both Tasks and Notes contribute to enhanced productivity and organisation, helping users stay on track and keep important information at their fingertips.

5.9 Collaboration and Sharing in Microsoft Outlook

Collaboration and sharing in Microsoft Outlook enable users to work together, share information, and stay connected with colleagues, friends, and family. Outlook offers various collaboration features that allow users to share emails, calendars, contacts, and tasks, facilitating seamless teamwork and efficient communication. In this chapter, we will explore how to collaborate and share information in Outlook, providing step-by-step instructions for each process.

5.9.1 Collaboration and Sharing Features in Outlook

Sharing Email Folders: Outlook allows users to share specific email folders with others, granting them access to view, edit, or manage the shared emails.

Sharing Calendars: Users can share their Outlook calendars with others, enabling them to view and even edit calendar events and appointments.

Sharing Contacts: Outlook facilitates the sharing of contact lists, making it easier for teams and groups to access essential contact information.

Assigning Tasks: Users can assign tasks to others and track their progress, promoting effective task management and collaboration.

5.9.2 Step-by-Step Instructions for Collaboration and Sharing in Outlook

Step 1: Share Email Folders

- Open Outlook and go to the "Mail" view.

- Right-click on the email folder you want to share (e.g., Inbox, Sent Items).

- Select "Share" from the context menu, then choose "Share [Folder Name]".

- In the "Properties" window, click on the "Add" button to select the people you want to share the folder with.

- Choose the desired permission level for the shared folder (e.g., "Editor" to allow editing, "Reviewer" for read-only access).

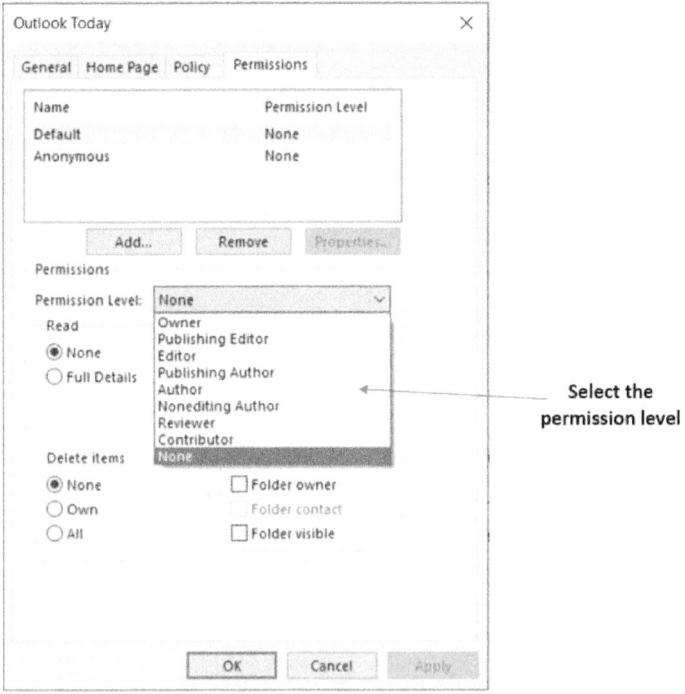

Select the
permission level

- Optionally, add a message to the invitation.

- Click "Send" to send the sharing invitation.

Step 2: Share Calendars

- Open Outlook and go to the "Calendar" view.

- Right-click on the calendar you want to share (e.g., "My Calendar").

- Select "Share" from the context menu, then choose "Share Calendar".

- In the "Calendar Properties" window, click on the "Add" button to select the people you want to share the calendar with.

- Choose the desired permission level for the shared calendar (e.g., "Can View All Details" or "Can Edit").

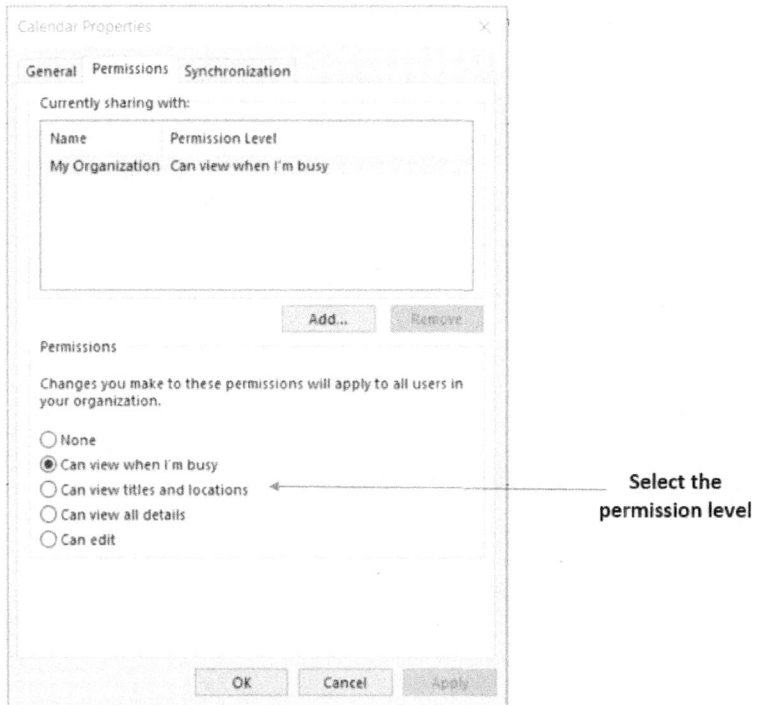

- Optionally, add a message to the invitation.

- Click "Send" to send the sharing invitation.

Step 3: Share Contacts

- Open Outlook and go to the "Contacts" view.

- Select the contact folder you want to share (e.g., "Contacts" or a custom folder).

- Go to the "Home" tab in the top menu.

- Click on the "Forward Contact" button in the "Share" group.

- Choose the sharing method (e.g., "As a Business Card" or "As an Outlook Contact").

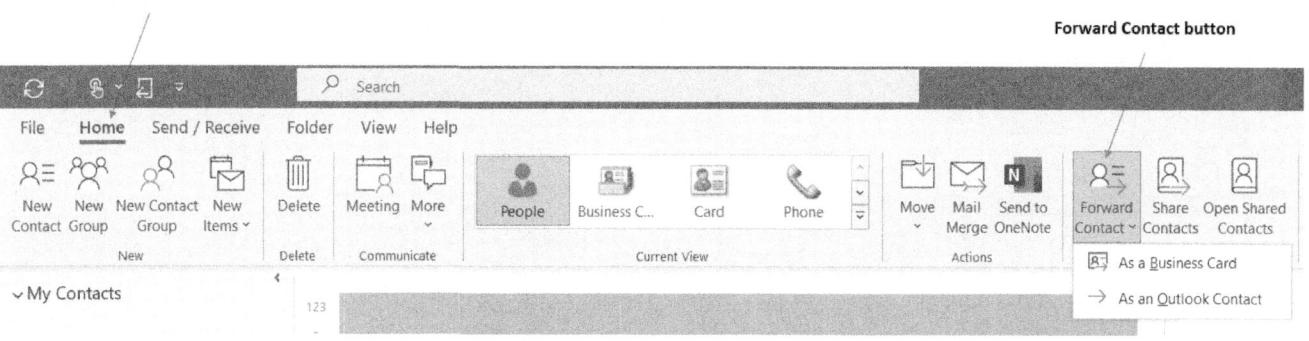

- Enter the recipient's email address or select them from your address book.

- Click "Send" to share the contact(s).

Step 4: Assign Tasks

- Open Outlook and go to the "Tasks" view.

- Create a new task or select an existing one that you want to assign.

- Go to the "Task" tab in the top menu.

- Click on the "Assign Task" button in the "Manage Task" group.

- Enter the recipient's email address or select them from your address book.

- Optionally, set the due date and add a message to the task assignment.

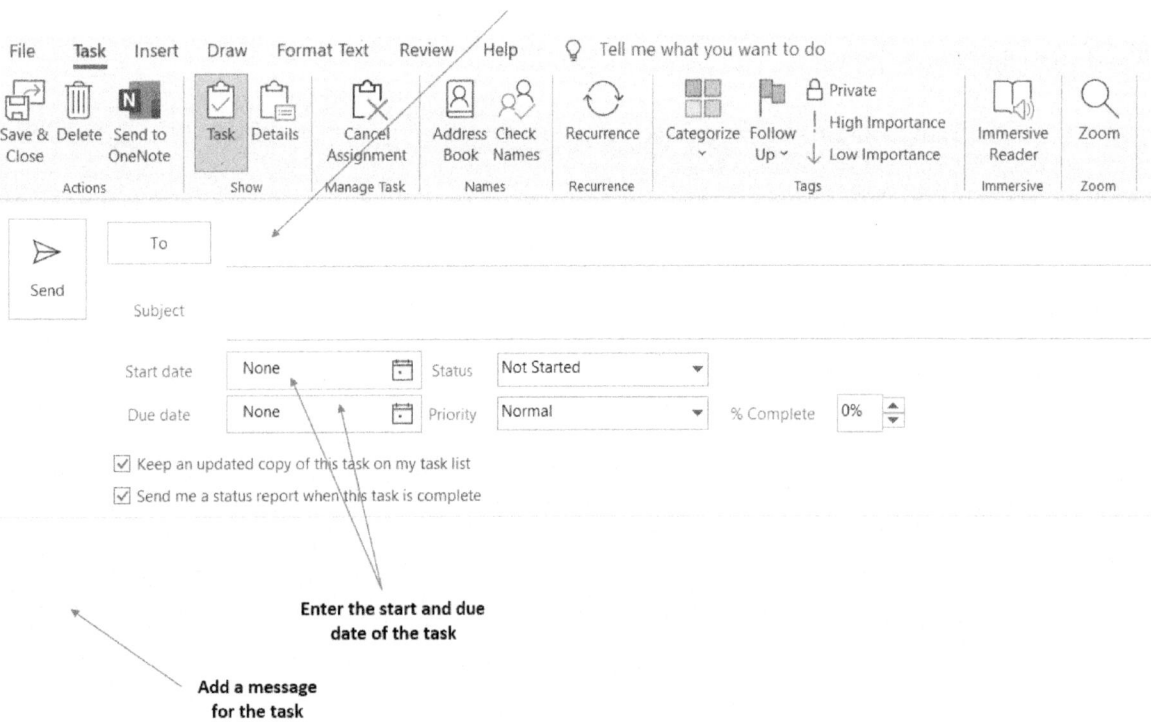

- Click "Send" to assign the task.

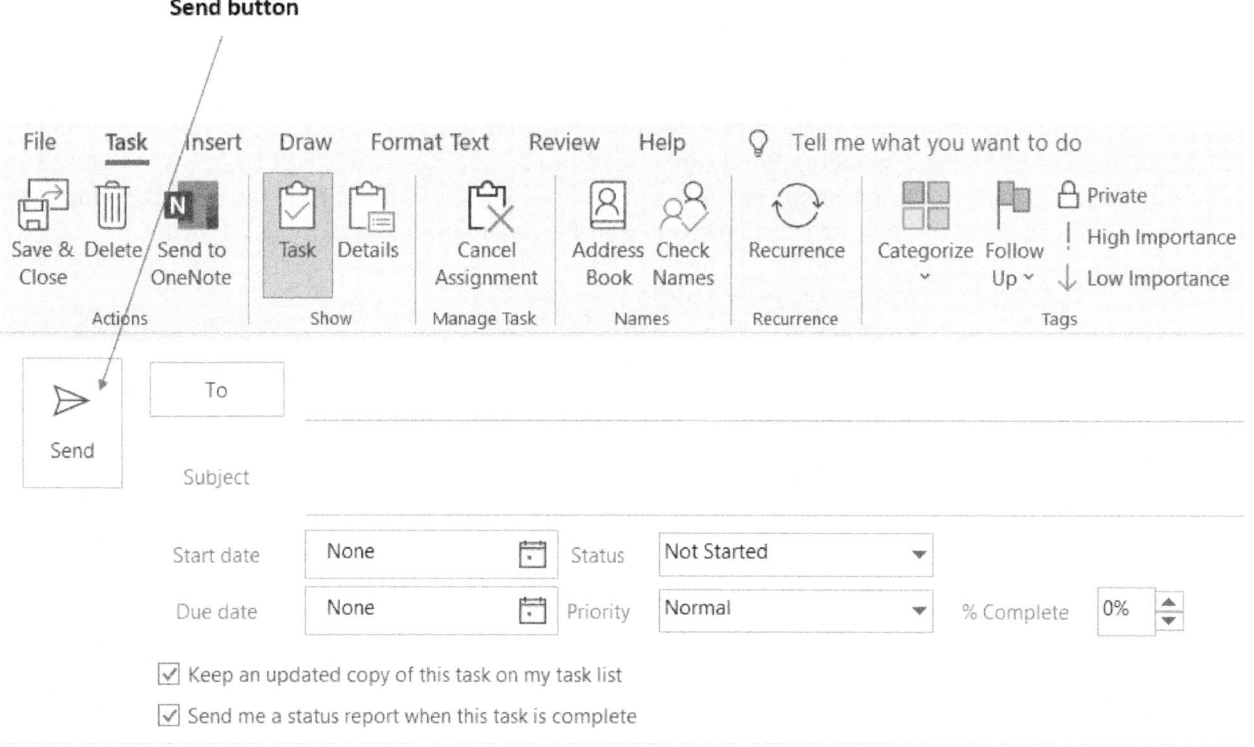

Send button

Step 5: Accept Shared Calendars, Contacts, and Tasks

- When someone shares a calendar, contact, or task with you, you will receive an email invitation.

- Open the email invitation and click "Accept" to access the shared information.

- The shared calendar will be added to your Outlook calendars list, shared contacts will appear in your contacts, and assigned tasks will appear in your tasks list.

Collaboration and sharing in Microsoft Outlook enhance teamwork and communication by allowing users to share emails, calendars, contacts, and tasks with others. By following the step-by-step instructions provided in this section, users can easily collaborate and share information in Outlook, whether it's sharing email folders, assigning tasks, or sharing calendars and contacts. Outlook's collaboration features promote seamless communication, efficient task management, and successful collaboration among individuals and teams, making it a valuable tool for both personal and professional use.

Chapter 6: Microsoft OneNote

Microsoft OneNote is a powerful note-taking and organisational tool developed by Microsoft. It is part of the Microsoft Office suite and is available on various platforms, including Windows, macOS, web, and mobile devices. OneNote is designed to help users capture, organise, and share information in a flexible and intuitive manner. In this chapter, we will explore what OneNote is, what it is used for, the benefits of using it, and provide step-by-step instructions on how to use it.

6.1 What is Microsoft OneNote?

Microsoft OneNote is a digital notebook application that allows users to gather and store various types of content, such as text, images, audio, video, and handwritten notes, in a single place. It uses a hierarchical structure based on notebooks, sections, and pages, making it easy to organise and navigate through different pieces of information. OneNote supports freeform notetaking, enabling users to create content on an open canvas and arrange it in a way that suits their preferences.

6.2 What is Microsoft OneNote Used For?

Note-Taking: OneNote serves as an electronic notebook, allowing users to take notes in meetings, classes, or during personal brainstorming sessions.

Organisation: OneNote enables users to organise their notes, ideas, and information into separate notebooks, sections, and pages, making it easy to find and access specific content.

Collaboration: OneNote supports real-time collaboration, allowing multiple users to work together on the same notebook simultaneously. This fosters teamwork and enhances productivity.

Information Collection: Users can clip web pages, articles, and images from the internet directly into OneNote using the web clipper, centralising information for future reference.

To-Do Lists and Task Management: OneNote can be used to create to-do lists, track tasks, and set reminders, helping users stay organised and manage their daily activities efficiently.

Research and Project Planning: OneNote is ideal for research and project planning, allowing users to gather information, create outlines, and organise resources in a structured manner.

Digital Sketching and Handwriting: OneNote supports digital inking, making it an excellent tool for sketching, handwriting, and annotating documents.

6.3 Benefits of Using Microsoft OneNote

Versatility: OneNote's flexible structure accommodates various content types, making it suitable for different tasks, such as note-taking, planning, and research.

Accessibility: OneNote is available on multiple platforms, including desktop, web, and mobile devices, allowing users to access their notes from anywhere with internet connectivity.

Integration: OneNote integrates seamlessly with other Microsoft Office applications, enhancing workflow and productivity.

Syncing and Backup: OneNote syncs automatically across devices, ensuring that users' notes are always up to date. Additionally, cloud storage options provide data backup and security.

Multimedia Support: OneNote's ability to handle various content types, including audio and video recordings, makes it a comprehensive tool for capturing information.

6.4 Creating and Organising Notebooks in Microsoft OneNote

Microsoft OneNote offers a flexible and organised way to create digital notebooks for various purposes. Notebooks in OneNote serve as containers to store related information, and they can be structured into sections and pages, allowing users to manage their content effectively. In this section, we will explore how to create and organise notebooks in OneNote, providing step-by-step instructions to help users get started.

6.4.1 Creating a New Notebook in OneNote

Step 1: Open Microsoft OneNote

- Launch Microsoft OneNote on your computer by clicking on the OneNote icon or searching for "Microsoft OneNote" in your operating system's search bar.

Step 2: Create a New Notebook

- In the OneNote application, go to the left-hand panel, where you will see the list of existing notebooks.

- Click on the "Notebooks" dropdown arrow to reveal the notebook options.

- Click on the "+ Add Notebook" option to create a new notebook.

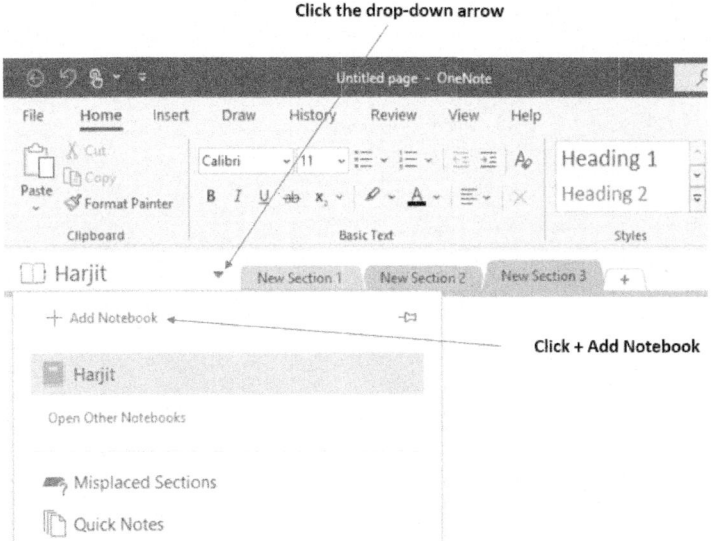

Step 3: Name the New Notebook

- Choose the desired location to save the notebook (e.g., OneDrive, your computer's hard drive).

- Enter the desired name for your notebook (e.g., "Personal Journal," "Project A Notes").

- Click "Create" to create the new notebook.

6.4.2 Organising Notebooks, Sections, and Pages

Step 1: Add Sections to a Notebook

- With your new notebook open, look for the "Add Section" tab located at the top of the application window.

- Click on the "+ Section" button to create a new section within the notebook.

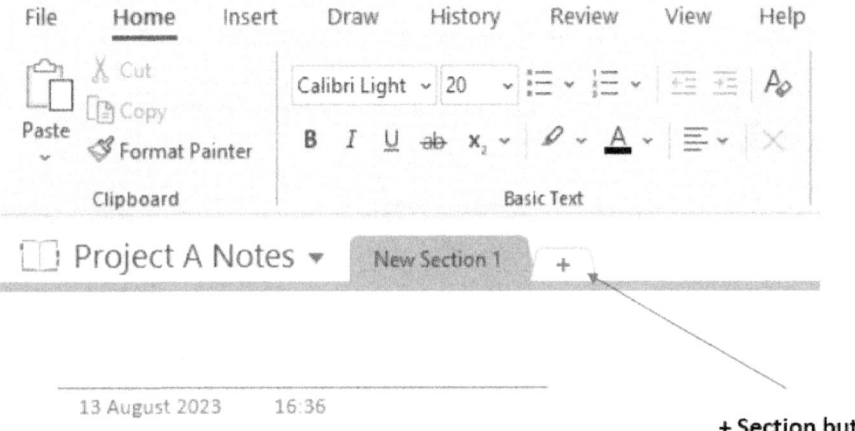

+ Section button

- Name the section appropriately (e.g., "Ideas," "Research," "Meetings").

Step 2: Create Pages within Sections

- Once you have a section created, go to the right-hand panel, where you will see a list of pages under that section.

- Click on the "+ Page" button to add a new page within the section.

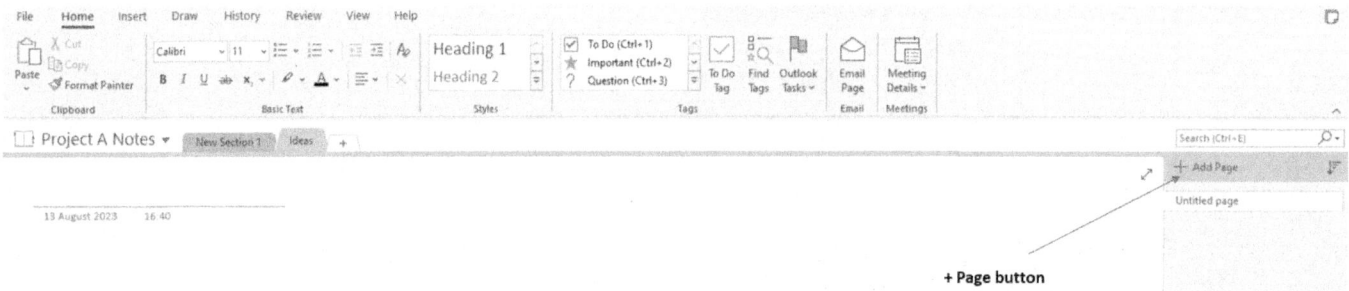

+ Page button

- Name the page accordingly (e.g., "Meeting Notes," "To-Do List").

Step 3: Organise Pages

- To rearrange pages within a section, click on a page and drag it to the desired position.

98

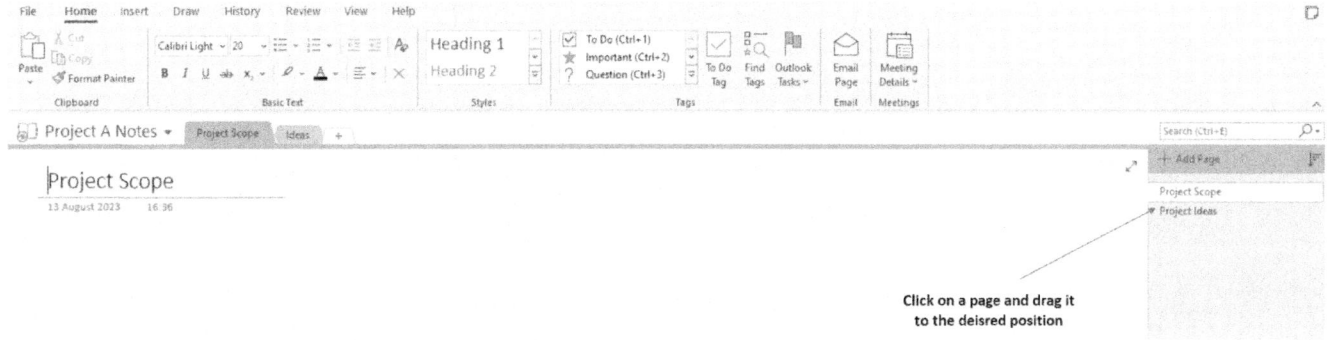

- To move pages between sections, click on a page, drag it to the section's tab, and release it.

Step 4: Group Sections (Optional)

- To create section groups for better organisation, right-click on a section tab.

- Choose "New Section Group" from the context menu.

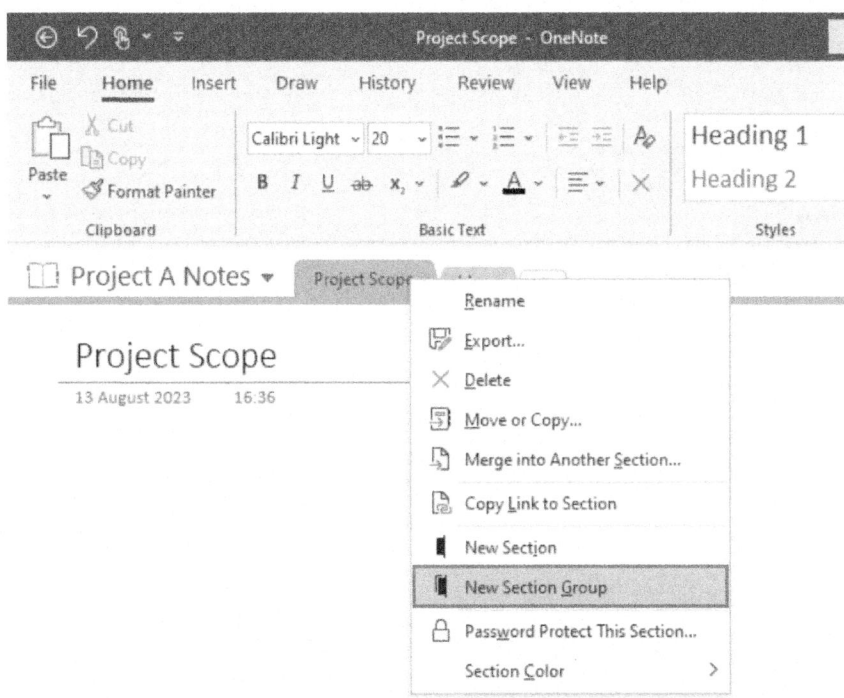

- Name the section group (e.g., "Project A," "Work").

Step 5: Move Sections into Section Groups (Optional)

- To move a section into a section group, click and drag the section tab onto the section group tab.

Step 6: Customise Sections with Colours (Optional)

- Right-click on a section tab and select "Section Colour".

- Choose a colour to assign to the section for visual organisation.

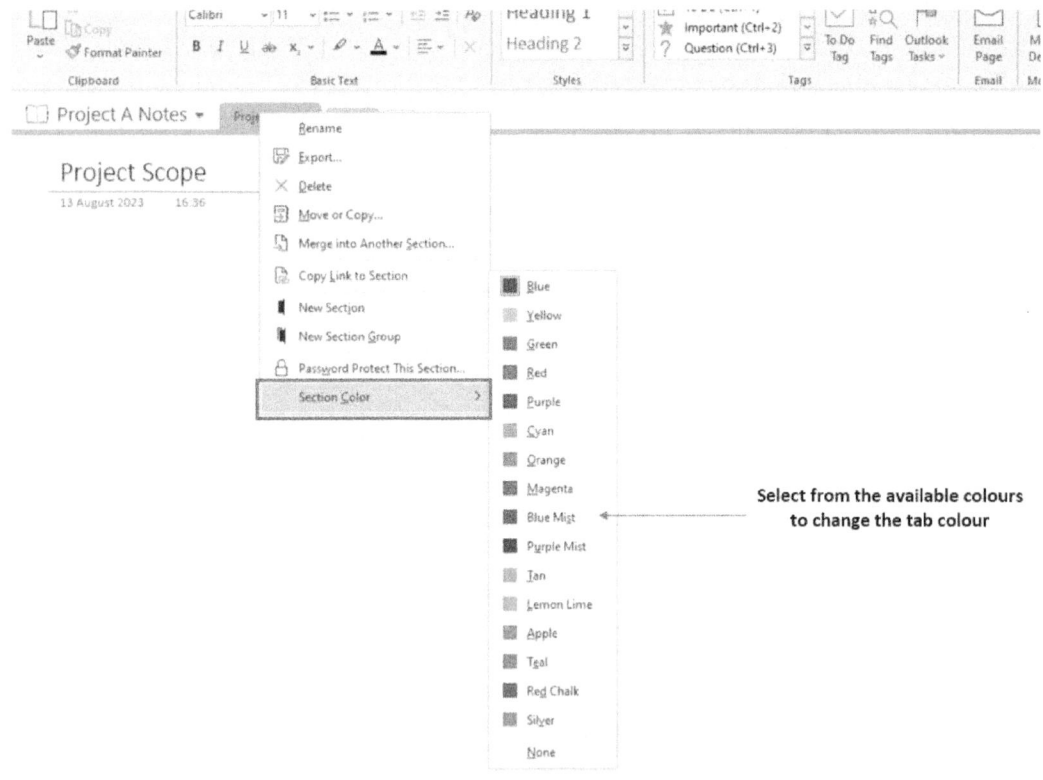

Select from the available colours to change the tab colour

6.4.3 Adding Data to Notebooks, Sections, and Pages

Step 1: Open the Desired Notebook and Section

- Click on the notebook name in the left-hand panel to open it.

- Click on the section tab to view the pages within that section.

Step 2: Add Text to a Page

- Double-click on a page to open it.

- Start typing or paste text onto the page.

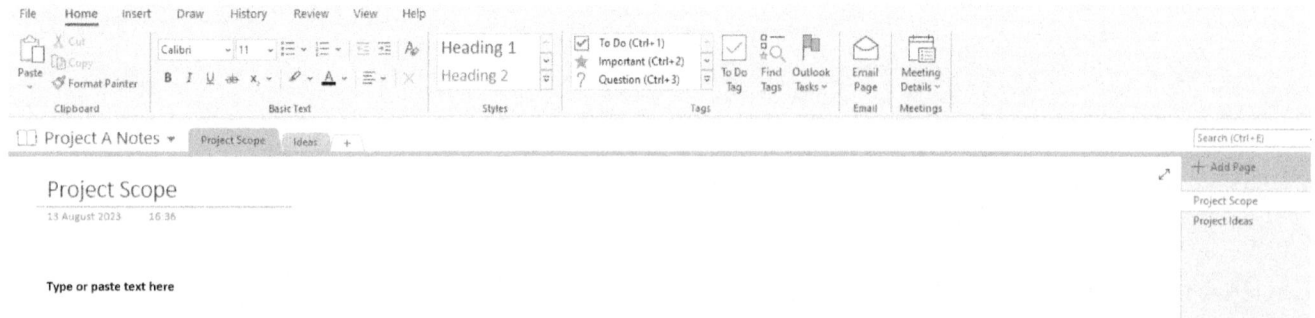

Step 3: Add Handwritten Notes (Optional)

- If using a compatible device, select the "Draw" tab at the top of the application window.

- Choose pen and ink colour from the available options

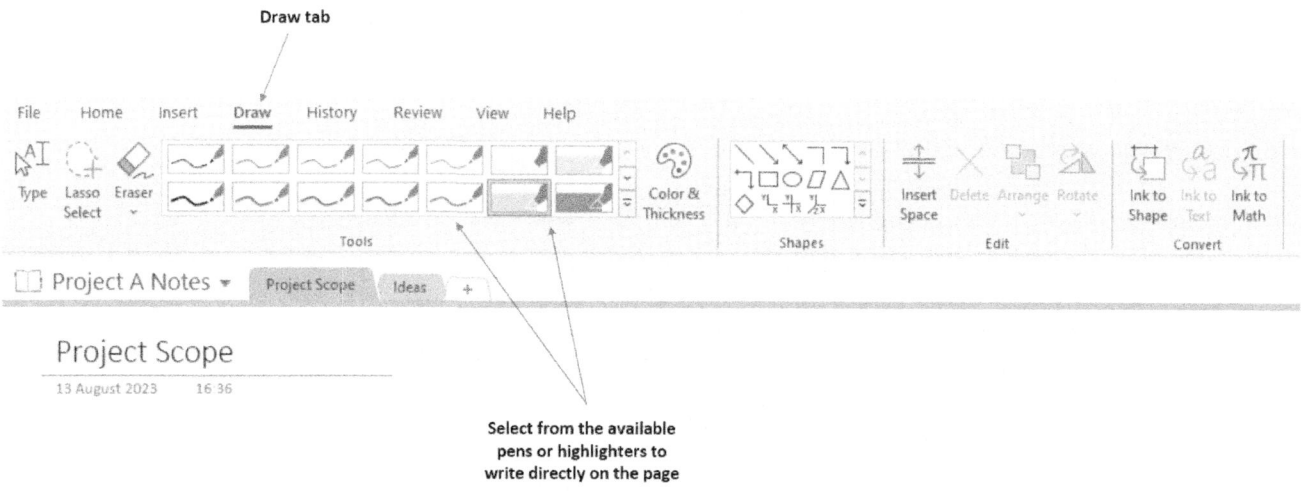

Use a stylus or touch input to draw or write directly on the page.

Creating and organising notebooks in Microsoft OneNote provides users with a powerful and structured way to store and manage information. By following the step-by-step instructions provided in this section, users can easily create new notebooks, add sections and pages, and customise the organisation to suit their needs. OneNote's flexibility allows for a personalized and efficient note-taking experience, making it an invaluable tool for various purposes, such as personal journaling, project planning, and academic notetaking. Whether organising information for work or personal use, Microsoft OneNote simplifies the process of creating and managing digital notebooks, enhancing productivity and information management for users.

6.5 Taking Notes and Adding Content in Microsoft OneNote

Microsoft OneNote provides users with a versatile and user-friendly platform for taking notes and adding various types of content. Whether it's text, images, audio, video, or hand-drawn sketches, OneNote allows users to capture information in a dynamic and organised manner. In this section, we will explore how to take notes and add content in OneNote by providing step-by-step instructions to demonstrate the process.

6.5.1 Getting Started with Notetaking in OneNote

Step 1: Open Microsoft OneNote

- Launch Microsoft OneNote on your computer by clicking on the OneNote icon or searching for "Microsoft OneNote" in your operating system's search bar.

Step 2: Accessing a Notebook

- In OneNote, choose the notebook where you want to take notes by clicking on its name in the left-hand panel.

- Once the notebook is open, select the section and page where you'd like to add your notes by clicking on their respective tabs.

6.5.2 Taking Text-Based Notes in OneNote

Step 1: Create a New Note

- On the desired page, click on an empty area to create a new note, or simply start typing to add text to the page.

Step 2: Organise Text with Headings

- Use headings to organise your notes hierarchically.

- Select the text you want to turn into a heading.

- In the "Home" tab, click on the appropriate heading level (e.g., "Heading 1" or "Heading 2").

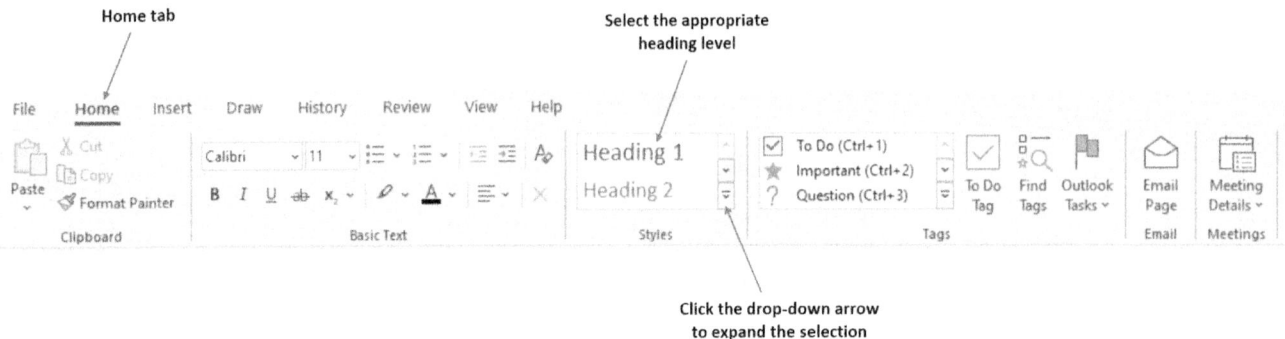

6.5.3 Adding Images to Notes in OneNote

Step 1: Insert an Image

- In the "Insert" tab at the top, click on "Pictures" to insert images.

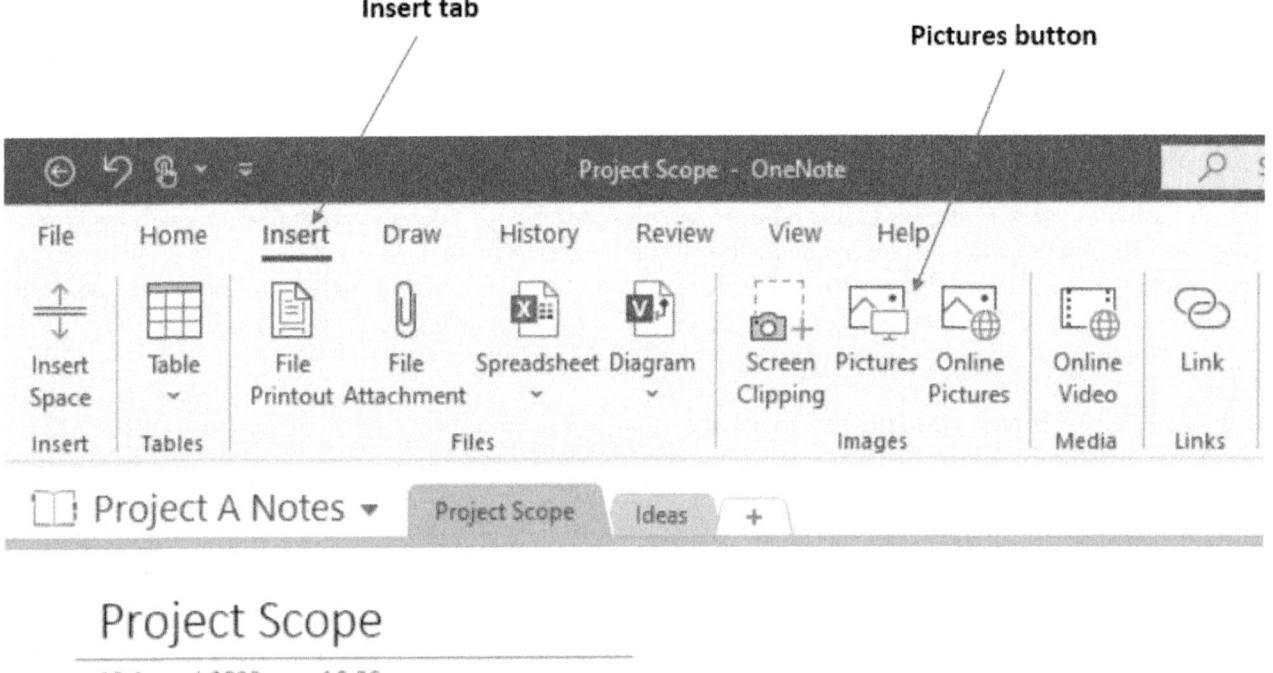

- Select the file and click "Insert".

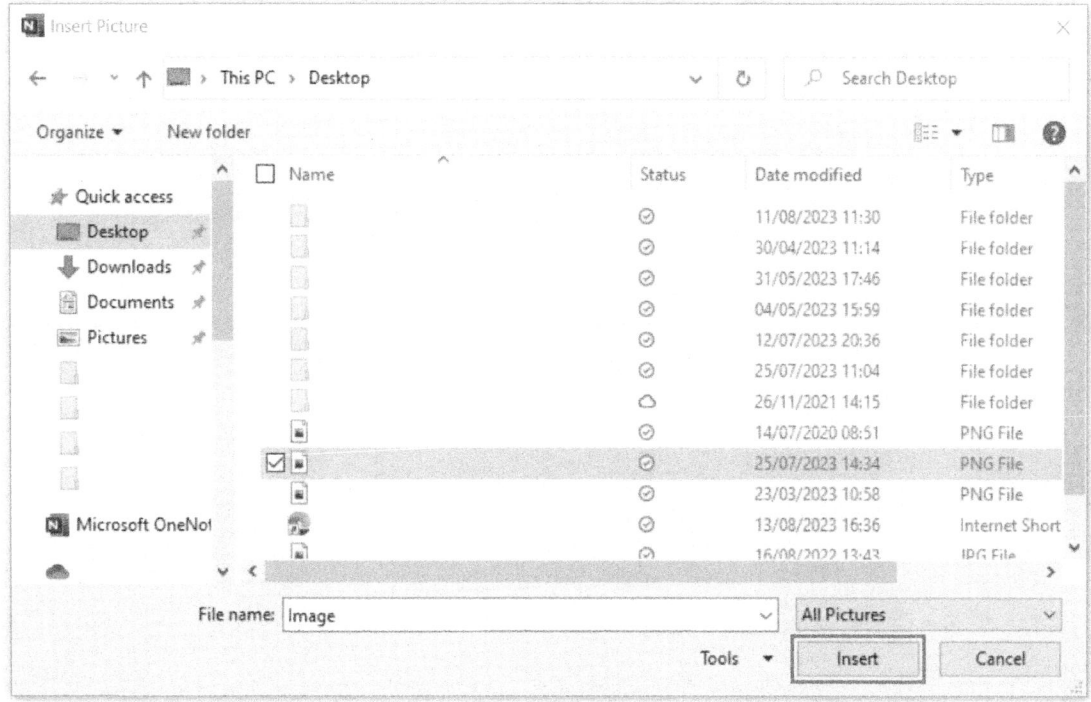

- Click on "All Files" to insert other files, such as PDFs or Word documents.

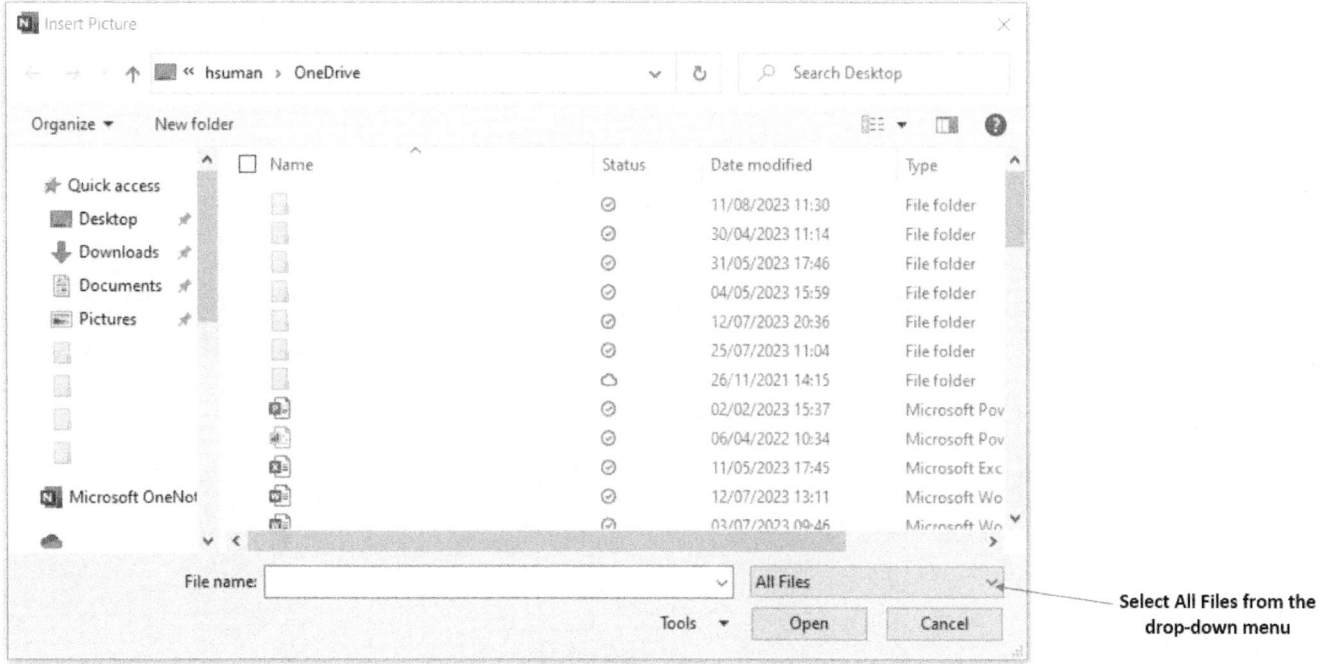

Select All Files from the drop-down menu

6.5.4 Recording Audio and Video in OneNote (Optional)

Step 1: Insert an Audio or Video Recording

- In the "Insert" tab, click on the "Record Audio" or " Record Video" button.

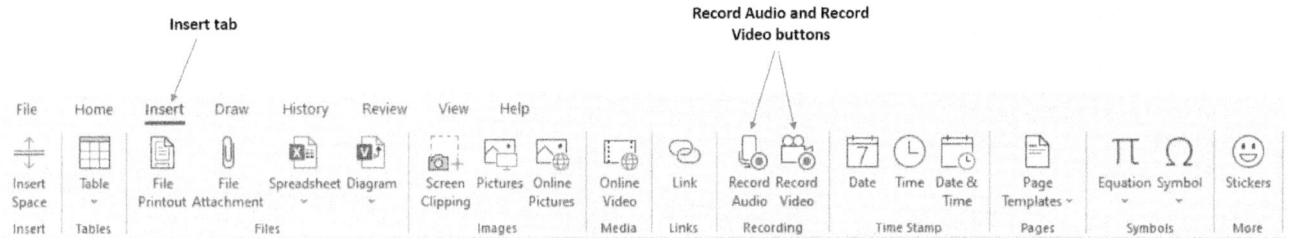

- If prompted, grant OneNote access to your microphone or camera.

- The audio or video file will be placed in the space.

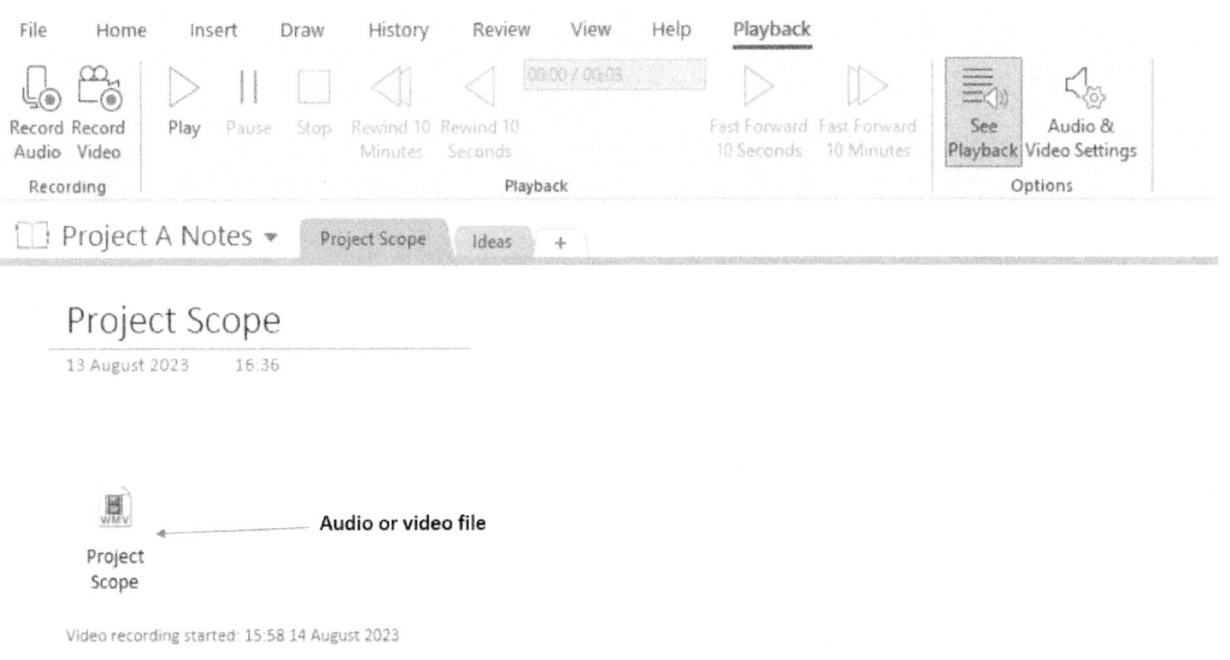

Step 2: Start Recording

- OneNote will start capturing the audio or video automatically.

- Click "Stop" when you're done recording.

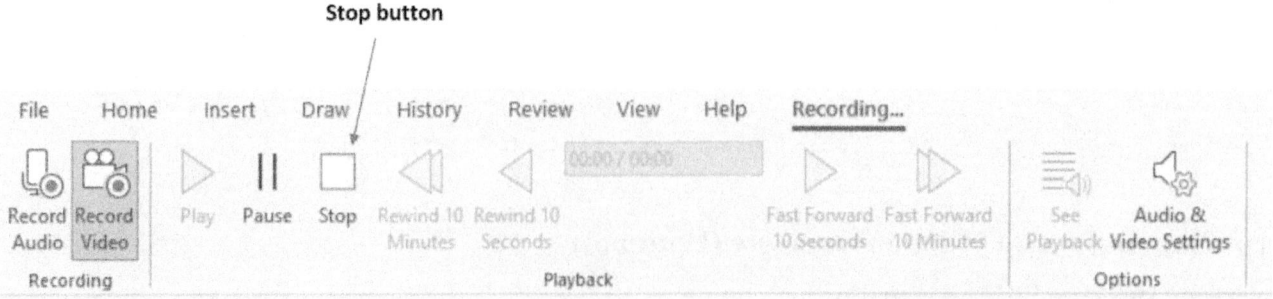

6.5.5 Attaching Files to Notes (Optional)

Step 1: Insert a File

- In the "Insert" tab, click on the "File Attachment" button in the "Files" group.

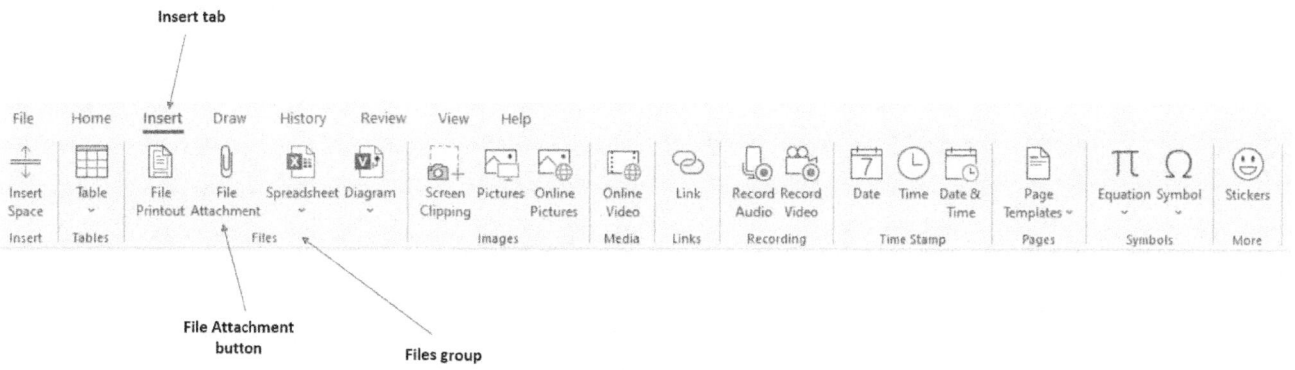

Step 2: Select the File

- Browse your computer or storage for the file you want to attach to your notes.

- Select the file and click "Insert".

Microsoft OneNote provides users with a comprehensive and intuitive platform for taking notes and adding various types of content. By following the step-by-step instructions provided in this section, users can easily create text-based notes, insert images, record audio and video, add handwritten sketches, and attach files to their notes. OneNote's flexibility and diverse features make it an invaluable tool for students, professionals, and individuals seeking an organised and dynamic way to capture and manage information effectively. Whether for meetings, lectures, research, or personal journaling, Microsoft OneNote simplifies the process of taking notes and enriches the note-taking experience with multimedia content and digital inking capabilities.

6.6 Using Tags and Templates in Microsoft OneNote

Microsoft OneNote offers users the ability to enhance organisation and productivity with tags and templates. Tags allow users to categorise and label specific content for easy reference, while templates provide pre-designed formats and layouts for various note-taking scenarios. In this section, we will explore how to use tags and templates in OneNote, by providing step-by-step instructions.

6.6.1 Utilising Tags in OneNote

Step 1: Open Microsoft OneNote

- Launch Microsoft OneNote on your computer by clicking on the OneNote icon or searching for "Microsoft OneNote" in your operating system's search bar.

Step 2: Access a Notebook and Page

- Choose the notebook where you want to add tags by clicking on its name in the left-hand panel.

- Once the notebook is open, select the section and page where you'd like to use tags by clicking on their respective tabs.

Step 3: Apply Tags to Content

- Highlight the text or select the content you want to tag (e.g., a paragraph, an image, a section title).

- In the "Home" tab at the top of the application window, click on the "Tag" drop-down menu.

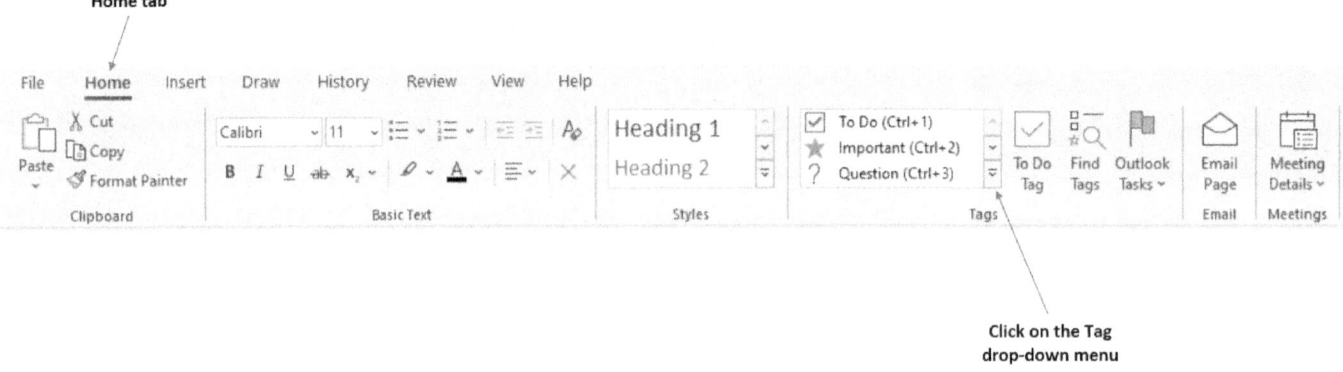

Step 4: Choose a Tag

- From the list of available tags, select the one that best represents the content (e.g., "To Do," "Important," "Idea").

Step 5: Review Tagged Content

- In the left-hand panel, click on the "Tags" icon to view a list of tagged content across all notebooks.

- Click on a specific tag to navigate to the page where it's applied.

6.6.2 Utilising Templates in OneNote

Step 1: Access Templates in OneNote

- In OneNote, go to the "Insert" tab at the top of the application window.

- Click on the "Page Templates" button in the "Pages" group.

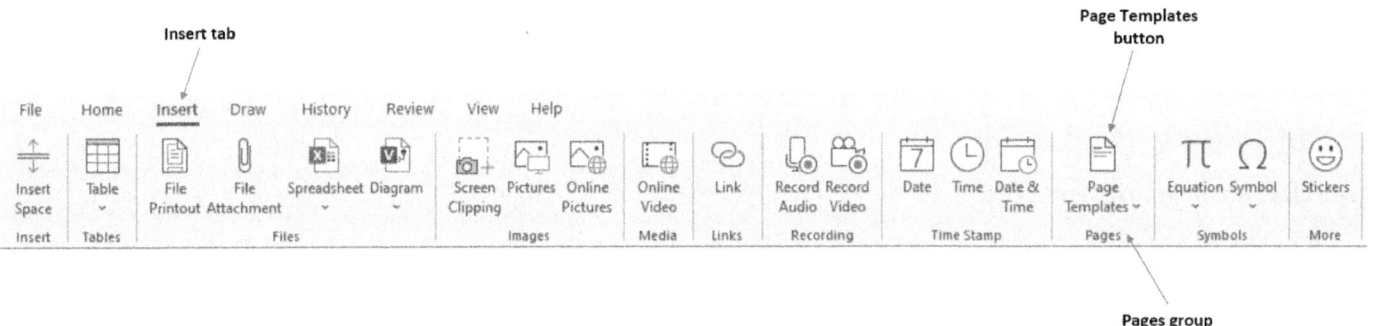

Step 2: Choose a Template Category

- Browse through the available template categories (e.g., Academic, Business, Planners).

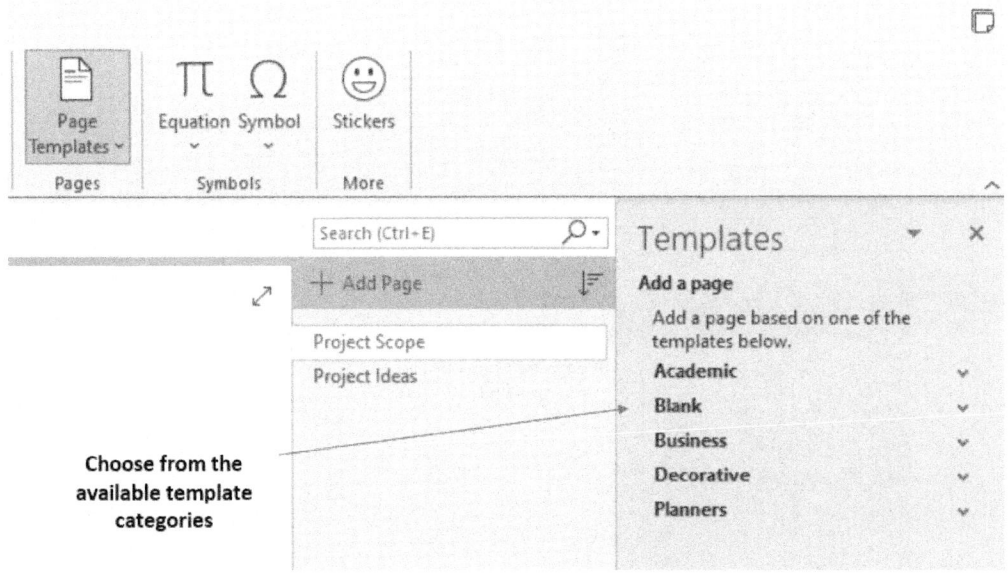

Choose from the available template categories

- Click on the category that matches your note-taking needs.

Step 3: Select a Template

- Within the chosen category, review the available templates.

- Click on the template that best suits your requirements.

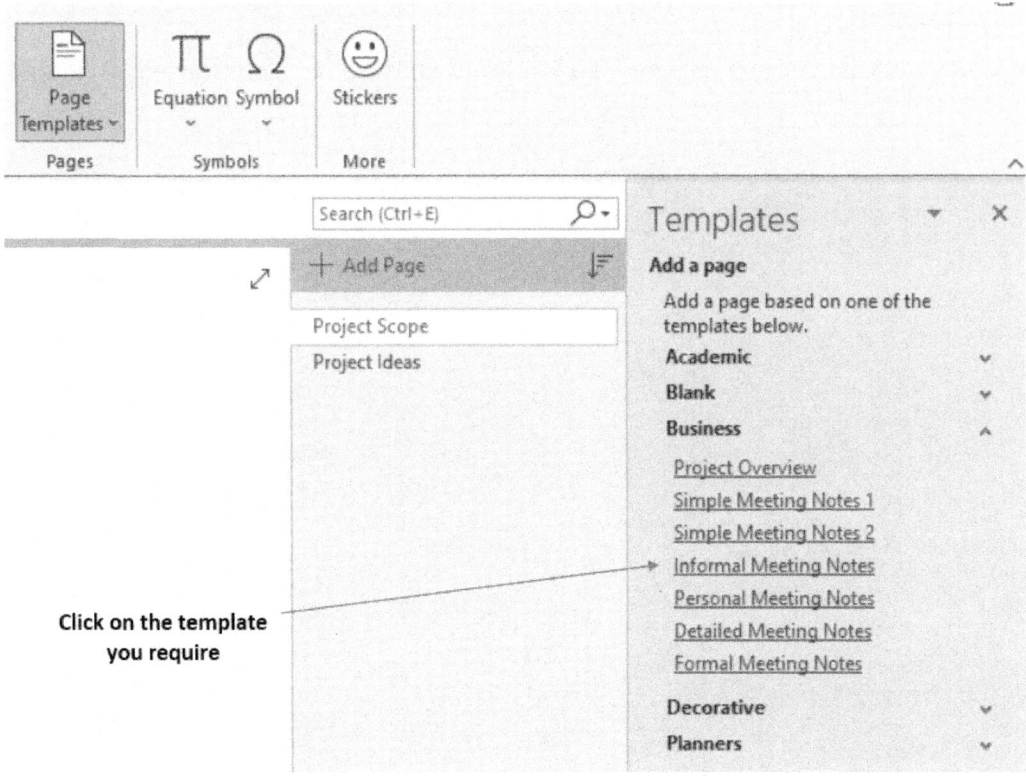

Click on the template you require

Step 4: Apply the Template

- OneNote will insert the chosen template as a new page in your current section.

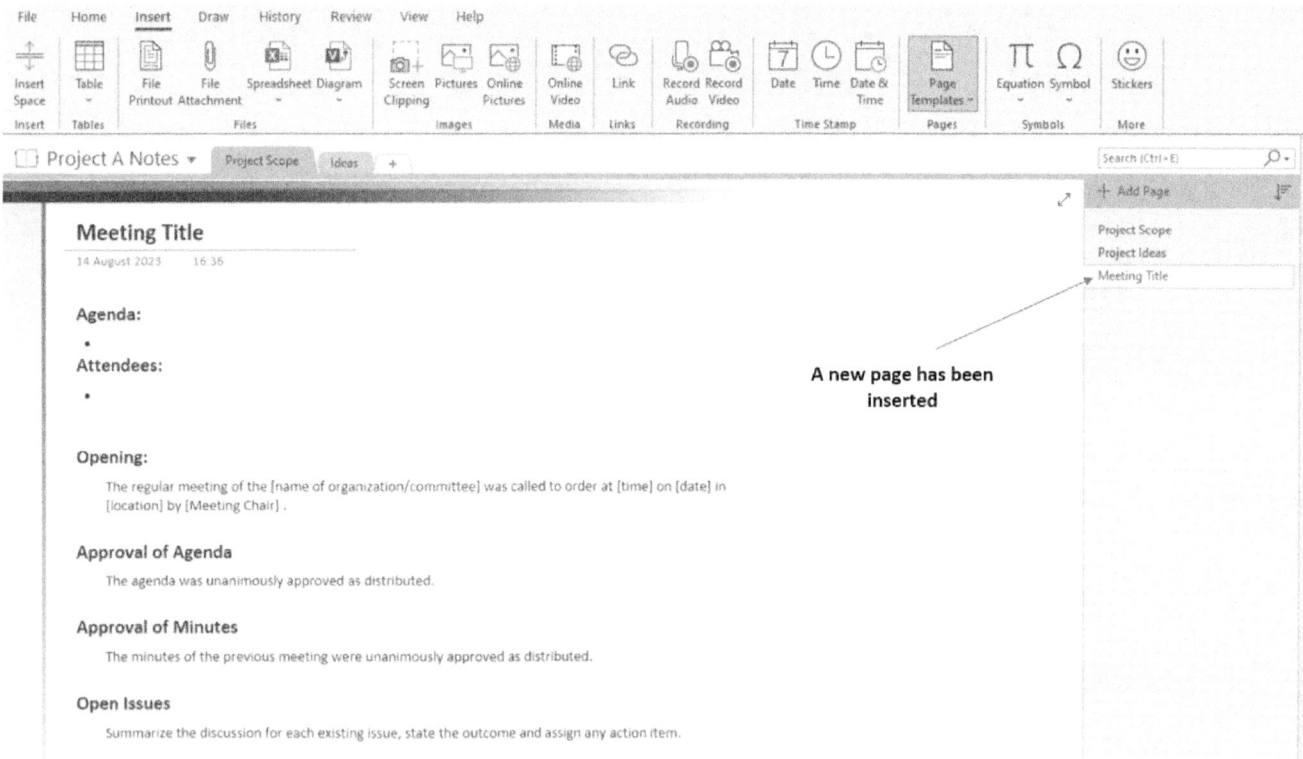

- Customise the template by adding your content, such as text, images, or other media.

Step 5: Save a Custom Template (Optional)

- After customising the template, go to the "Page Templates" button again and choose "Save Current Page as a Template".

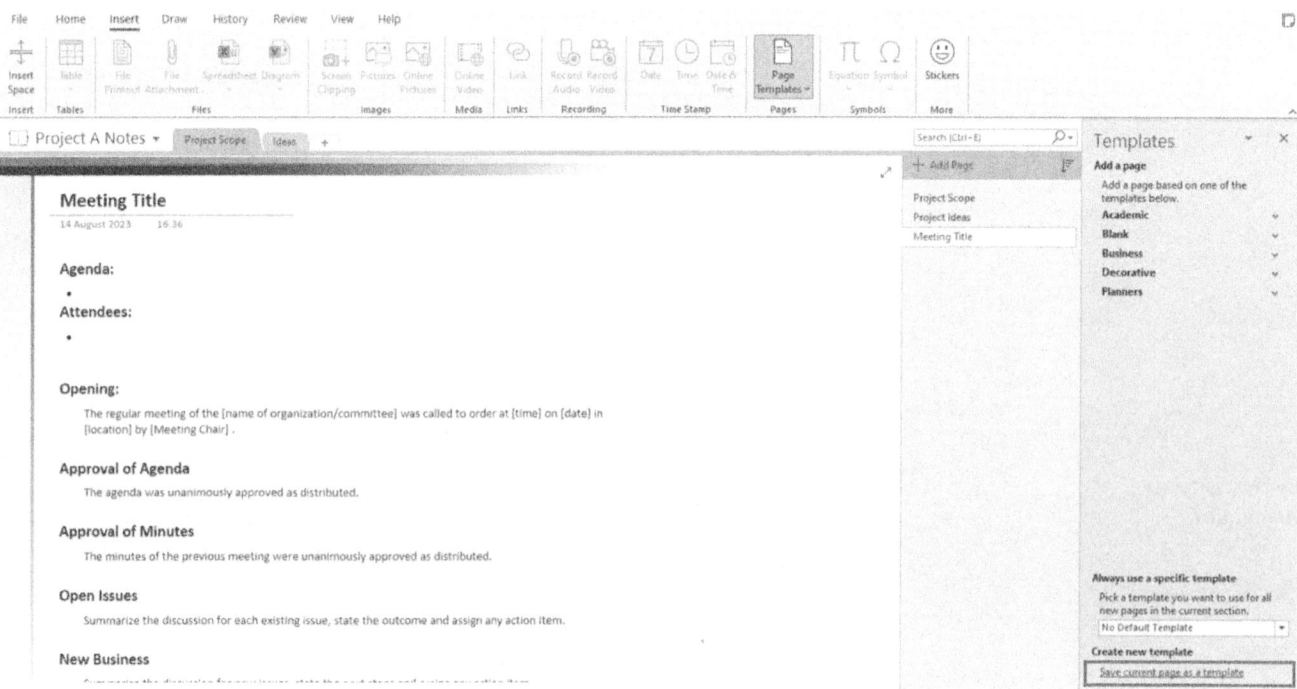

- Name the template and select the category to which it belongs.

- Click "Save" to add your custom template to the template gallery under "My Templates".

6.6.3 Using Quick Notes (Optional)

Step 1: Access Quick Notes

- In OneNote, click on the "Note" icon in the system tray or press the shortcut keys (Windows: Windows Key + N, macOS: Shift + Command + N).

Step 2: Create a Quick Note

- A small window will pop up, allowing you to type or paste quick notes.

- Write your note and click "Close" when done.

Step 3: Review and Organise Quick Notes

- Quick Notes are automatically saved to a designated "Quick Notes" section within your default notebook.

- Periodically review and organise these notes by moving them to the appropriate sections or pages.

Tags and templates in Microsoft OneNote are powerful tools that help users organise, categorise, and streamline their note-taking process. By following the step-by-step instructions provided in this section, users can easily apply tags to content, access and use various pre-designed templates, and create quick notes for rapid information capture. OneNote's tagging and templating features enhance productivity and simplify the organisation of notes for various purposes, such as academic research, business planning, or personal journaling. Whether using tags for quick identification or templates for standardised note-taking formats, Microsoft OneNote empowers users to take efficient and organised digital notes, fostering a more productive and effective note-taking experience.

6.7 Collaboration and Sharing in Microsoft OneNote

Microsoft OneNote's collaboration and sharing features make it easy for users to work together on notebooks, share information, and stay connected with colleagues, friends, and family. Whether it's collaborating on a project, sharing notes for a meeting, or co-editing study materials, OneNote's real-time collaboration capabilities facilitate seamless teamwork. In this section, we will explore how to collaborate and share notebooks in Microsoft OneNote, providing step-by-step instructions to help users engage in effective collaboration.

6.7.1 Collaborating on Notebooks in OneNote

Step 1: Open Microsoft OneNote

- Launch Microsoft OneNote on your computer by clicking on the OneNote icon or searching for "Microsoft OneNote" in your operating system's search bar.

Step 2: Access the Notebook for Collaboration

- Choose the notebook you want to collaborate on by clicking on its name in the left-hand panel.

- Once the notebook is open, select the section and page where you want to collaborate by clicking on their respective tabs.

Step 3: Share the Notebook with Collaborators

- Click on the "File" tab in the top left corner and then "Share".

- Enter the email addresses or names of the people you want to collaborate with.

- Optionally, customise the sharing permissions by clicking on the "Can Edit" drop-down menu to select "Can View" or "Can Edit".

- Include a message to your collaborators (optional).

- Click on the "Share" button to send the sharing invitation.

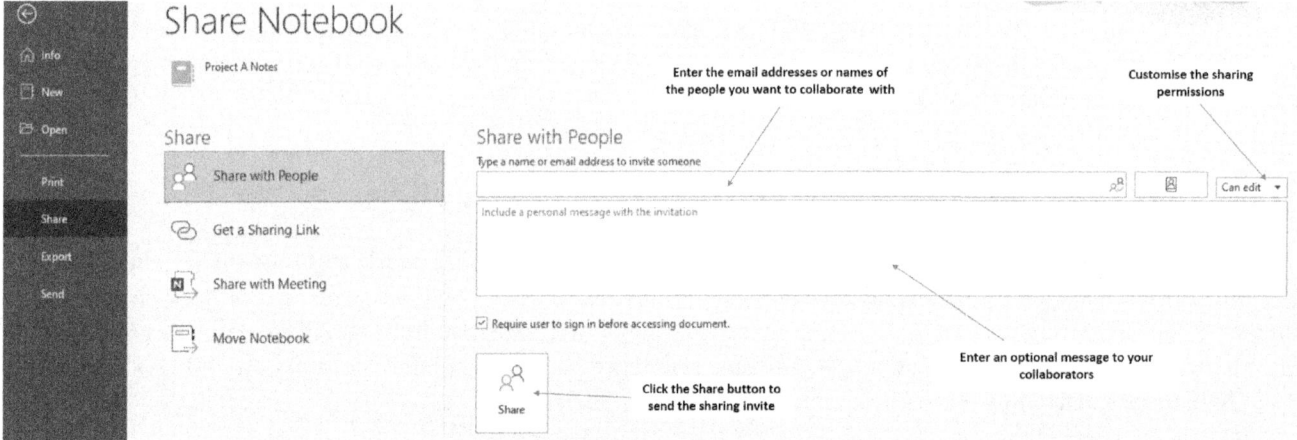

Step 4: Collaborate in Real-Time

- Once the notebook is shared, collaborators will receive an email invitation with a link to access the notebook.

- When collaborators open the link, they can view or edit the shared notebook in real-time.

- Collaborators' changes and updates will be instantly visible to all other participants.

6.7.2 Using Version History

Step 1: Access Version History

- In the "History" tab, click on the "Page Versions" button drip-down menu and then select "Page Versions".

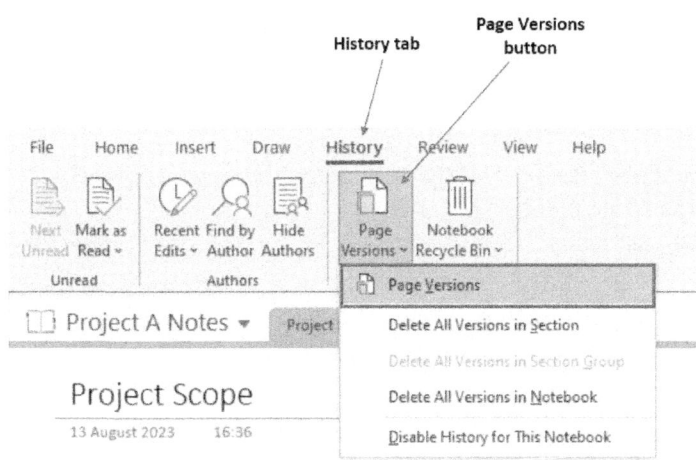

Step 2: Review Page Versions

- The "Page Versions" pane will open, showing the different versions of the page with timestamps.

- Click on a specific version to view its content.

Step 3: Restore a Previous Version (Optional)

- If you want to revert to a previous version, click on the version you wish to restore.

- OneNote will prompt you to confirm the restoration. Click on the prompt.

- Click "Restore Version" to revert the page to the selected version.

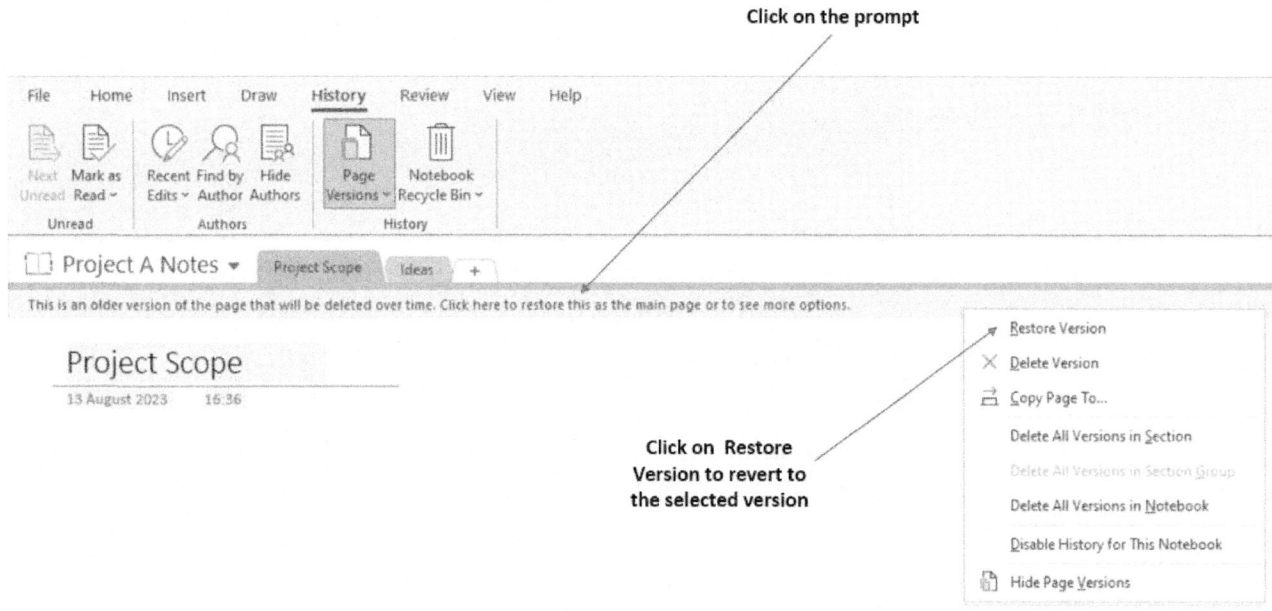

6.7.3 Using the Collaboration Pane

Step 1: Open the Collaboration Pane

- In the top-right corner of the OneNote window, click on the "View" tab.

- In the "Show" group, click on "Collaboration".

Step 2: View Collaborator Activity

- The "Collaboration" pane will open, showing the list of collaborators currently working on the shared notebook.

- You can see who is currently editing or viewing the notebook.

Step 3: Jump to Collaborator's Location (Optional)

- To jump to a collaborator's location in the notebook, click on their name in the "Collaboration" pane.

Collaboration and sharing in Microsoft OneNote enable users to work together seamlessly on notebooks, share information, and engage in real-time co-editing. By following the step-by-step instructions provided in this section, users can easily share notebooks with collaborators, grant appropriate permissions, access version history, and monitor collaborator activity using the collaboration pane. OneNote's collaboration features foster teamwork, enhance productivity, and facilitate effective communication among individuals and teams. Whether collaborating on projects, sharing meeting notes, or co-authoring study materials, Microsoft OneNote provides a robust platform for productive collaboration and information sharing.

Chapter 7: Microsoft Teams

Microsoft Teams is a collaborative communication and teamwork platform developed by Microsoft. It is designed to facilitate seamless communication, collaboration, and project management within organisations and teams. Teams integrates various Office 365 services, such as chat, video conferencing, file sharing, and app integration, into a single interface, providing users with a centralised hub for teamwork. In this chapter, we will explore what Microsoft Teams is, what it is used for, the benefits of using it, and provide step-by-step instructions on how to use this powerful collaboration tool.

7.1 What is Microsoft Teams?

Microsoft Teams is a unified communication and collaboration platform that allows users to work together in real-time, regardless of their physical location. Teams provides a digital workspace where members of an organisation or team can communicate, share files, conduct meetings, and collaborate on projects in a secure and efficient manner. It serves as a hub for teamwork, bringing together various collaboration tools into a single application.

7.2 What is Microsoft Teams Used For?

Team Communication: Teams offers real-time chat functionality, allowing team members to have quick and informal conversations, share updates, and exchange information instantly.

Video Conferencing: Teams enables high-quality video and audio conferencing, making it easy for teams to conduct virtual meetings and stay connected, even when working remotely.

File Sharing and Collaboration: Teams provides a centralised location for sharing and collaborating on files, ensuring everyone has access to the latest versions and edits.

Project Management: Teams facilitates project planning and management with features like task assignment, file organisation, and integrated apps for enhanced productivity.

App Integration: Teams integrates with various third-party applications, enabling users to bring their favourite tools and services directly into the Teams interface.

Security and Compliance: Teams adheres to rigorous security and compliance standards, ensuring that sensitive data and communications are protected.

7.3 Benefits of Using Microsoft Teams

Enhanced Team Communication: Teams provides a seamless communication experience, allowing team members to stay connected and collaborate effortlessly.

Increased Productivity: By centralising communication, files, and apps in one platform, Teams streamlines workflows and enhances overall productivity.

Real-Time Collaboration: Teams supports real-time co-authoring, enabling multiple users to work simultaneously on the same documents and files.

Remote Work Facilitation: Teams is particularly valuable for remote and distributed teams, as it provides a virtual workspace where teams can collaborate as if they were in the same room.

Access to Integrated Services: Teams integrates with popular Office 365 services, making it easy to access tools like Word, Excel, and SharePoint within the platform.

Secure and Compliant: Microsoft Teams prioritises security and compliance, ensuring that data and communications are protected in accordance with industry standards.

7.4 Joining and Creating Teams in Microsoft Teams

Microsoft Teams allows users to join existing teams and create new ones, fostering seamless collaboration and communication within organisations and groups. Joining teams enables users to participate in ongoing projects and discussions, while creating teams empowers users to initiate new collaborative initiatives. In this section, we will explore how to join and create teams in Microsoft Teams, providing step-by-step instructions.

7.4.1 Joining a Team in Microsoft Teams

Step 1: Open Microsoft Teams

- Launch Microsoft Teams on your computer or device by clicking on the Teams icon or searching for "Microsoft Teams" in your operating system's search bar.

Step 2: Access the Teams Tab

- In the left-hand navigation panel, click on the "Teams" tab to view a list of available teams.

- Teams you are a part of will be listed under "Your teams," while other teams will appear under "Discover more teams".

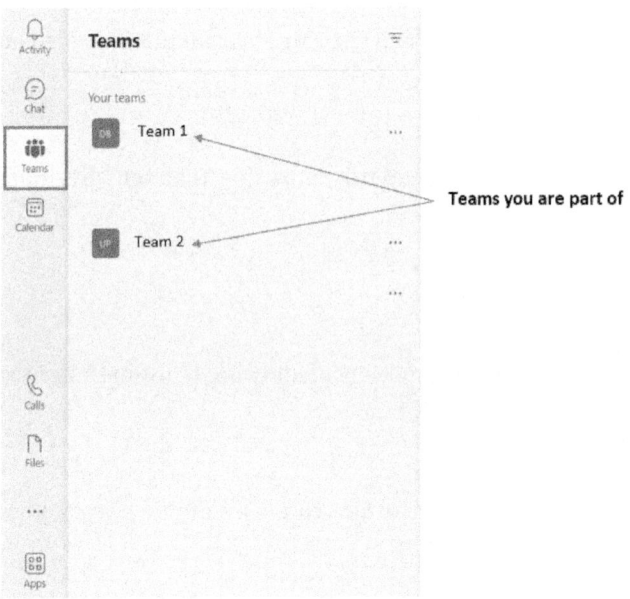

Step 3: Join a Team

- At the bottom of the "Your teams" section, click on the "+ Join or create a team" button.

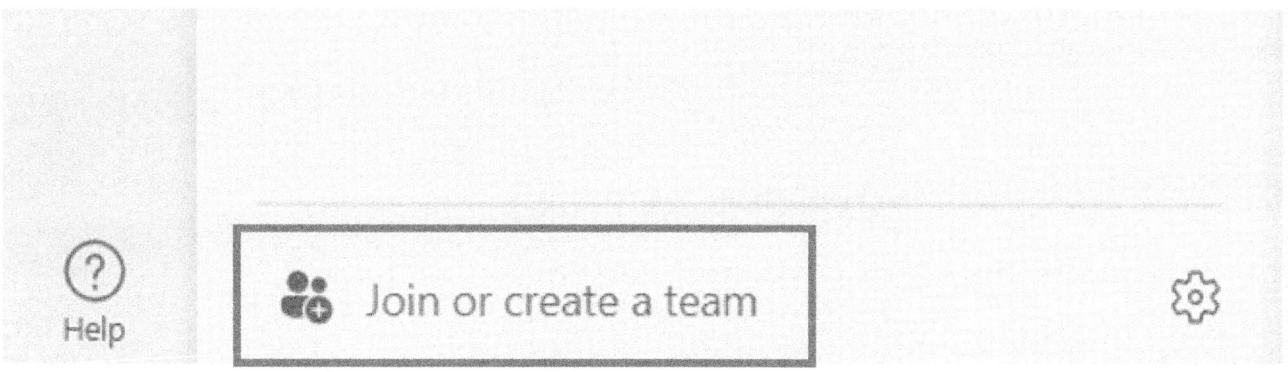

- At the top right, type a specific team name in the search box and press Enter.

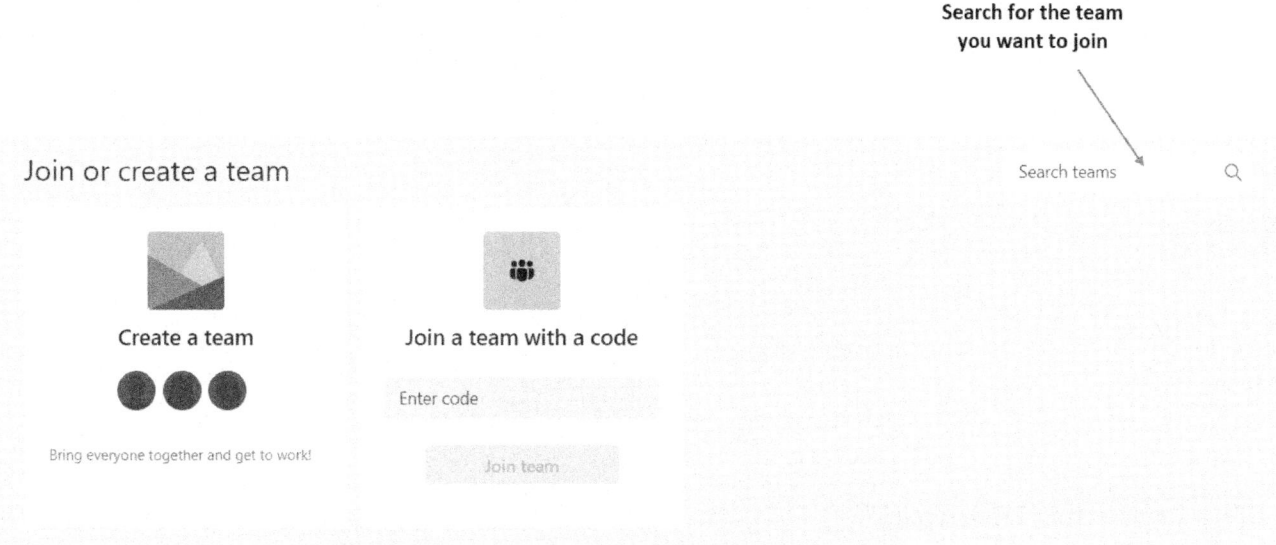

- Find the team you are looking for and then select "Join Team".

Step 4: Request to Join (If Private)

- If the team is private, you will need to request to join by clicking on the "Request to join" button.

- Optionally, provide a brief message explaining why you want to join the team.

- Click "Send" to send your join request to the team's owners.

Step 5: Access the Joined Team

- Once your request is approved (if applicable), the team will appear under "Your teams," indicating that you have successfully joined.

7.4.2 Creating a Team in Microsoft Teams

Step 1: Open Microsoft Teams

- Launch Microsoft Teams on your computer or device by clicking on the Teams icon or searching for "Microsoft Teams" in your operating system's search bar.

Step 2: Access the Teams Tab

- In the left-hand navigation panel, click on the "Teams" tab.

- At the bottom of the "Your teams" section, click on the "+ Join or create a team" button.

Step 3: Create a New Team

- Hover over the "Create a team" and click the "Create team" button.

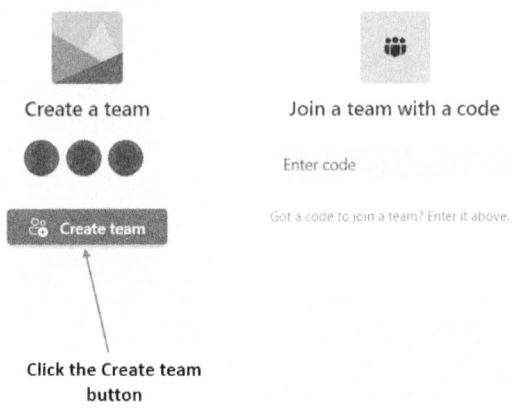

- For this example, select "From scratch".

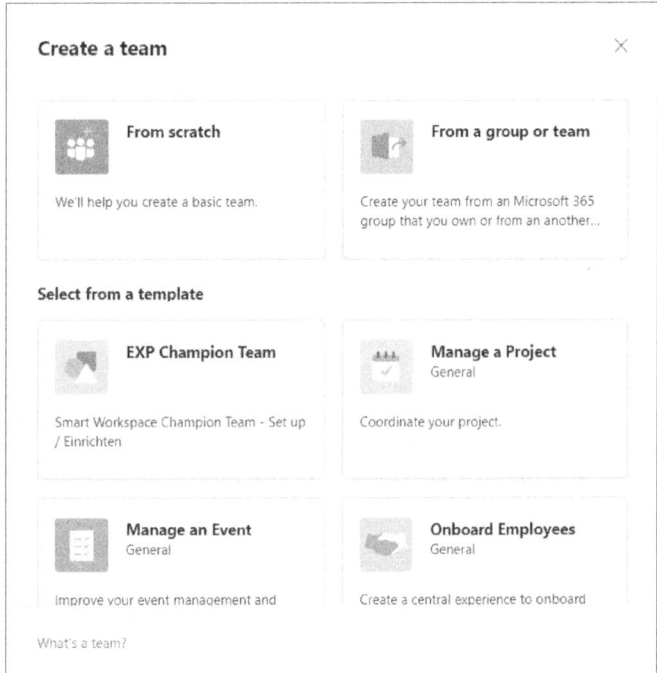

Step 4: Select a Team Type

- Decide what kind of team that you want this to be, whether it is for internal use, restricted or public by selecting one of the options in the drop-down menu.

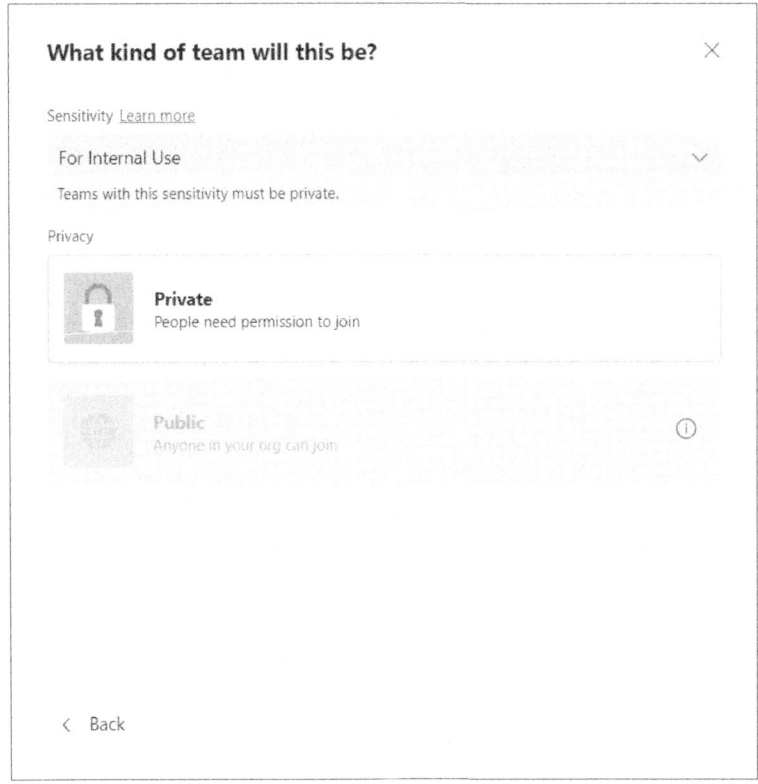

Step 5: Name the Team

- Enter a name for the new team in the "Team name" field.

- Optionally, provide a brief description of the team's purpose in the "Description" field.

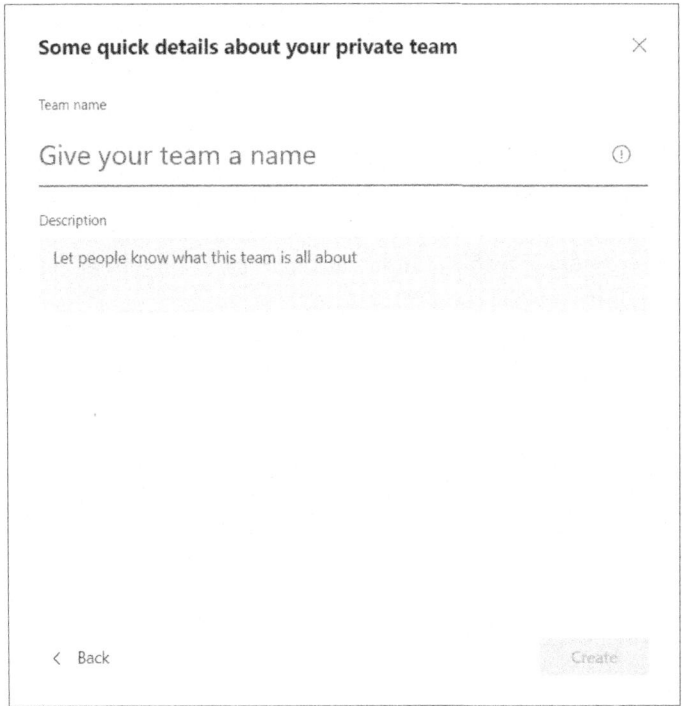

Step 6: Create the Team

- Click on the "Create" button to create the new team.

Step 7: Add Members (Optional)

- Optionally, you can add members to the team immediately by entering their names or email addresses in the "Add members" field.

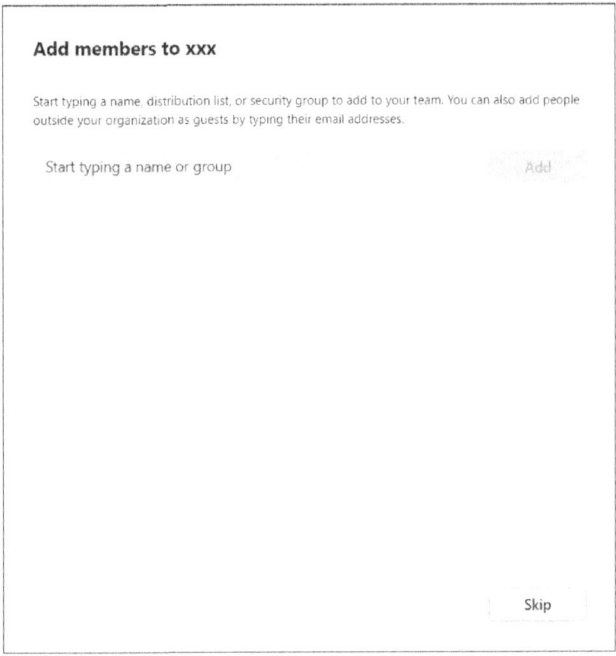

- You can also add members later.

Step 8: Access the New Team

- The new team will now appear under "Your teams," and you can start collaborating and communicating with the team members.

Joining and creating teams in Microsoft Teams facilitate seamless collaboration and communication among individuals and groups. By following the step-by-step instructions provided in this section, users can easily join existing teams to participate in ongoing projects and discussions. Additionally, users can create new teams to initiate new collaborative initiatives and invite team members to join. Microsoft Teams' flexibility and user-friendly interface empower users to engage in effective teamwork, making it a valuable tool for modern-day collaboration within organisations and groups.

7.5 Communicating with Team Members in Microsoft Teams

Microsoft Teams offers various communication features that enable team members to connect, share information, and collaborate efficiently. From real-time chat to audio and video calls, Teams provides a versatile platform for seamless communication within organisations and teams. In this section, we will explore how to communicate with team members in Microsoft Teams by providing step-by-step instructions.

7.5.1 Sending Messages in Microsoft Teams

Step 1: Open Microsoft Teams

- Launch Microsoft Teams on your computer or device by clicking on the Teams icon or searching for "Microsoft Teams" in your operating system's search bar.

Step 2: Access a Team

- In the left-hand navigation panel, click on the "Teams" tab to view your list of teams.

- Select the team you want to communicate with by clicking on its name.

Step 3: Create a Channel (Optional)

- Right-click the team where you want to create a channel and select "Add channel" from the menu.

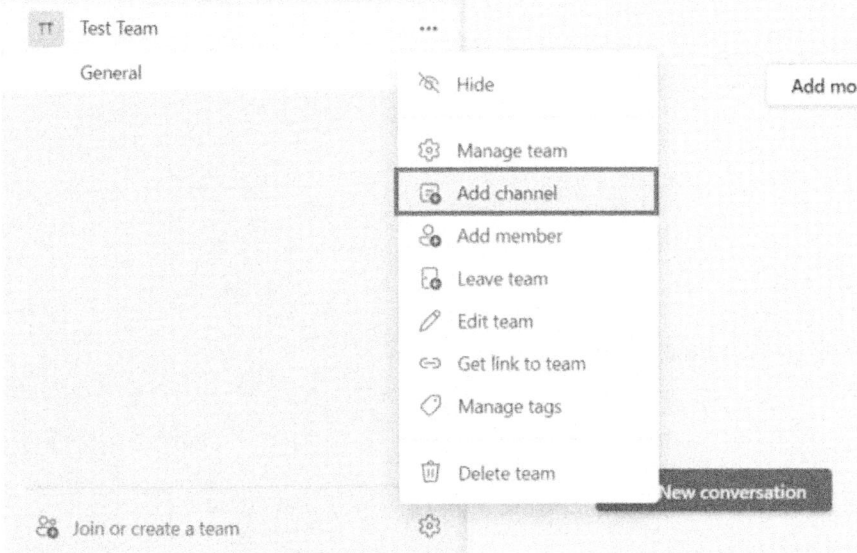

- Enter the channel name, an optional description and select the privacy from the drop-down menu and then click the "Add" button.

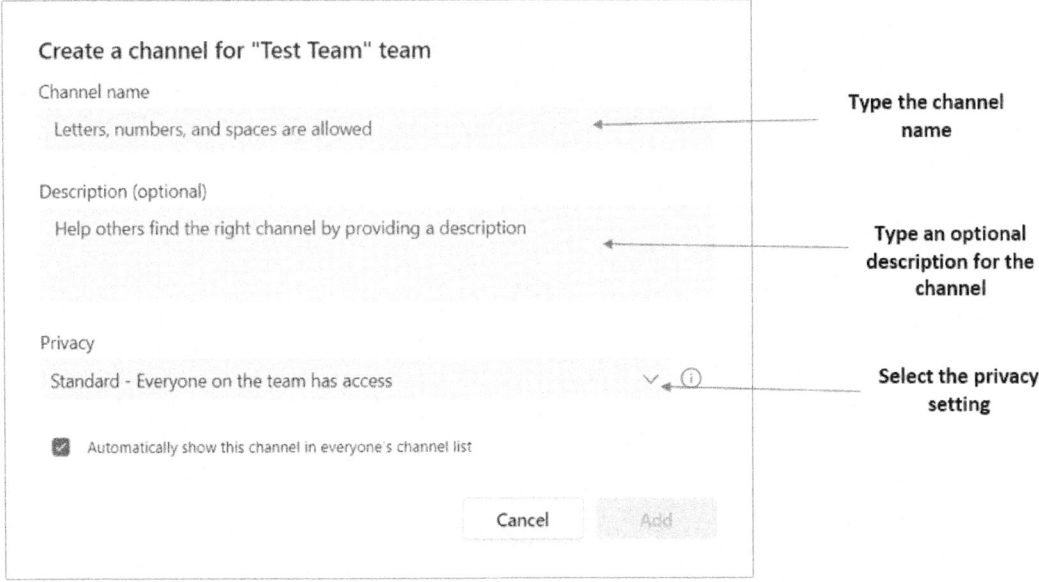

Step 4: Access the Channel

- In the selected team, click on the channel where you want to send a message.

- If you want to send a message to the entire team, click on the "General" channel.

Step 5: Compose and Send a Message

- At the bottom of the channel, click on the "New conversation" button.

- Type your message in the message box.

- You can also use the formatting options to add emphasis, bulleted lists, or hyperlinks by clicking the "Format" button.

Format button

- When ready, click on the paper plane icon or press "Enter" to send the message.

Step 6: View Sent Messages

- Your message will appear in the channel conversation, visible to all team members in that channel.

7.5.2 Starting a Chat with a Team Member

Step 1: Open Microsoft Teams

- Launch Microsoft Teams on your computer or device by clicking on the Teams icon or searching for "Microsoft Teams" in your operating system's search bar.

Step 2: Access the Chat Tab

- In the left-hand navigation panel, click on the "Chat" tab to access your chat list.

- Your chat list will display recent conversations and contacts.

Step 3: Start a New Chat

- Click on the "New chat" button at the top of the chat list to start a new conversation.

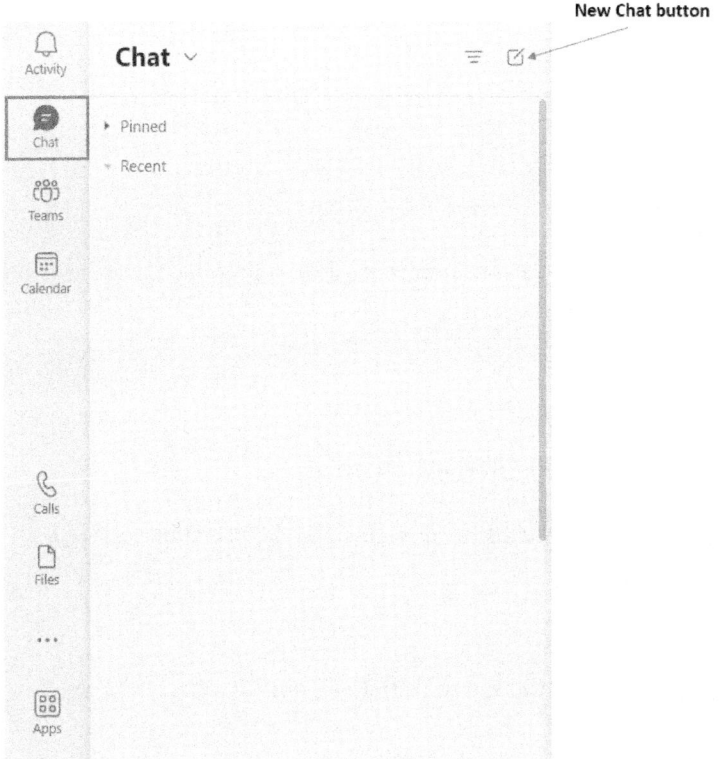

- In the "To:" field, type the name or email address of the team member you want to chat with.

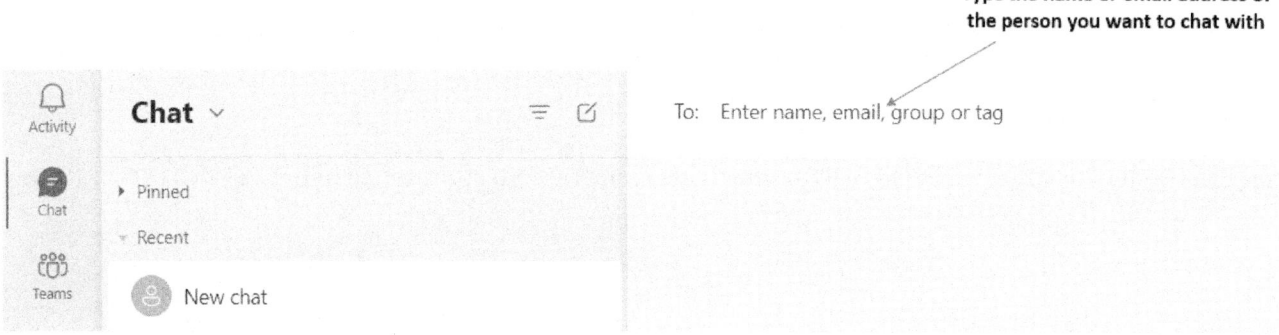

Step 4: Compose and Send a Message

- In the chat window, type your message in the message box.

- Use the formatting options if needed, such as bold or italic text.

- Click on the paper plane icon or press "Enter" to send the message.

Step 5: View Sent Messages

- Your message will appear in the chat conversation, visible to the recipient.

7.5.3 Initiating an Audio or Video Call

Step 1: Open Microsoft Teams

- Launch Microsoft Teams on your computer or device by clicking on the Teams icon or searching for "Microsoft Teams" in your operating system's search bar.

Step 2: Access the Chat Tab

- In the left-hand navigation panel, click on the "Chat" tab to access your chat list.

- Select the chat with the team member you want to call or start a new chat (as described in the previous section).

Step 3: Initiate an Audio Call

- In the chat window, click on the "Audio call" button (phone icon) at the top to initiate an audio call.

- The recipient will receive a notification and can choose to accept or decline the call.

Step 4: Initiate a Video Call

- In the chat window, click on the "Video call" button (video camera icon) at the top to initiate a video call.

- The recipient will receive a notification and can choose to accept or decline the call.

Step 5: Conduct the Call

- Once the call is connected, you can communicate with your team member via audio or video, depending on the type of call initiated.

Step 6: End the Call

- To end the call, click on the "Leave" button (red button) at the top of the call window.

Communicating with team members in Microsoft Teams is straightforward and efficient, thanks to its built-in messaging, chat, and audio/video calling capabilities. By following the step-by-step instructions provided in this section, users can easily send messages in channels, start chats with team members, and initiate audio or video calls. Microsoft Teams' robust communication features empower teams to collaborate seamlessly and stay connected, regardless of their physical location. Whether for quick updates, in-depth discussions, or face-to-face meetings, Teams provides a comprehensive platform for effective and real-time communication within organisations and teams.

7.6 Sharing Files and Collaborating on Documents in Microsoft Teams

Microsoft Teams offers a powerful platform for sharing files and collaborating on documents, enabling team members to work together efficiently and access important resources from a centralised location. With seamless integration with OneDrive and SharePoint, Teams simplifies file sharing, version control, and real-time collaboration. In this section, we will explore how to share files and collaborate on documents in Microsoft Teams, with step-by-step instructions.

7.6.1 Sharing Files in Microsoft Teams

Step 1: Open Microsoft Teams

- Launch Microsoft Teams on your computer or device by clicking on the Teams icon or searching for "Microsoft Teams" in your operating system's search bar.

Step 2: Access a Team and Channel

- In the left-hand navigation panel, click on the "Teams" tab to view your list of teams.

- Select the team and channel where you want to share a file by clicking on their respective names.

Step 3: Click on the Files Tab

- At the top of the channel, click on the "Files" tab to access the files shared within that channel.

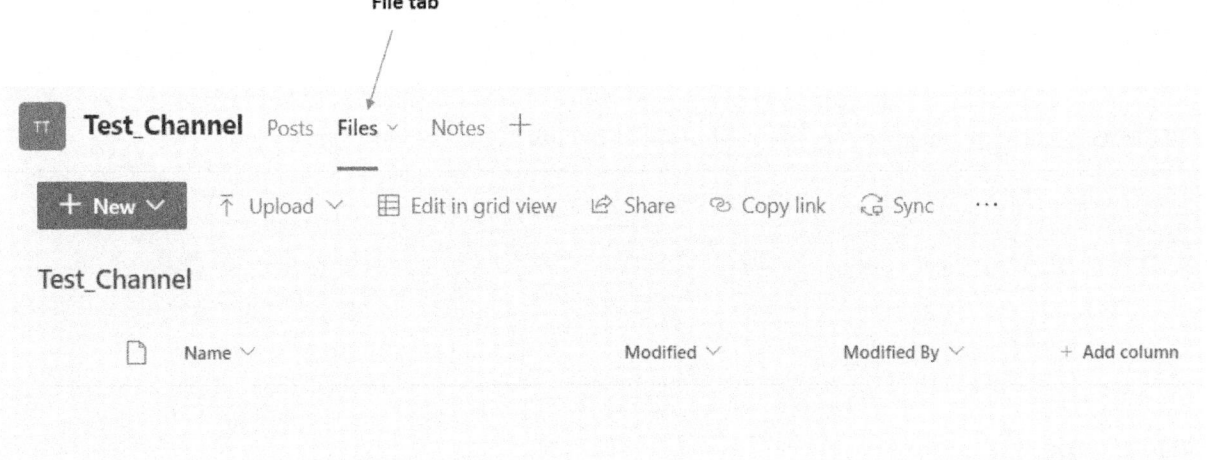

- You will see a list of files and folders in the channel's file repository.

Step 4: Upload a File

- To upload a new file, click on the "Upload" button at the top of the Files tab and then "Files".

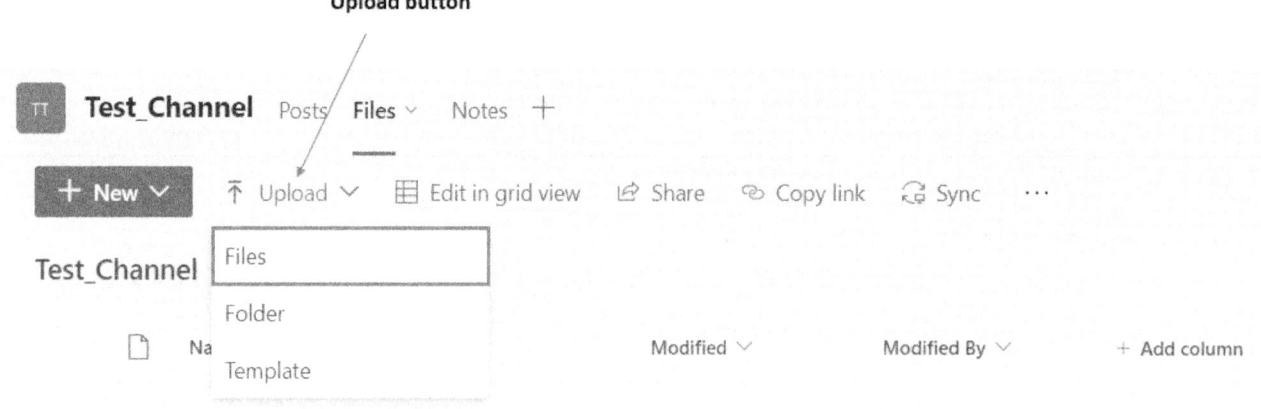

Upload button

- Browse your computer or storage to select the file you want to upload.

- Click "Open" to begin the upload.

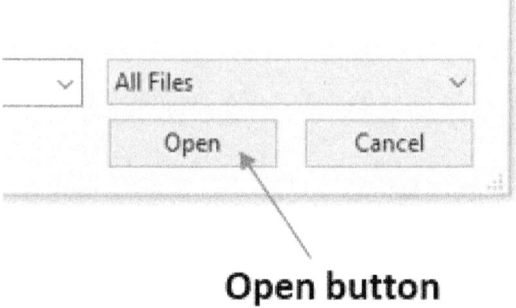

Open button

Step 5: Share a File

- Once the file is uploaded, it will be added to the channel's file repository.

- Click on the file to open the file preview.

- To share the file with the team, click on the "Share" button at the top-right corner of the file preview.

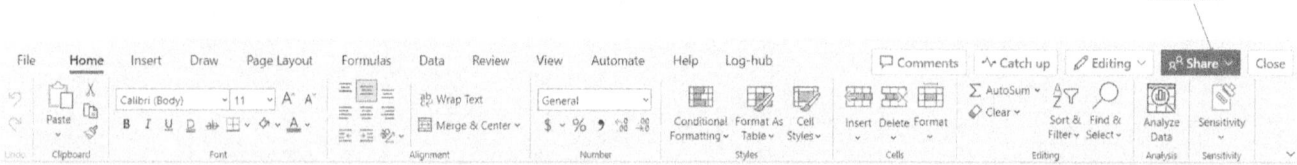

Step 6: Choose Sharing Options

- In the sharing window, enter the name or email address of the people you want to share the file with and enter a message.

- Optionally, you can set permissions to "View" or "Edit" by clicking the drop-down menu next to the pencil.

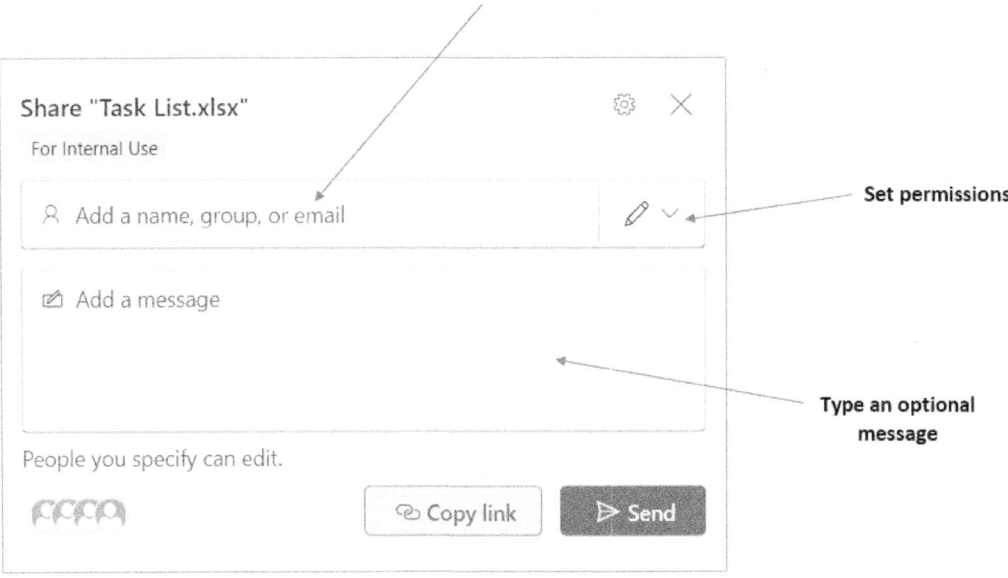

Enter the name or email address of the people you want to share the file with

Set permissions

Type an optional message

Step 7: Send the File

- Click on the "Send" button to share the file with the selected recipients.

- The file link will be sent to the selected team members through a Teams message.

7.6.2 Collaborating on Documents in Microsoft Teams

Step 1: Open Microsoft Teams

- Launch Microsoft Teams on your computer or device by clicking on the Teams icon or searching for "Microsoft Teams" in your operating system's search bar.

Step 2: Access a Team and Channel

- In the left-hand navigation panel, click on the "Teams" tab to view your list of teams.

- Select the team and channel where the document you want to collaborate on is located.

Step 3: Click on the Files Tab

- At the top of the channel, click on the "Files" tab to access the files shared within that channel.

- You will see a list of files and folders in the channel's file repository.

Step 4: Open the Document

- Click on the document you want to collaborate on to open it in file preview.

- The document will open in a new tab, and you can start editing it.

Step 5: Collaborate in Real-Time

- Multiple team members can open the same document simultaneously and edit it in real-time.

- Each user's changes will be instantly visible to others collaborating on the document.

Step 6: Save and Update the Document

- As you make changes to the document, Microsoft Teams will automatically save the changes in real-time.

- All collaborators will have access to the latest version of the document.

Step 7: Access Version History (Optional)

- To access the version history of the document, select the file. Click on the ellipsis on the top menu and then select "Open in SharePoint".

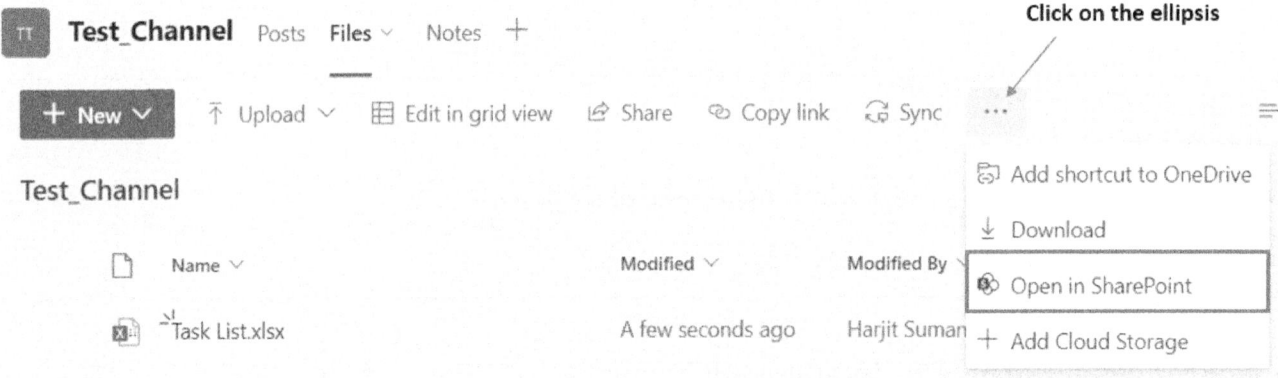

- The document will open in SharePoint.

- Select the file in SharePoint. In the top menu, click on the ellipsis and from the menu select "Version history".

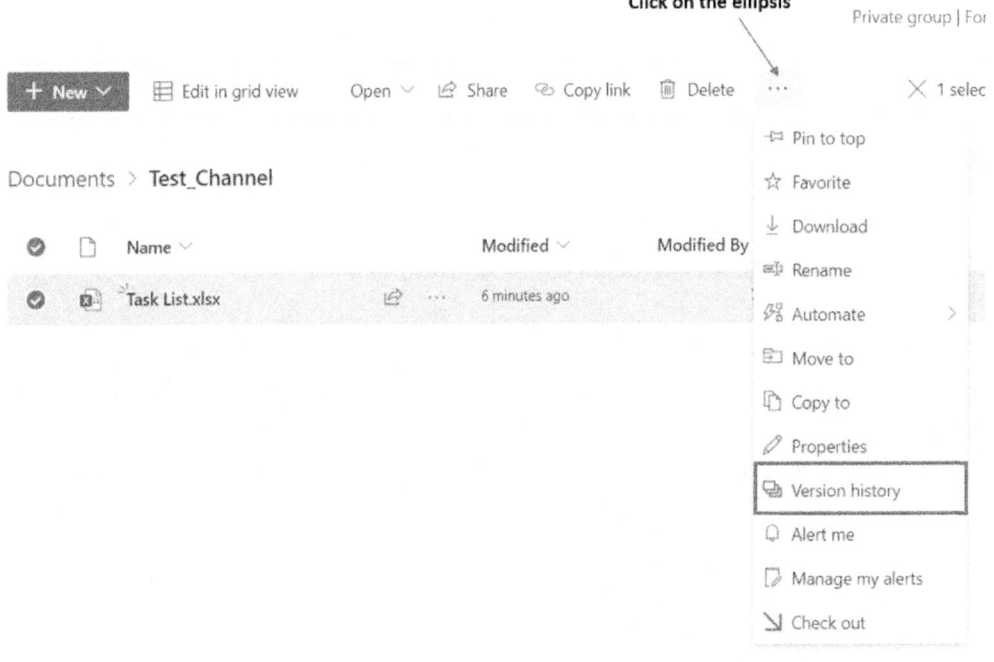

Sharing files and collaborating on documents in Microsoft Teams streamlines teamwork and enhances productivity within organisations and teams. By following the step-by-step instructions provided in this section, users can easily upload and share files in Teams channels, set sharing permissions, and collaborate in real-time on shared documents. Microsoft Teams' integration with OneDrive and SharePoint simplifies file management and version control, ensuring that all team members have access to the latest documents and updates. Whether sharing project files, presentation materials, or important resources, Teams provides a comprehensive platform for efficient file sharing and seamless document collaboration.

7.7 Hosting Meetings and Video Conferences in Microsoft Teams

Microsoft Teams offers robust features for hosting meetings and video conferences, making it easy for teams to collaborate, discuss ideas, and conduct virtual meetings with ease. Whether it's a quick team huddle or a large-scale video conference, Teams provides a versatile platform for seamless communication and collaboration. In this section, we will explore how to host meetings and video conferences in Microsoft Teams.

7.7.1 Hosting a Meeting in Microsoft Teams

Step 1: Open Microsoft Teams

- Launch Microsoft Teams on your computer or device by clicking on the Teams icon or searching for "Microsoft Teams" in your operating system's search bar.

Step 2: Access the Calendar Tab

- In the left-hand navigation panel, click on the "Calendar" tab to access your schedule and upcoming meetings.

- The calendar will display your scheduled meetings for the day.

Step 3: Schedule a New Meeting

- Click on the "New meeting" button at the top-right corner of the calendar to schedule a new meeting.

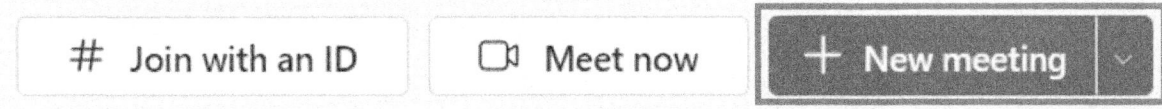

- The "New Meeting" window will open.

Step 4: Enter Meeting Details

- In the "New event" window, enter the meeting title, channel, location, and a brief description.

- Add participants by typing their names or email addresses in the "Add required attendees" field. You can also invite optional attendees by typing their names in the "+ Optional" field.

- Choose the date and time for the meeting using the date and time pickers.

- Optionally, set the duration of the meeting using the "End time" picker.

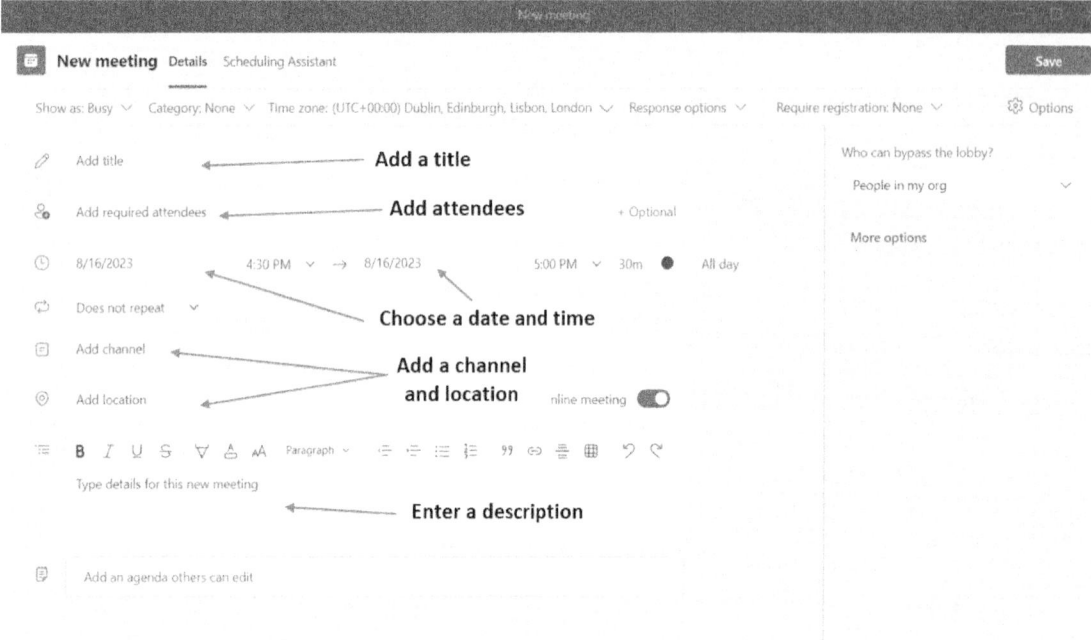

Step 5: Send the Meeting Invitation

- Click on the "Save" button at the top-right corner of the "New Meeting" window to schedule the meeting.

- An invitation with the meeting details will be sent to all participants.

7.7.2 Hosting a Video Conference in Microsoft Teams

Step 1: Open Microsoft Teams

- Launch Microsoft Teams on your computer or device by clicking on the Teams icon or searching for "Microsoft Teams" in your operating system's search bar.

Step 2: Access the Calendar Tab

- In the left-hand navigation panel, click on the "Calendar" tab to access your schedule and upcoming meetings.

- The calendar will display your scheduled meetings for the day.

Step 3: Join the Video Conference

- Locate the scheduled video conference in the calendar and click on it to view the meeting details.

- Click on the "Join" button to join the video conference at the scheduled time.

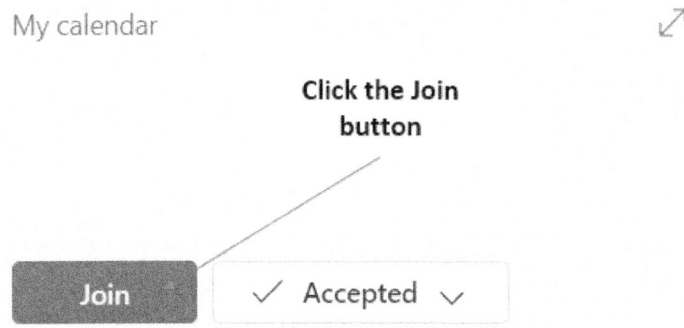

Step 4: Join the Video Conference

- Click on the "Join now" button to enter the video conference.

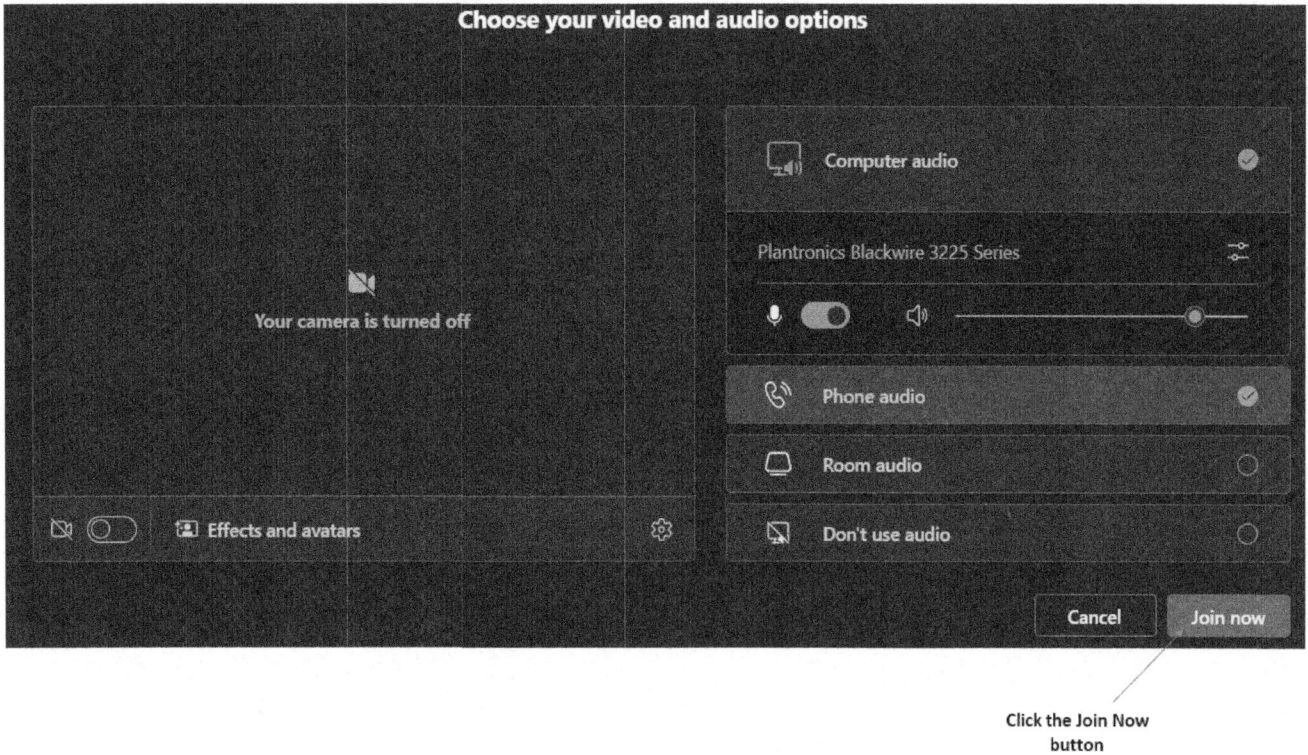

- You will be able to see and hear other participants, and they will see and hear you.

Step 5: Meeting Controls

- During the video conference, use the meeting controls at the top of the screen to mute/unmute your microphone, turn your camera on/off, and share your screen if needed.

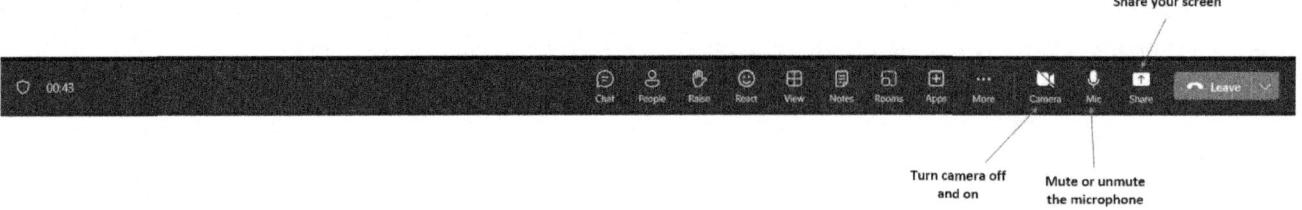

Share your screen

Turn camera off
and on

Mute or unmute
the microphone

Step 6: End the Video Conference

- To end the video conference, click on the "Leave" button at the top of the screen.

Hosting meetings and video conferences in Microsoft Teams is a straightforward process, empowering teams to collaborate and communicate effectively. By following the step-by-step instructions provided in this section, users can easily schedule meetings, invite participants, and conduct video conferences seamlessly. Microsoft Teams' integrated calendar and meeting features streamline communication, allowing teams to huddle virtually, discuss ideas, and make decisions efficiently. Whether conducting team meetings, client presentations, or cross-departmental discussions, Teams provides a comprehensive platform for hosting meetings and video conferences with ease and convenience.

7.8 Integrating with Other Apps in Microsoft Teams

Microsoft Teams offers a wide range of app integrations that enhance productivity and streamline workflows. By integrating with other apps, Teams users can bring their favourite tools and services directly into the Teams interface, enabling seamless collaboration and communication. In this section, we will explore how to integrate other apps with Microsoft Teams, by providing step-by-step instructions.

7.8.1 Accessing the Teams App Store

Step 1: Open Microsoft Teams

- Launch Microsoft Teams on your computer or device by clicking on the Teams icon or searching for "Microsoft Teams" in your operating system's search bar.

Step 2: Access the App Store

- In the left-hand navigation panel, click on the "Apps" tab to access the Teams app store.

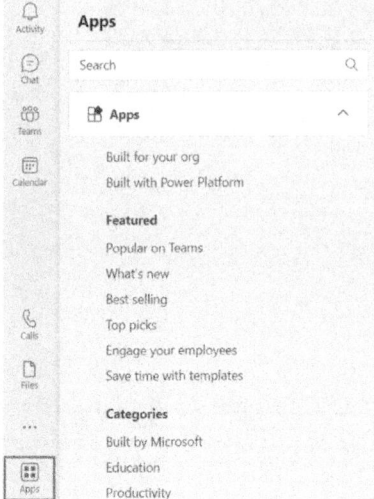

- The app store displays a wide range of available integrations and apps.

7.8.2 Integrating Apps with Microsoft Teams

Step 1: Browse the App Store

- In the app store, you can browse various app categories, such as Productivity, Education, Project Management, and more.

- Use the search bar to find specific apps or browse through the featured and recommended apps.

Step 2: Install an App

- To install an app, click on its tile to view more information.

- Click on the "Add" button to add the app to your Teams workspace.

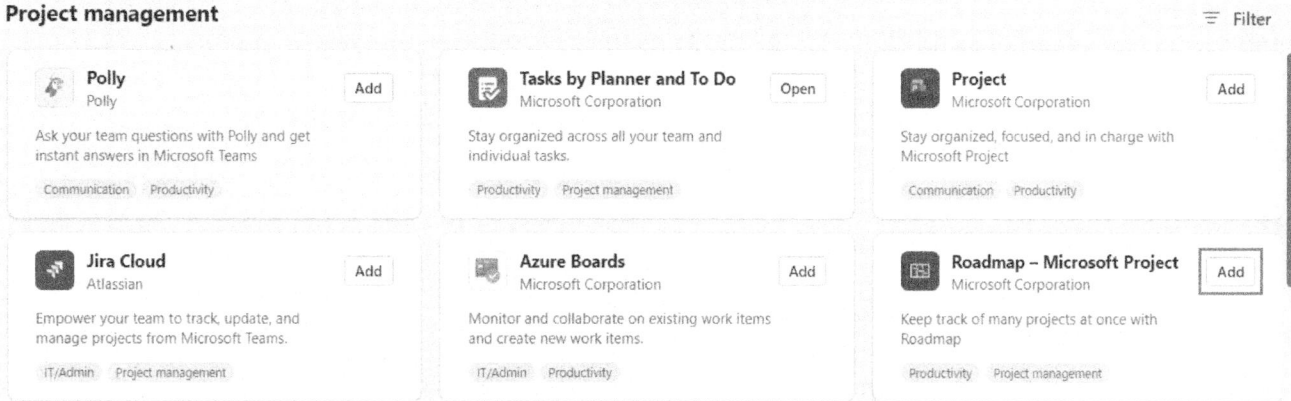

Step 3: Configure the App (If Needed)

- Some apps may require configuration or setup after installation.

- Follow the on-screen instructions to set up the app and connect it to your Teams account.

Step 4: Access the App

- Once the app is installed and configured, it will be available in the left-hand navigation panel under the "Apps" tab.

- Click on "Manage your apps" at the bottom to view the app.

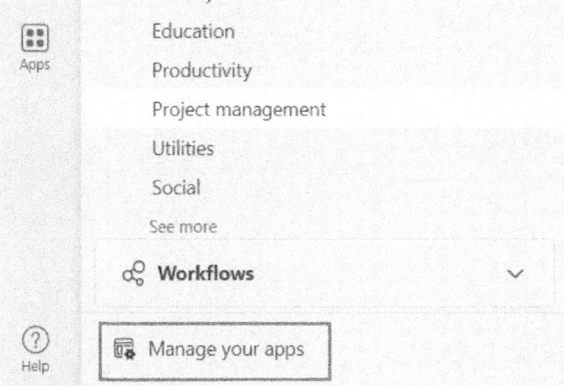

Click on the app's icon to access its features and functions.

7.8.3 Example: Integrating Trello with Microsoft Teams

Step 1: Install the Trello App

- In the app store, search for "Trello" using the search bar.

- Click on the Trello app tile to view more details.

- Click on the "Add" button to add Trello to your Teams workspace.

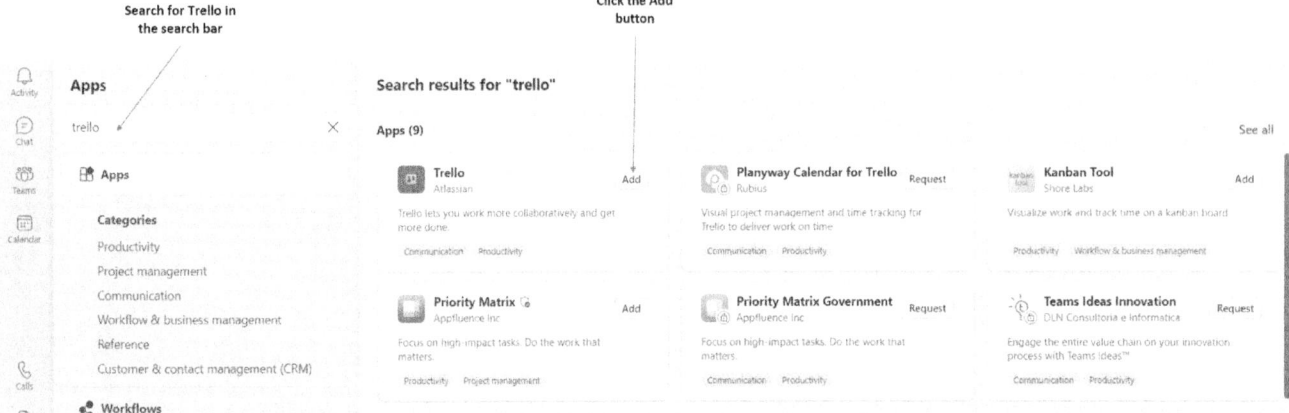

Step 2: Configure Trello Integration

- After installing Trello, follow the on-screen instructions to connect your Trello account to Teams.

Step 3: Access Trello from Teams

- Once the integration is complete, you will see the Trello icon in the left-hand navigation panel.

- Click on the Trello icon to access your Trello boards and cards directly from Teams.

Step 4: Collaborate with Trello in Teams

- From the Trello interface in Teams, you can view and manage your Trello boards, create new cards, and collaborate with team members seamlessly.

Integrating other apps with Microsoft Teams enhances productivity, communication, and collaboration within organisations and teams. By following the step-by-step instructions provided in this section, users can easily explore and install apps from the Teams app store and seamlessly integrate them into their Teams workspace. Microsoft Teams' robust app integrations allow users to bring their favourite tools and services directly into the Teams interface, streamlining workflows and empowering teams to work more efficiently. Teams provides a comprehensive platform for integrating and utilising various apps, making it a valuable tool for modern-day collaboration and productivity.

Chapter 8: Microsoft OneDrive

Microsoft OneDrive is a cloud-based file storage and synchronisation service provided by Microsoft as part of the Office 365 suite. It offers users a secure and convenient way to store, access, and share files from anywhere, on any device. OneDrive is designed to simplify file management and enhance collaboration, making it a versatile tool for individuals and businesses alike. In this chapter, we will explore what Microsoft OneDrive is, what it is used for, the benefits of OneDrive, and provide step-by-step instructions of how to use this powerful cloud storage service.

8.1 What is Microsoft OneDrive?

Microsoft OneDrive is a cloud-based storage service that allows users to store files and documents in the cloud instead of relying solely on local storage. It seamlessly syncs files across devices, enabling users to access their files from desktop computers, laptops, tablets, and smartphones with ease. OneDrive integrates with Microsoft Office applications and offers robust sharing and collaboration features, making it a comprehensive solution for file management and teamwork.

8.2 What is Microsoft OneDrive Used For?

Cloud Storage: OneDrive provides users with ample cloud storage to store files, photos, videos, and documents, reducing the need for physical storage devices.

File Synchronisation: OneDrive automatically syncs files across devices, ensuring that the latest versions are accessible from any device connected to the internet.

File Sharing: Users can easily share files and folders with others, allowing for seamless collaboration and real-time updates.

Collaboration: OneDrive integrates with Microsoft Office applications, facilitating real-time co-authoring of documents and spreadsheets with team members.

File Backup: OneDrive serves as an efficient file backup solution, protecting important data from hardware failures or accidental deletions.

Access Anywhere: OneDrive allows users to access their files from any device with an internet connection, providing flexibility and productivity on the go.

8.3 Benefits of Using Microsoft OneDrive

Accessibility: OneDrive ensures that files are accessible from any device, eliminating the need to carry physical storage devices and enabling remote work.

Version Control: OneDrive keeps track of file versions, allowing users to restore previous versions if needed and preventing accidental data loss.

Security: OneDrive employs robust security measures, ensuring that files are encrypted during transmission and storage, providing data protection.

Integration: OneDrive seamlessly integrates with Microsoft Office applications, streamlining productivity and file management within the familiar Office environment.

File Sharing Controls: OneDrive allows users to set permissions and control who can view, edit, or share specific files, maintaining data privacy and security.

Scalability: OneDrive offers scalable storage options, accommodating the growing storage needs of individuals and organisations.

8.4 Uploading and Managing Files in Microsoft OneDrive

Microsoft OneDrive provides a user-friendly interface for uploading and managing files in the cloud, making it easy to access and organise documents, photos, and other files from any device. In this section, we will explore how to upload and manage files in Microsoft OneDrive with step-by-step instructions.

8.4.1 Uploading Files to Microsoft OneDrive

Step 1: Open Microsoft OneDrive

- Access Microsoft OneDrive by visiting the OneDrive website or launching the OneDrive app on your computer or device.

Step 2: Sign Into Your Account

- Enter your Microsoft account credentials (email and password) to sign into your OneDrive account.

- If you don't have a Microsoft account, you can create one for free.

Step 3: Access the Upload Button

- In the OneDrive interface, click on the "Upload" button located at the top of the screen.

- A drop-down menu will appear with upload options.

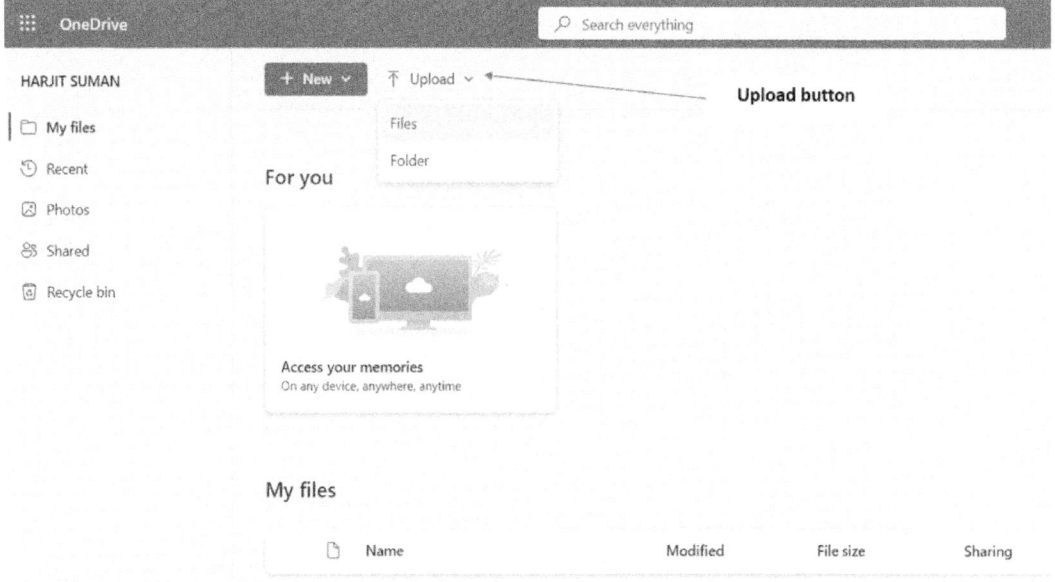

Step 4: Upload Files

- Click on "Files" in the drop-down menu to browse and select files from your local storage.

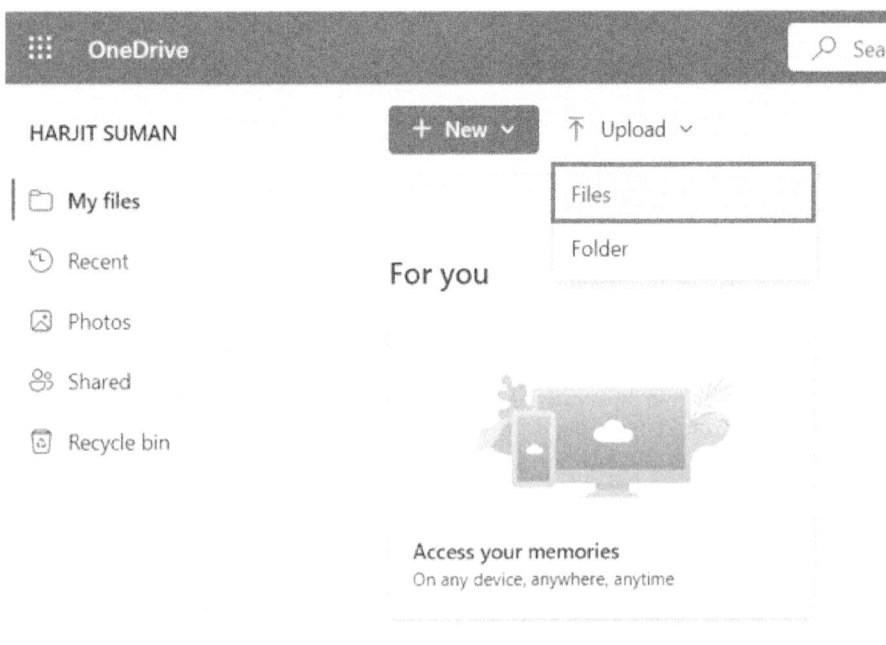

- Select one or multiple files to upload to your OneDrive.

- Click "Open" to begin the upload process.

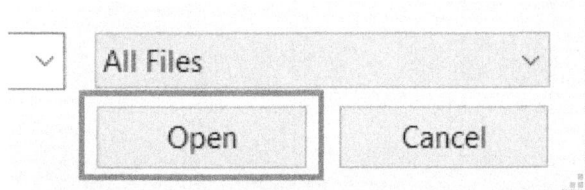

Step 5: Monitor Upload Progress

- The selected files will start uploading to your OneDrive.

- You can monitor the upload progress, and once it's complete, the files will be available in your OneDrive storage.

8.4.2 Managing Files in Microsoft OneDrive

Step 1: Access Your OneDrive

- Open Microsoft OneDrive and sign into your account.

Step 2: View and Organise Files

- In the OneDrive interface, you will see a list of files and folders in your storage.

- You can organise files into folders or create new folders to keep your files organised.

Step 3: Create a New Folder

- To create a new folder, click on the "New" button at the top of the screen.

- Select "Folder" from the drop-down menu.

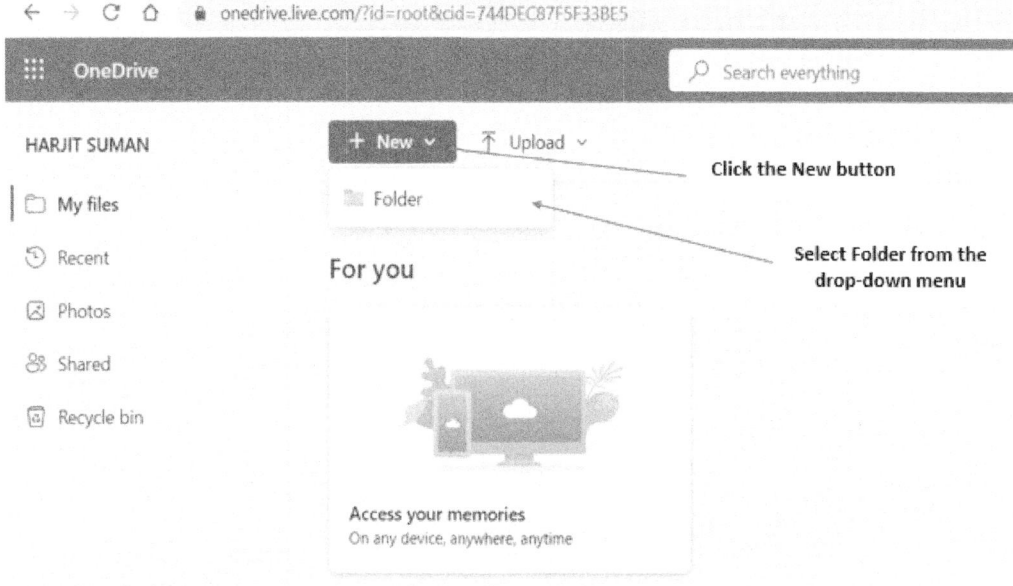

- Enter a name for the folder and click "Create".

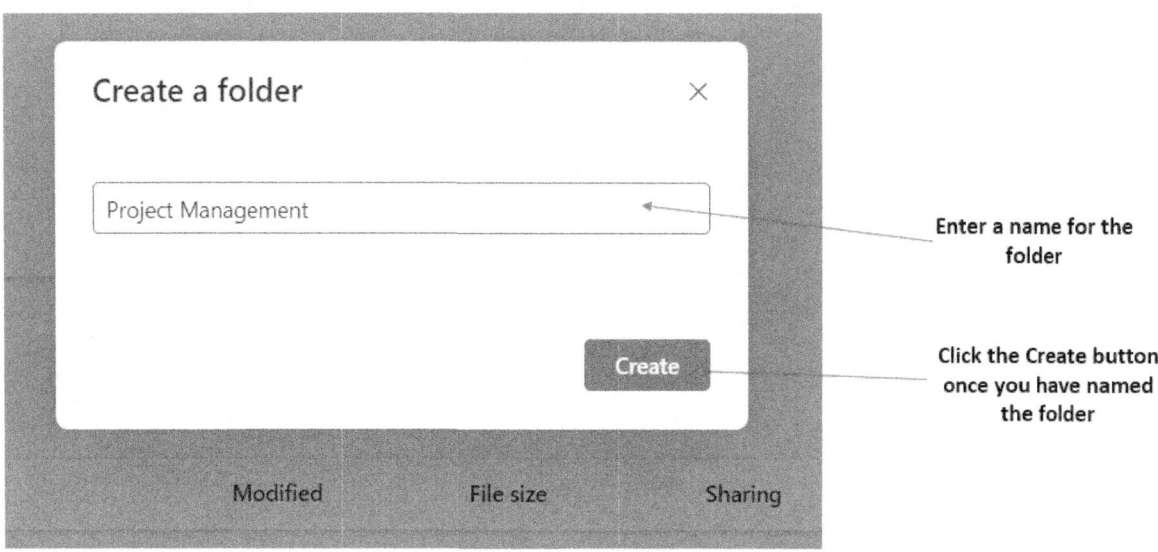

Step 4: Move Files to a Folder

- To move files into a folder, select the files you want to move by checking the boxes next to their names.

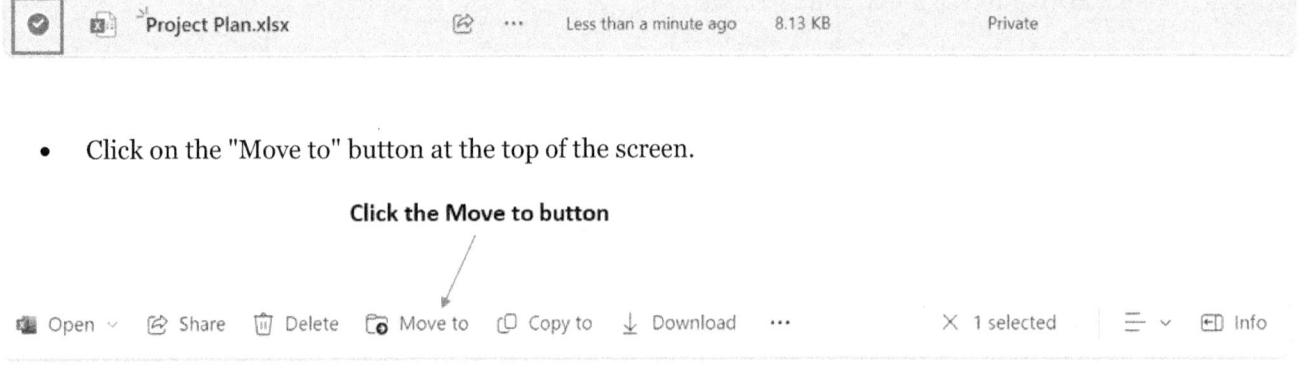

- Click on the "Move to" button at the top of the screen.

Click the Move to button

- Select the destination folder from the list, and then click the "Move here" button. The files will be moved to the selected folder.

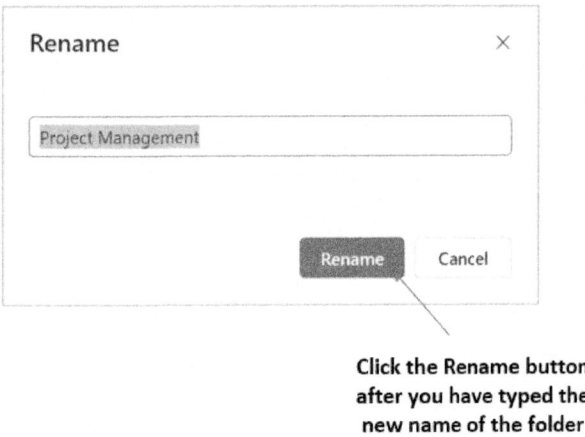

Step 5: Rename Files or Folders

- To rename a file or folder, right-click on its name and select "Rename".

- Enter the new name and press the "Rename" button to save the changes.

Rename   ×

Project Management

Rename   Cancel

**Click the Rename button
after you have typed the
new name of the folder**

Step 6: Delete Files or Folders

- To delete files or folders, select them by checking the boxes next to their names.

- Click on the "Delete" button at the top of the screen.

Click the Delete button

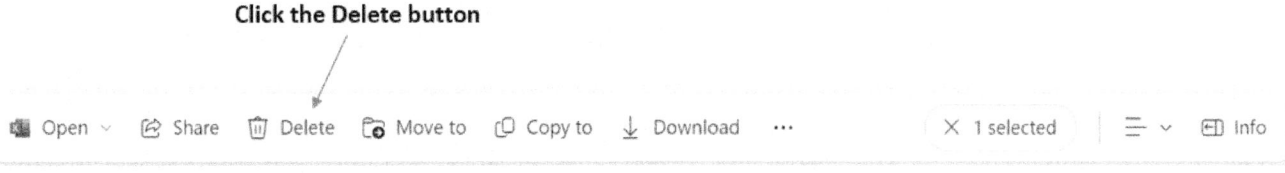

- Confirm the deletion when prompted.

Step 7: Restore Deleted Files (If Needed)

- If you accidentally deleted a file, click on the "Recycle bin" link in the left-hand navigation panel.

- Select the file you want to restore and click on the "Restore" button.

Click the Restore button

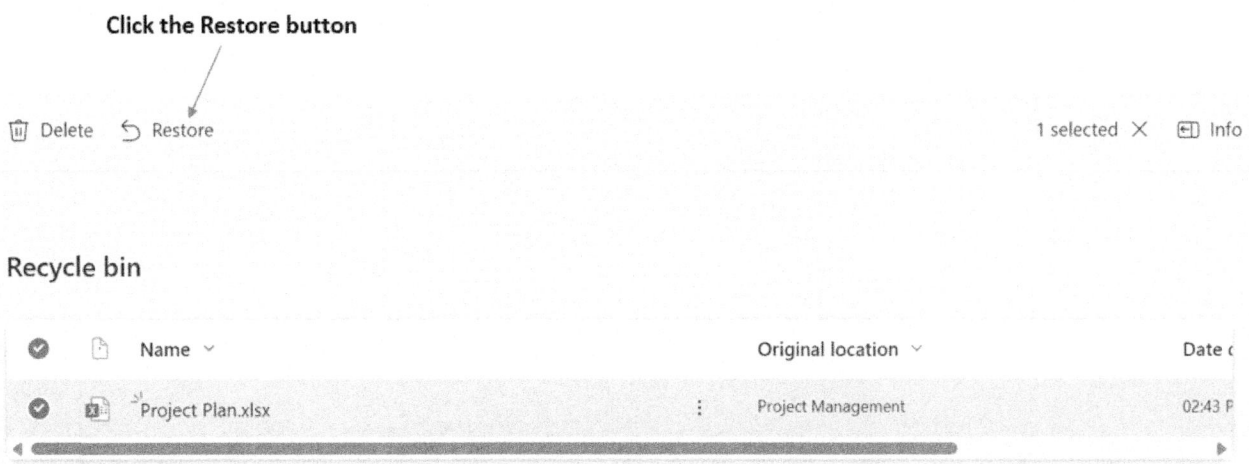

Uploading and managing files in Microsoft OneDrive is a straightforward process that allows users to store, organise, and access their files conveniently in the cloud. By following the step-by-step instructions provided in this section, users can easily upload files to their OneDrive and manage their files by creating folders, moving files, renaming items, and deleting unwanted files. Microsoft OneDrive's user-friendly interface and robust file management features make it an excellent tool for individuals and businesses seeking efficient cloud storage and file organisation solutions. Whether it's documents, photos, or other files, OneDrive simplifies file management and enhances accessibility, ensuring that your files are securely stored and easily accessible from any device with an internet connection.

8.5 Sharing Files and Folders in Microsoft OneDrive

Microsoft OneDrive offers powerful sharing capabilities that enable users to collaborate with others by granting them access to specific files or folders. With flexible sharing options and permissions settings, OneDrive ensures that data is shared securely and efficiently. In this section, we will explore how to share files and folders in Microsoft OneDrive by providing step-by-step instructions.

8.5.1 Sharing Files in Microsoft OneDrive

Step 1: Open Microsoft OneDrive

- Access Microsoft OneDrive by visiting the OneDrive website or launching the OneDrive app on your computer or device.

Step 2: Sign Into Your Account

- Enter your Microsoft account credentials (email and password) to sign into your OneDrive account.

- If you don't have a Microsoft account, you can create one for free.

Step 3: Locate the File to Share

- In the OneDrive interface, browse and locate the file you want to share.

- Hover your mouse over the file to reveal the selection checkboxes.

Step 4: Start Sharing

- Click on the checkbox next to the file you want to share to select it.

- At the top of the screen, click on the "Share" button.

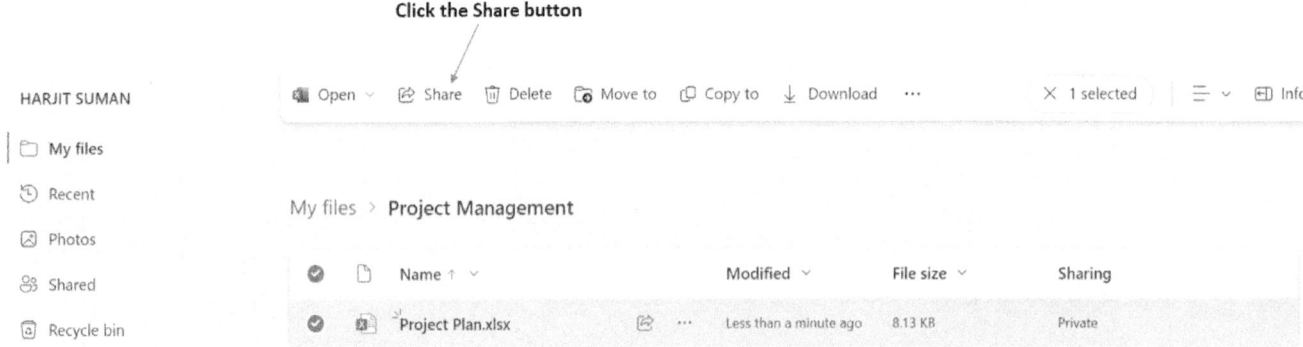

Step 5: Choose Sharing Options

- The sharing options will appear. By default, the file is set to "Anyone with the link can edit".

- Click on the "Anyone with the link can edit" to change the sharing settings.

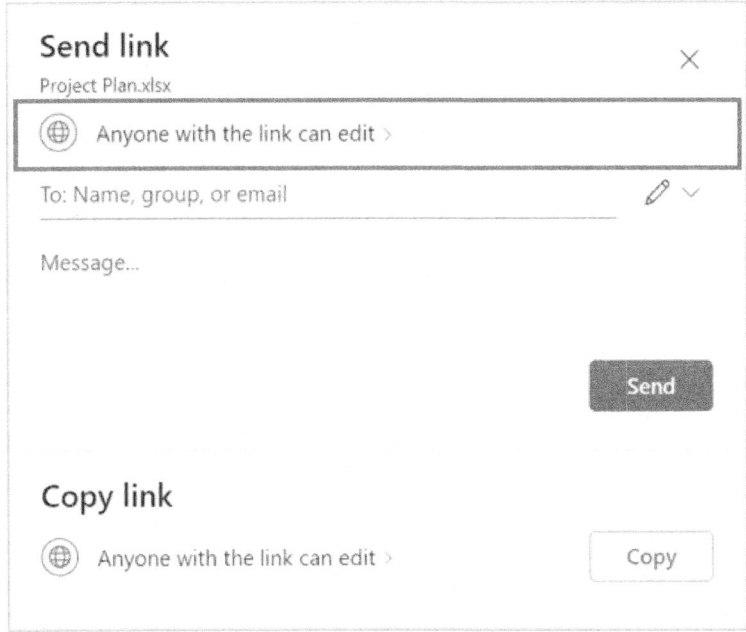

Step 6: Select Sharing Permission

- Choose one of the sharing options:

  - "Anyone" allows anyone who has the link to access the file.

  - "Specific people" allows you to invite specific individuals by entering their email addresses.

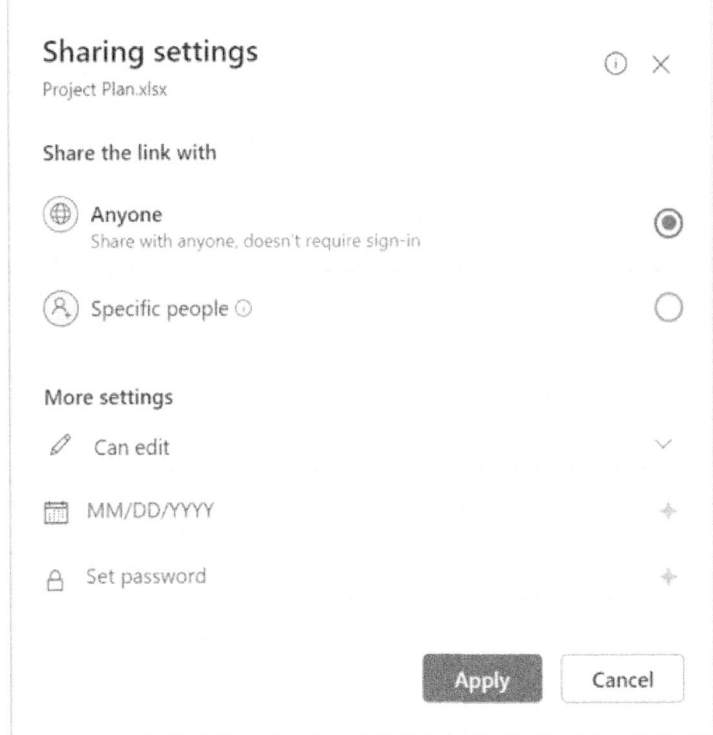

Step 7: Set Editing Permissions

- Depending on the sharing option you selected, you can choose whether recipients can "View" or "Edit" the file.

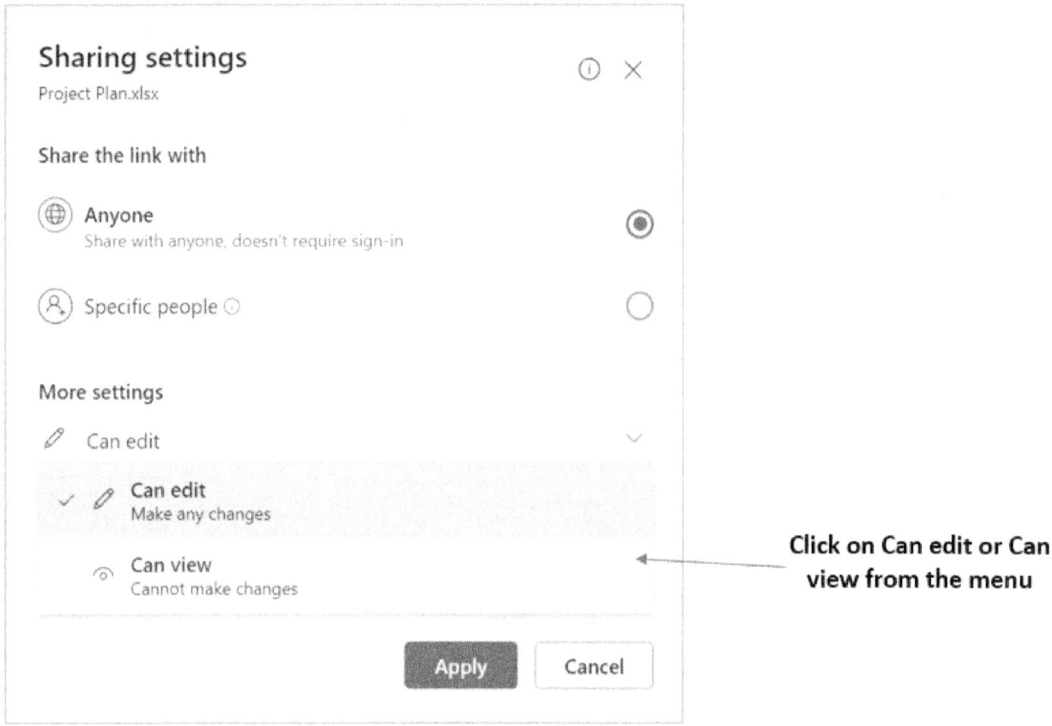

- If you select "Edit," recipients will be able to make changes to the file.

- Click on the "Apply" button once you have set the permissions.

Step 8: Add a Personal Message (Optional)

- You can include a personal message with the invitation in the "Message" field and entering your message.

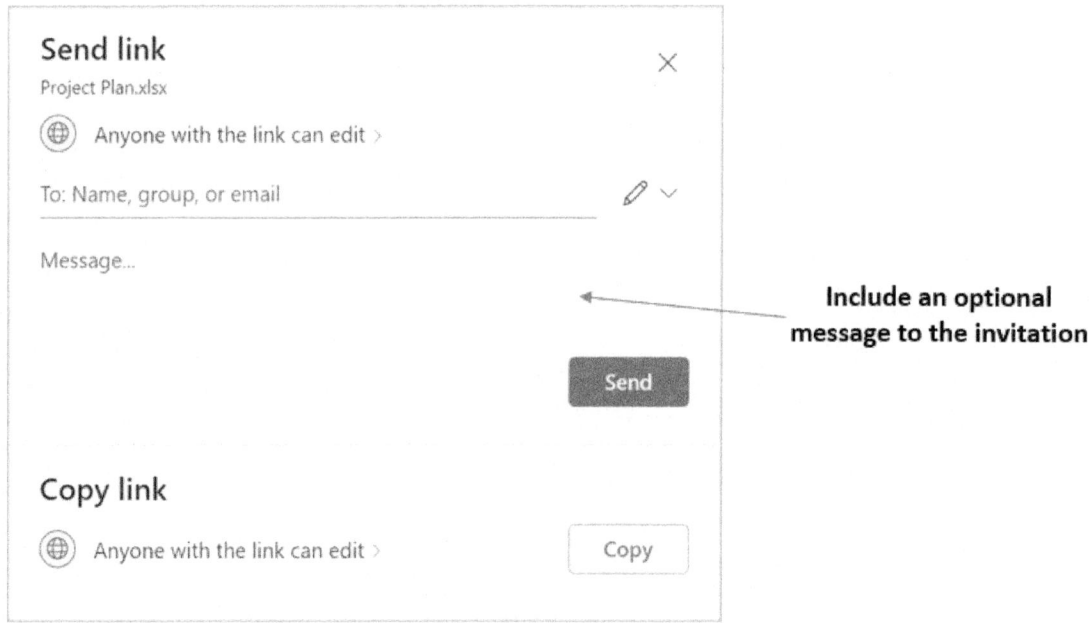

Step 9: Send the Sharing Invitation

- Click on the "Send" button to send the sharing invitation to the selected recipients.

- The recipients will receive an email with a link to access the shared file.

8.5.2 Sharing Folders in Microsoft OneDrive

Step 1: Open Microsoft OneDrive

- Access Microsoft OneDrive by visiting the OneDrive website or launching the OneDrive app on your computer or device.

Step 2: Sign Into Your Account

- Enter your Microsoft account credentials (email and password) to sign into your OneDrive account.

- If you don't have a Microsoft account, you can create one for free.

Step 3: Locate the Folder to Share

- In the OneDrive interface, browse and locate the folder you want to share.

- Hover your mouse over the folder to reveal the selection checkboxes.

Step 4: Start Sharing

- Click on the checkbox next to the folder you want to share to select it.

- At the top of the screen, click on the "Share" button.

Step 5: Choose Sharing Options

- The sharing options will appear. By default, the folder is set to "Anyone with the link can edit".

- Click on the "Anyone with the link can edit" to change the sharing settings.

Step 6: Select Sharing Permission

- Choose one of the sharing options:

    o "Anyone" allows anyone who has the link to access the folder.

    o "Specific people" allows you to invite specific individuals by entering their email addresses.

Step 7: Set Editing Permissions

- Depending on the sharing option you selected, you can choose whether recipients can "View" or "Edit" the folder.

- If you select "Edit," recipients will be able to make changes to the files inside the folder.

Step 8: Add a Personal Message (Optional)

- You can include a personal message with the invitation in the "Message" field and entering your message.

Step 9: Send the Sharing Invitation

- Click on the "Send" button to send the sharing invitation to the selected recipients.

- The recipients will receive an email with a link to access the shared folder.

8.5.3 Managing Shared Files and Folders

Step 1: Open Microsoft OneDrive

- Access Microsoft OneDrive by visiting the OneDrive website or launching the OneDrive app on your computer or device.

Step 2: Sign Into Your Account

- Enter your Microsoft account credentials (email and password) to sign into your OneDrive account.

- If you don't have a Microsoft account, you can create one for free.

Step 3: Access Shared with Me (Files)

- In the OneDrive interface, click on "Shared" in the left-hand navigation panel to access files shared with you.

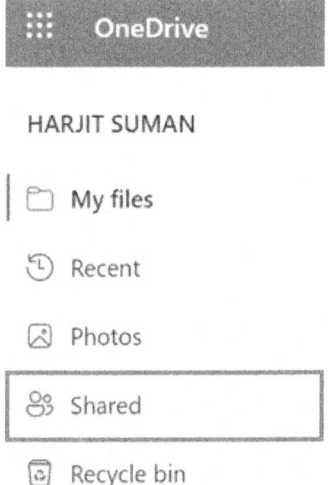

- The "Shared with you" view will display all the files and folders shared by others with your account.

Step 4: Access Shared by You (Folders)

- To view the files and folders you have shared with others, click on "Shared by you" tab at the top of the screen.

Step 5: Manage Shared Files

- To manage files shared with you, select the file, and then select the appropriate action, such as "Open", "Download," or "Remove from shared list" at the top of the screen.

Step 6: Manage Shared Folders

- To manage folders shared with you, select the appropriate action, such as "Open," "Download," or "Remove from shared list" at the top of the screen.

Step 7: Stop Sharing (Files and Folders)

- To stop sharing a file or folder you shared with others, locate the file/folder in your OneDrive.

- Right-click on the file/folder and select "Manage access".

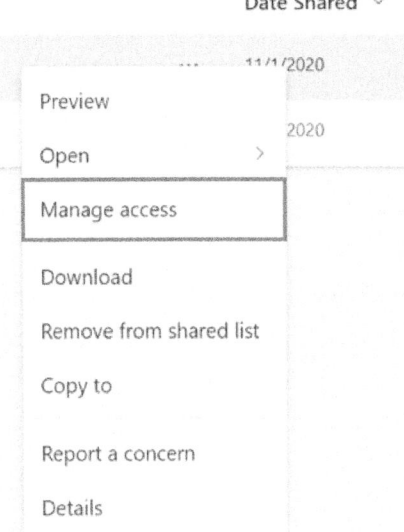

- In the sharing settings, click on the "Stop sharing" button to revoke access.

Sharing files and folders in Microsoft OneDrive is a straightforward process that enables users to collaborate effectively and securely. By following the step-by-step instructions provided in this section, users can easily share files and folders with specific individuals or teams, set permissions, and manage shared files and folders. Microsoft OneDrive's robust sharing capabilities enhance productivity, allowing users to collaborate seamlessly and access shared files from any device with an internet connection. Whether for personal use, project collaboration, or team coordination, OneDrive's flexible sharing features make it a powerful cloud storage solution for individuals and businesses alike.

8.6 OneDrive Sync and Mobile App in Microsoft OneDrive

Microsoft OneDrive offers a convenient way to access and sync your files across devices, ensuring that you have the latest version of your files on your computer and mobile devices. In this section, we will provide step-by-step instructions on how to set up OneDrive Sync on your computer and use the OneDrive mobile app.

8.6.1 Setting Up OneDrive Sync on Your Computer

Step 1: Open Microsoft OneDrive on Your Computer

- If you don't have the OneDrive desktop app installed, download it from the Microsoft website and follow the installation instructions.

- Launch the OneDrive app on your computer.

Step 2: Sign Into Your Microsoft Account

- Enter your Microsoft account credentials (email and password) to sign into your OneDrive account.

- If you don't have a Microsoft account, you can create one for free.

Step 3: Choose Folders to Sync

- After signing in, the OneDrive setup wizard will prompt you to choose which folders you want to sync to your computer.

- Select the folders you want to sync or choose the "Sync all files and folders" option.

- Click "Next" to proceed.

Step 4: Set Up OneDrive Sync

- In the next step, you can choose to use OneDrive as your default location for storing files and documents.

- Select the appropriate option and click "Next".

Step 5: Choose Your OneDrive Folder Location

- In this step, you can select the location on your computer where you want to store your OneDrive folder.

- You can choose the default location or specify a custom folder path.

- Click "Next" to continue.

Step 6: Finish Setup

- Review your settings and click "Done" to complete the OneDrive setup.

- OneDrive will begin syncing the selected folders to your computer.

8.6.2 Using the OneDrive Mobile App

Step 1: Download the OneDrive Mobile App

- Open the App Store (iOS) or Google Play Store (Android) on your mobile device.

- Search for "OneDrive" in the app store and download the official Microsoft OneDrive app.

Step 2: Sign Into Your Microsoft Account

- Launch the OneDrive app on your mobile device.

- Enter your Microsoft account credentials (email and password) to sign into your OneDrive account.

- If you don't have a Microsoft account, you can create one for free.

Step 3: Access Your Files

- Once signed in, you will see your OneDrive files and folders on the mobile app.

- Navigate through your files and folders to find the file you want to access.

Step 4: Upload Files to OneDrive

- To upload files from your mobile device to OneDrive, tap the "Upload" button in the app.

- Choose the file or photo you want to upload from your device's storage.

Step 5: Download and Access Files Offline

- To access files offline, tap the three-dot menu next to the file and select "Make available offline".

- The file will be downloaded to your device and accessible without an internet connection.

Step 6: Share Files from OneDrive

- To share a file with others, tap and hold the file you want to share.

- Select the "Share" option from the context menu.

- Choose how you want to share the file (e.g., via email, link, or other apps).

Step 7: Enable Camera Upload (Optional)

- To automatically upload photos and videos from your mobile device's camera roll to OneDrive, tap the "Me" or "Profile" tab in the app.

- Go to "Settings" and then "Camera Upload".

- Turn on "Camera Upload" to enable automatic syncing of your photos and videos to OneDrive.

Setting up OneDrive Sync on your computer and using the OneDrive mobile app allows you to access, manage, and share your files seamlessly across devices. By following the step-by-step instructions provided in this section, you can easily set up OneDrive on your computer, select folders for syncing, and use the OneDrive mobile app to access files on the go. OneDrive's cross-platform compatibility and real-time sync ensure that you have the latest version of your files available on your computer and mobile devices, promoting productivity and collaboration wherever you are. Whether you need to access important documents while traveling or share files with colleagues from your smartphone, the OneDrive mobile app empowers you to stay connected and productive in today's mobile-centric world.

8.7 Collaboration and Version History in Microsoft OneDrive

Microsoft OneDrive offers robust collaboration features that enable users to work together on files and documents in real-time, facilitating seamless teamwork and enhancing productivity. Additionally, OneDrive keeps track of version history, allowing users to access and restore previous versions of files, ensuring data integrity and preventing accidental data loss. In this section, we will provide step-by-step instructions on how to collaborate with others and utilise version history in Microsoft OneDrive.

8.7.1 Collaboration in Microsoft OneDrive

Step 1: Open Microsoft OneDrive

- Access Microsoft OneDrive by visiting the OneDrive website or launching the OneDrive app on your computer or device.

Step 2: Sign Into Your Account

- Enter your Microsoft account credentials (email and password) to sign into your OneDrive account.

- If you don't have a Microsoft account, you can create one for free.

Step 3: Select a File to Collaborate On

- In the OneDrive interface, browse and locate the file you want to collaborate on.

- Click on the file to open it in the appropriate application (e.g., Word, Excel, PowerPoint).

Step 4: Invite Collaborators

- While the file is open in the application, click on the "Share" button in the top right corner and then select "Share" from the menu.

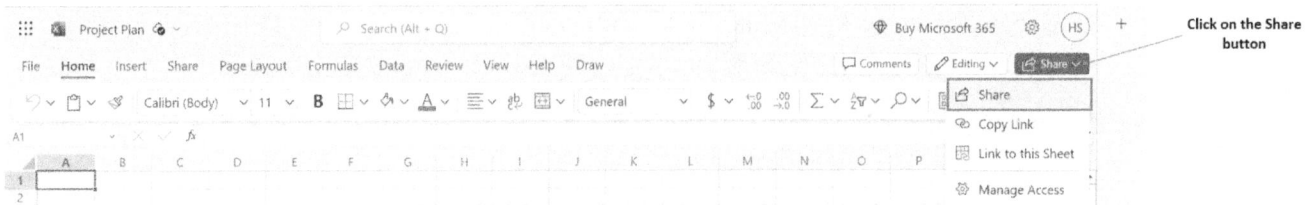

- In the sharing pane, enter the email addresses of the people you want to collaborate with.

- Choose the permission level for each collaborator (e.g., "Can edit" or "Can view").

- Optionally, include a personal message with the invitation.

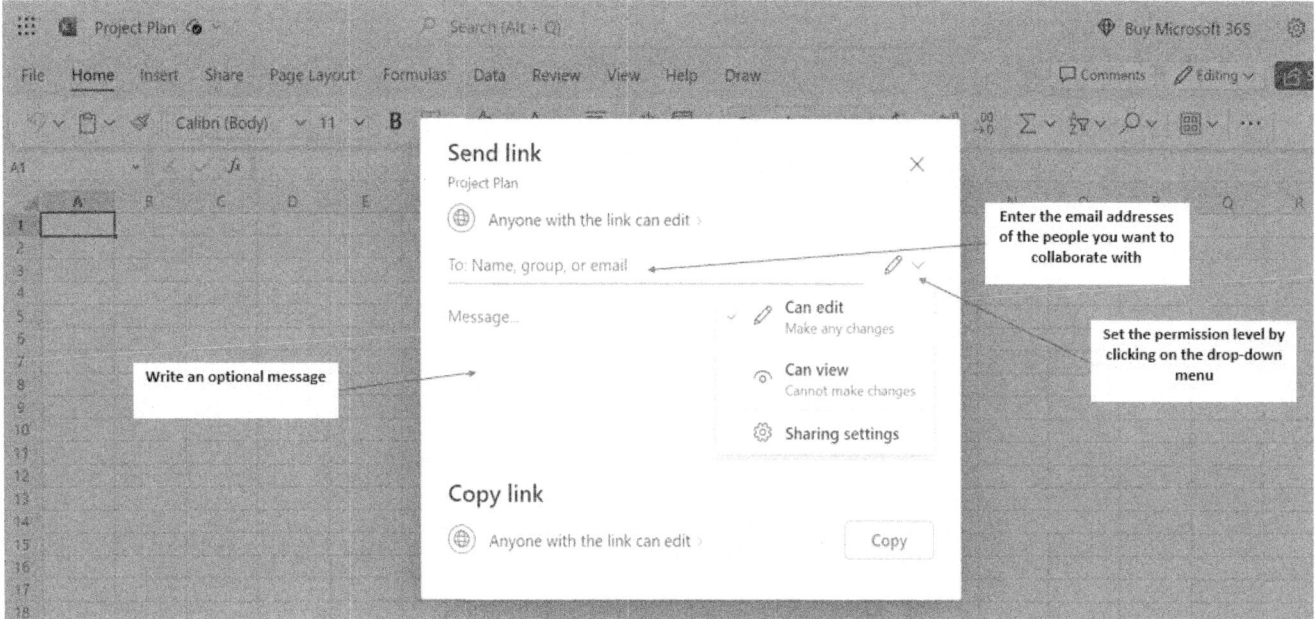

- Click on the "Send" button to send the collaboration invitation.

Step 5: Collaborate in Real-Time

- Once the invited collaborators accept the invitation and open the file, you can work together in real-time.

- Changes made by each collaborator are automatically synced and visible to others.

Step 6: Review Changes and Comments

- Collaborators can leave comments within the document to provide feedback or ask questions.

- Review and address the comments as necessary to facilitate effective collaboration.

Step 7: Save and Close the File

- After finishing collaboration, save the changes made to the document.

- Close the file to end the real-time collaboration session.

8.7.2 Version History in Microsoft OneDrive

Step 1: Open Microsoft OneDrive

- Access Microsoft OneDrive by visiting the OneDrive website or launching the OneDrive app on your computer or device.

Step 2: Sign Into Your Account

- Enter your Microsoft account credentials (email and password) to sign into your OneDrive account.

- If you don't have a Microsoft account, you can create one for free.

Step 3: Locate the File with Version History

- In the OneDrive interface, browse and locate the file for which you want to access version history.

- Right-click on the file and select "Version history" from the context menu.

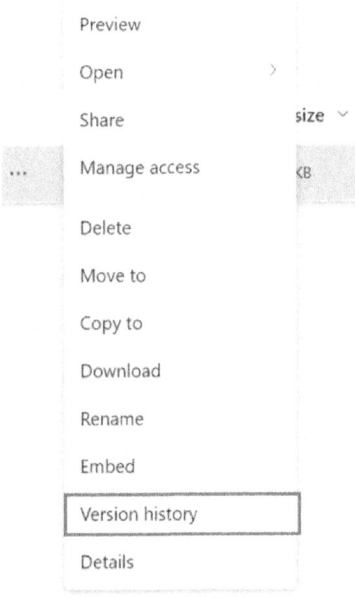

Step 4: Access Version History

- The version history pane will appear, displaying a list of previous versions of the file.

- Each version includes a timestamp and information about who made the changes.

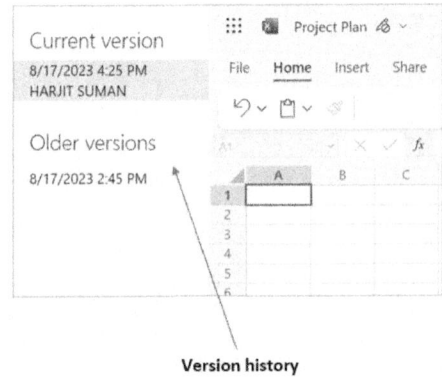

Version history

Step 5: View Previous Versions

- Click on a specific version to preview it in the right-hand pane.

- The preview will display the content of the file at that point in time.

Step 6: Restore Previous Version (If Needed)

- To restore a previous version of the file, select the version you want to revert to.

- Click on the "Restore" button to replace the current version with the selected version.

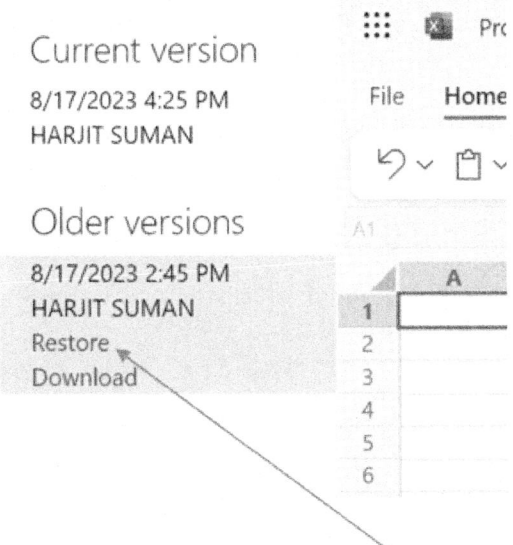

**Click on the Restore button
to restore previous version**

Collaboration and version history in Microsoft OneDrive empower users to work together effectively and maintain data integrity. By following the step-by-step instructions provided in this section, users can easily collaborate with others in real-time on files, inviting collaborators and managing permissions. Additionally, the version history feature ensures that users can access and restore previous versions of files, allowing for data recovery and maintaining the accuracy of shared documents. Microsoft OneDrive's powerful collaboration tools and version control capabilities make it a valuable platform for teamwork, enabling seamless collaboration and efficient file management across individuals and teams.

Chapter 9: Microsoft Access

Microsoft Access is a powerful and user-friendly database management system developed by Microsoft. It is part of the Microsoft Office suite and is designed to help individuals and businesses efficiently store, manage, and analyse large volumes of data. In this chapter, we will explore what Microsoft Access is, what it is used for, the benefits of using it, and provide step-by-step instructions on how to use this versatile database application.

9.1 What is Microsoft Access?

Microsoft Access is a relational database management system (RDBMS) that allows users to create and manage databases. It provides a graphical user interface (GUI) that simplifies the process of designing and working with databases, making it accessible to users with varying levels of technical expertise. Access utilises a combination of tables, queries, forms, and reports to organise and present data, allowing users to interact with their data in meaningful ways.

9.2 What is Microsoft Access Used For?

Data Storage and Organisation: Microsoft Access allows users to store large amounts of data in a structured manner, facilitating efficient data organisation and retrieval.

Data Analysis and Reporting: Access provides powerful tools for querying and filtering data, enabling users to perform complex data analysis and generate comprehensive reports.

Building Forms for Data Entry: Users can create custom forms in Access to simplify data entry and ensure data accuracy.

Developing Applications: Access can be used to develop small-scale business applications, such as inventory management systems, project trackers, and customer relationship management (CRM) solutions.

Integrating with Other Office Applications: Access seamlessly integrates with other Microsoft Office applications, allowing users to import and export data between Access and Excel, Word, and other Office programs.

9.3 Benefits of Using Microsoft Access

User-Friendly Interface: Access offers a visually intuitive interface, making it easy for beginners to start working with databases.

Customisability: Users can tailor their databases, forms, and reports to meet specific business needs and workflows.

Quick Data Analysis: Access provides quick and efficient data analysis capabilities through queries and reports, enabling users to gain valuable insights from their data.

Data Security: Access allows users to set permissions and access controls to ensure data security and privacy.

Scalability: While suitable for small to medium-sized databases, Access can handle growing data volumes and is a stepping stone to more advanced database systems for larger-scale projects.

Time and Cost Savings: Access enables users to create their database solutions without the need for extensive programming knowledge, saving time and costs associated with custom software development.

9.4 Creating and Managing Databases in Microsoft Access

Microsoft Access allows users to create and manage databases to efficiently store, organise, and analyse data. In this section, we will walk you through the process of creating and managing a database in Microsoft Access with step-by-step instructions.

9.4.1 Creating a New Database

Step 1: Open Microsoft Access

- Launch Microsoft Access from the Start menu or desktop shortcut.

Step 2: Choose a Database Template (Optional)

- Upon opening Access, you will see the "New" tab.

- Access offers various pre-designed database templates for common tasks like asset tracking, task management, or nutrition tracking.

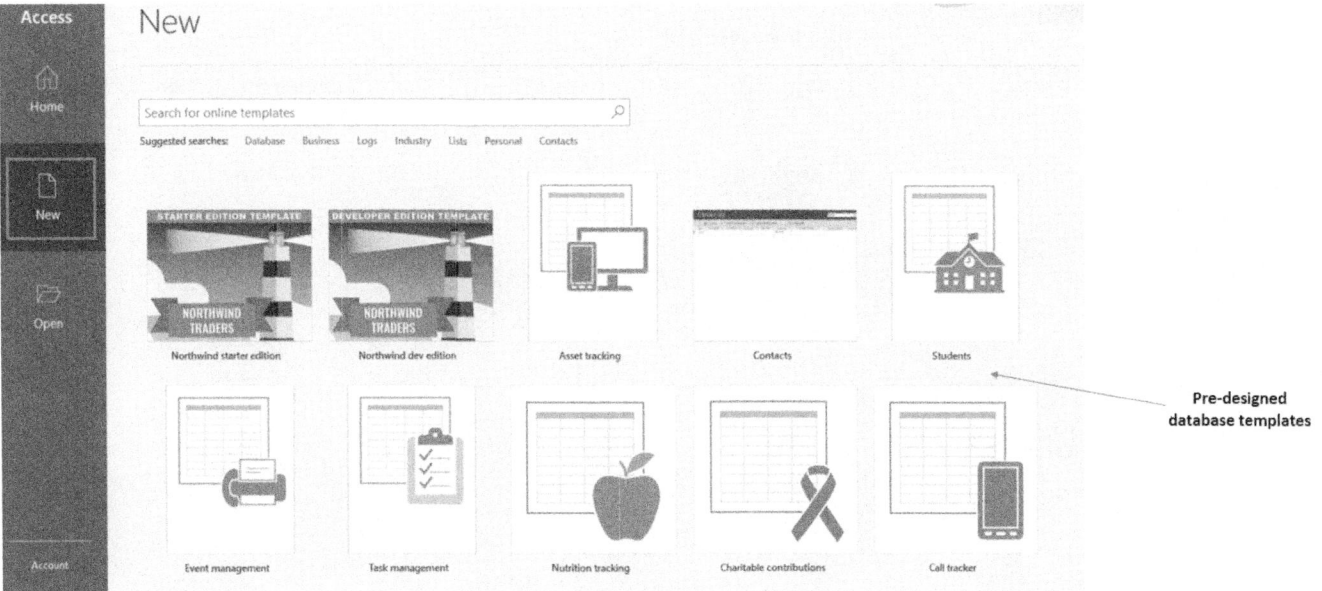

- If you want to use a template, select the appropriate one and click "Create".

Step 3: Create a Blank Database

- If you prefer to create a new database from scratch, click on the "Blank database" option.

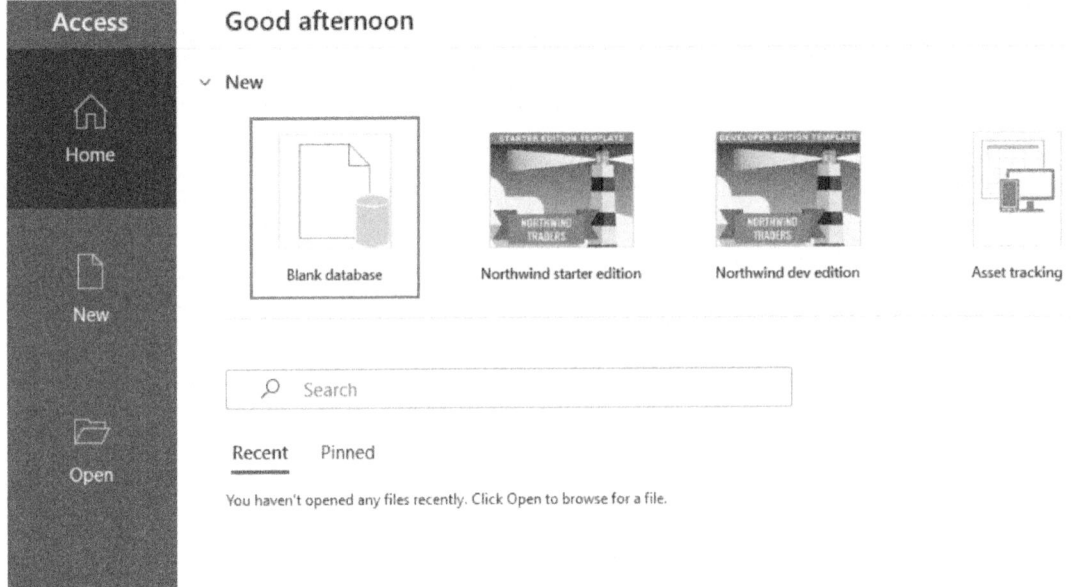

- Choose a location to save the database and give it a meaningful name.

- Click "Create" to proceed.

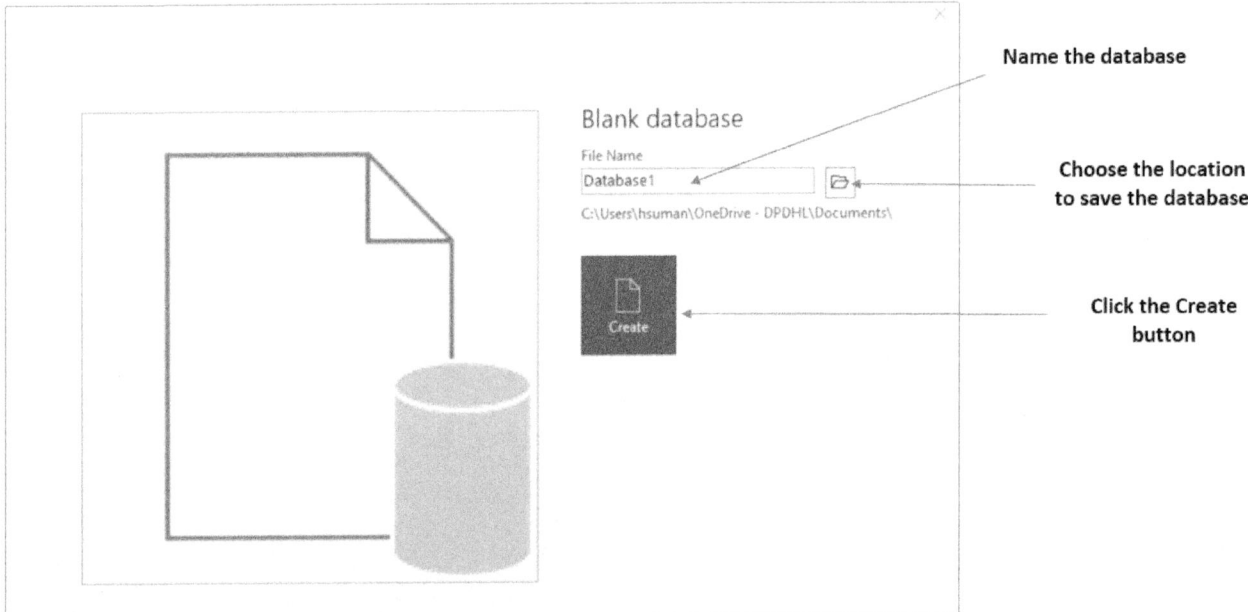

9.4.2 Navigating the Access Interface

Step 1: Explore the Access Interface

- Once the database is created, you will be taken to the main Access interface.

- The interface consists of a Ribbon at the top with various tabs, a Navigation pane on the left, and the main workspace in the centre.

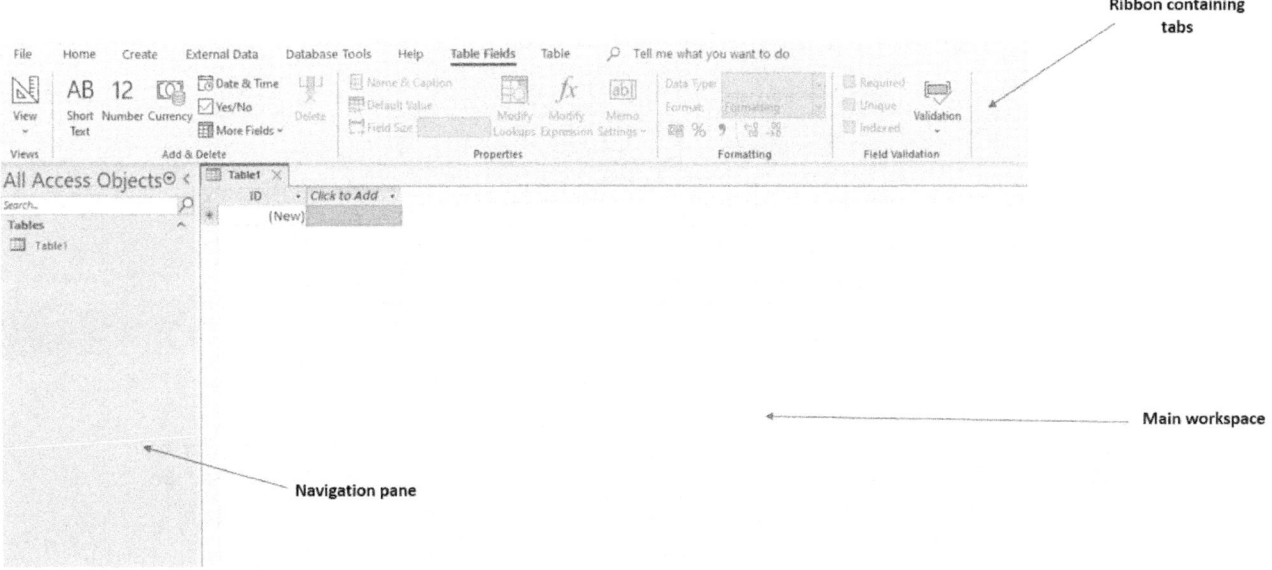

Step 2: Understanding the Navigation Pane

- The Navigation pane lists all the objects in your database, such as tables, queries, forms, and reports.

- Click on the arrow next to each section to expand or collapse the objects.

9.4.3 Creating Tables to Store Data

Step 1: Create a New Table

- Access will automatically create a table for you.

- To create a new table, in the "Create" tab, click on the "Table" button in the "Tables" group in the ribbon.

- Access will create a new table and open the "Datasheet View" to design the table.

Step 2: Define Data Types for Fields

- Click the "Click to Add" field heading and select a data type from the menu.

- When selecting a data type, select the smallest or shortest field that us required for your data. For example, don't choose "Long Text" if the text is only going to be two or three characters long.

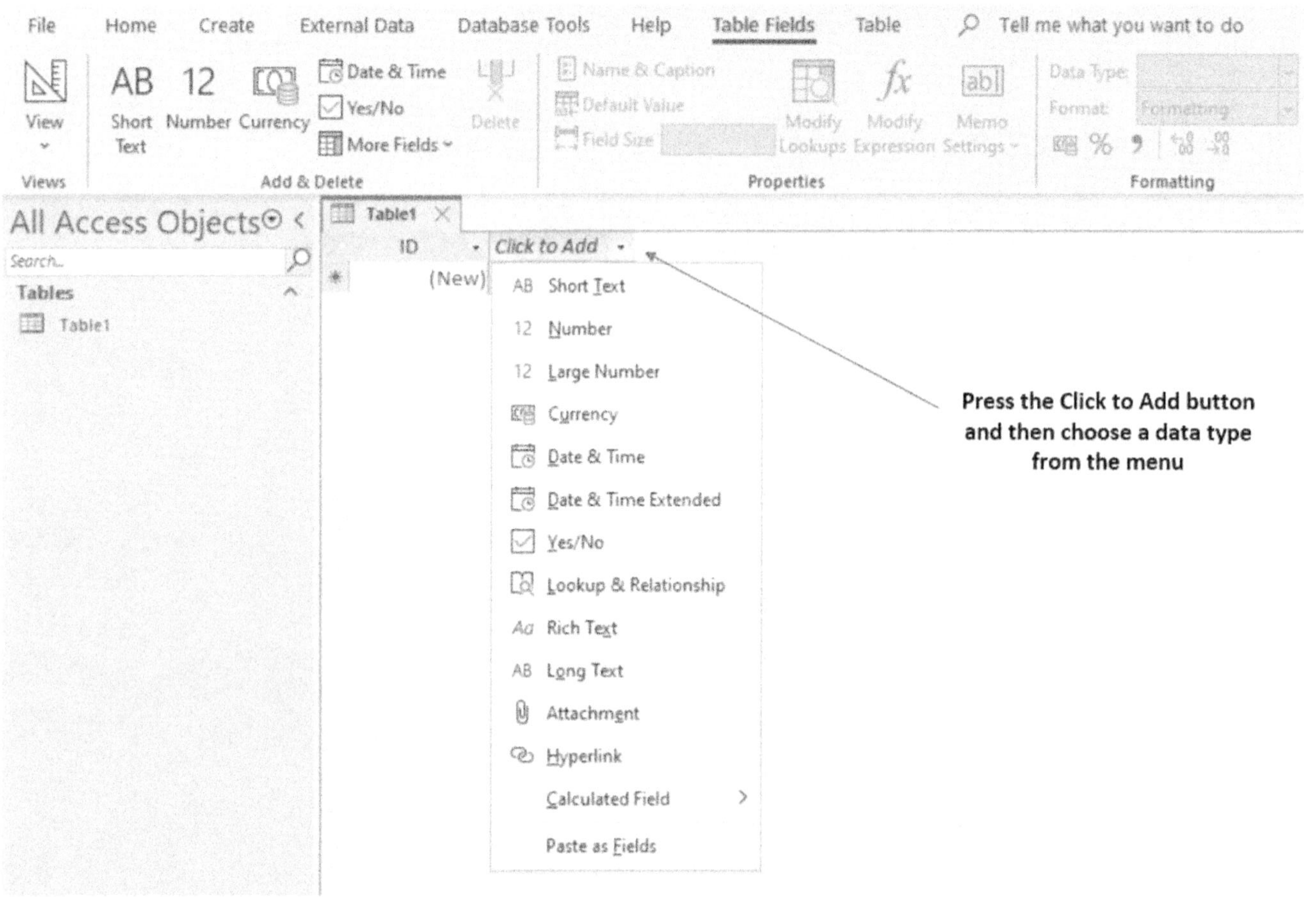

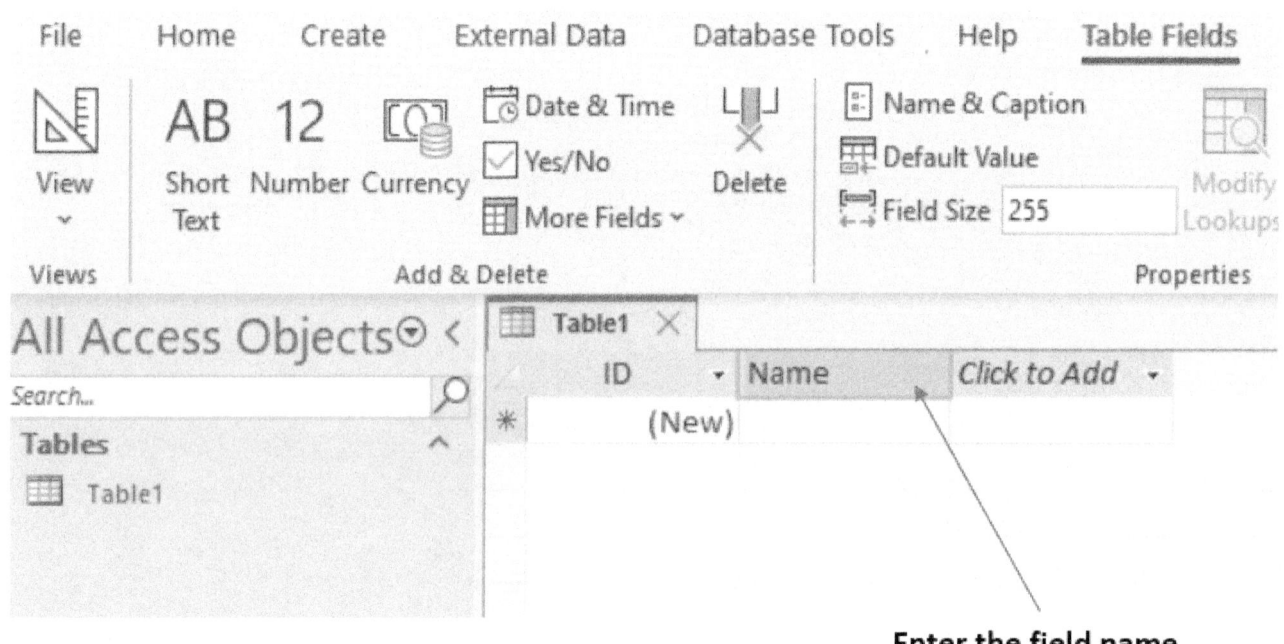

Step 3: Type a name for the field

- Enter the name of the field.

Enter the field name

Step 4: Add the Remaining Fields (Columns) to the Table

- Repeat steps 2 and 3 to add the remaining fields to your table. Ensure each field has a unique name that describes the type of data it will store (e.g., "ID," "Name," "Email Address," etc.).

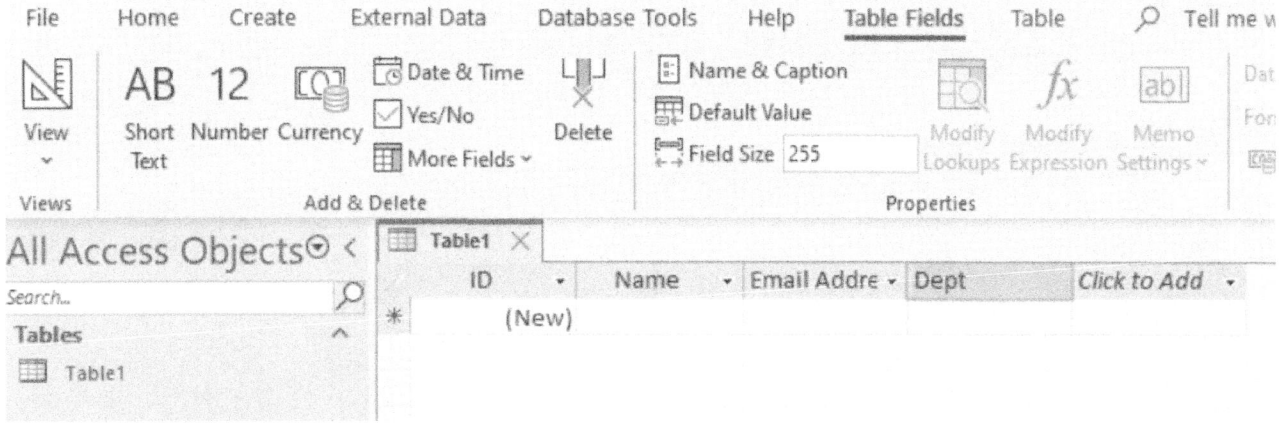

Step 5: Save the Table

- Once you have added all the fields, press "Ctrl + S" or click on the "Save" button in the Ribbon.

- Give the table a name and click "OK" to save it.

9.4.4 Entering Data into the Table

Step 1: Navigate to Datasheet View

- In the Navigation pane, click on the table you just created to select it.

- Access will open the table in "Datasheet View," ready for data entry.

Step 2: Enter Data

- Begin entering data into the table, row by row, field by field.

- Use the "Tab" key to move to the next field, and the "Enter" key to move to the next row.

- Enter sample data into each field to populate the table.

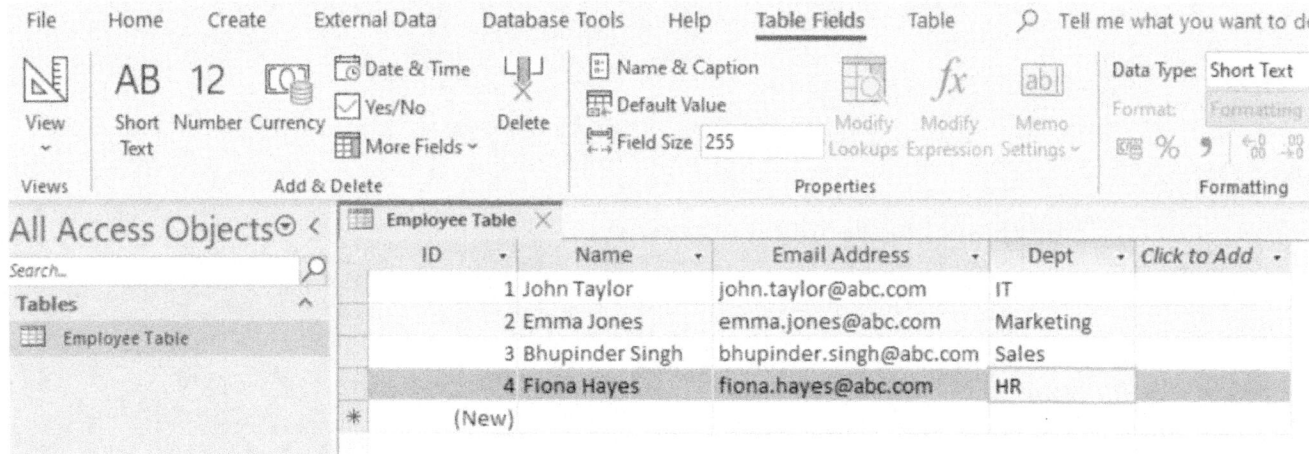

9.4.5 Modifying Table Structure (Adding, Deleting, or Renaming Fields)

Step 1: Enter Design View

- To modify the table structure, right-click on the table in the Navigation pane.

- Select "Design View" from the context menu.

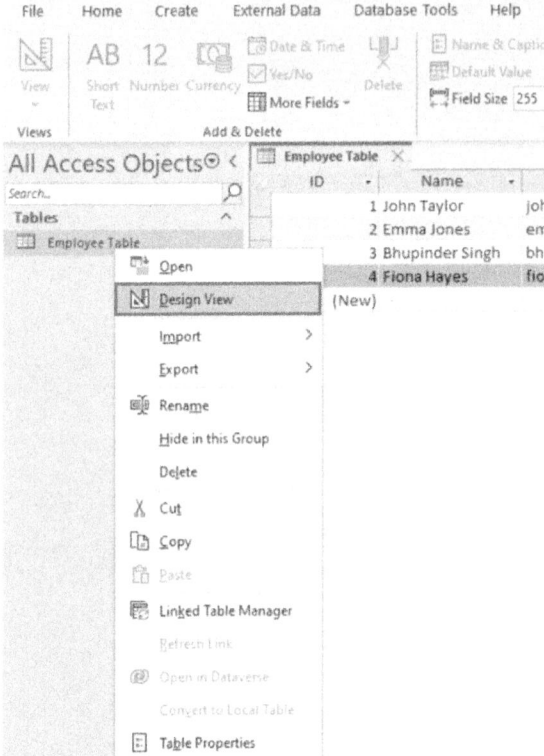

Step 2: Add a New Field

- In the table design, move the cursor to the first empty row in the "Field Name" column.

- Enter the name of the new field.

- Choose the appropriate data type for the new field from the "Data Type" column.

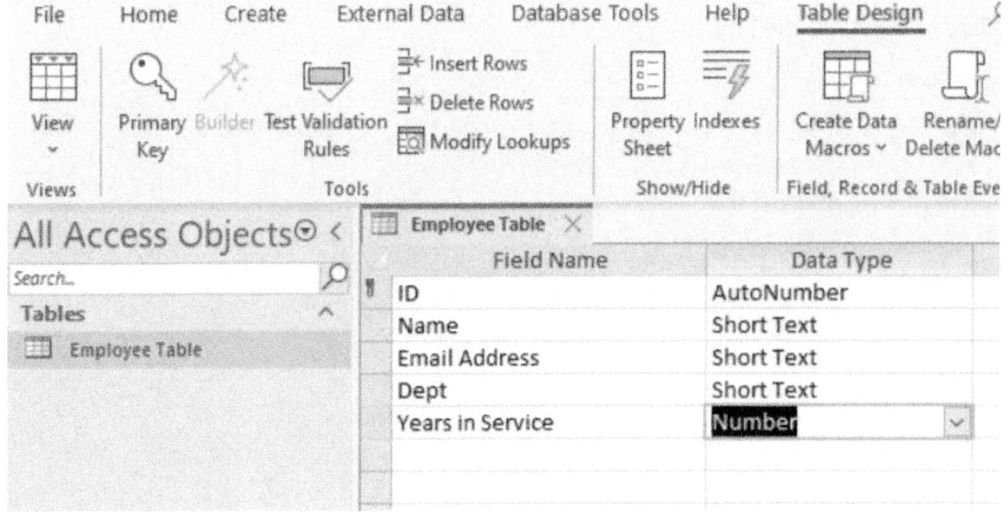

Step 3: Delete a Field

- To delete a field, select the entire row corresponding to that field.

- Press the "Delete" key on your keyboard.

Step 4: Rename a Field

- To rename a field, click on the field's name in the "Field Name" column and edit it.

Step 5: Save the Table

- Once you have made the necessary changes, press "Ctrl + S" or click on the "Save" button in the Ribbon.

- Click on the "Datasheet View" button at the bottom right of the screen to return to the datasheet view.

9.4.6 Deleting a Table

Step 1: Delete a Table

- In the Navigation pane, right-click on the table you want to delete.

- Select "Delete" from the context menu.

Creating and managing databases in Microsoft Access is a fundamental process that allows users to store, organise, and manage their data efficiently. By following the step-by-step instructions provided in this section, beginners can easily create new databases, design tables with appropriate fields, and enter sample data. Additionally, they can modify the table structure by adding, deleting, or renaming fields as needed. Understanding these basic concepts is essential for effectively working with Access and leveraging its database management capabilities for better data organisation and analysis.

9.5 Entering and Editing Data in Microsoft Access

Entering and editing data in Microsoft Access is a crucial aspect of managing databases effectively. In this section, we will guide you through with step-by-step instructions the process of entering and editing data in existing Access tables.

9.5.1 Entering Data into an Existing Table

Step 1: Open Microsoft Access

- Launch Microsoft Access from the Start menu or desktop shortcut.

Step 2: Open the Existing Database

- In the Access interface, click on "Open" from the left pane and open the database that contains the table you want to enter data into.

Step 3: Navigate to the Table

- In the Navigation pane, click on the "Tables" section to see a list of available tables.

- Select the table you want to work with.

Step 4: Enter Data

- Access will open the table in "Datasheet View," ready for data entry.

- Move to the first empty row at the bottom of the table.

- Start entering data into each field (column) of the table, row by row.

- Use the "Tab" key to move to the next field and the "Enter" key to move to the next row.

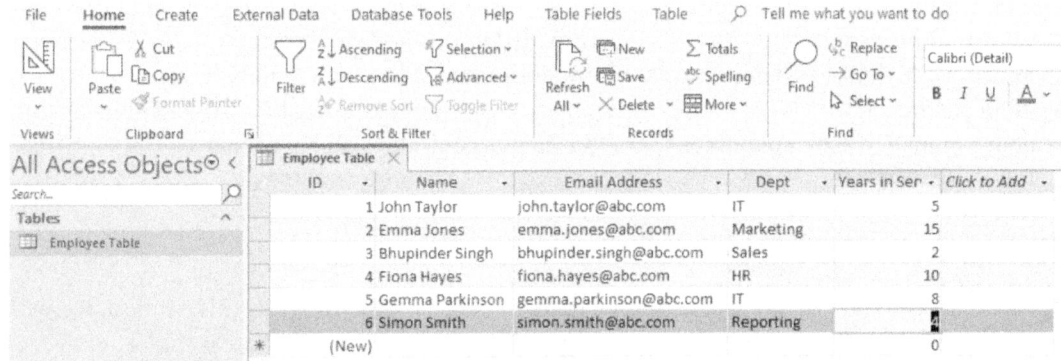

Step 5: Save the Changes

- Once you have entered the data, press "Ctrl + S" or click on the "Save" button in the Ribbon to save the changes to the table.

9.5.2 Editing Data in an Existing Table

Step 1: Navigate to the Table

- In the Navigation pane, click on the "Tables" section to see a list of available tables.

- Select the table you want to edit.

Step 2: Access Datasheet View

- Access will open the table in "Datasheet View," displaying the existing data.

- Locate the record (row) containing the data you want to edit.

Step 3: Edit the Data

- Click on the cell (field) containing the data you want to edit.

- Modify the data as needed.

- Press "Tab" to move to the next field.

Step 4: Save the Changes

- Once you have finished editing the data, press "Ctrl + S" or click on the "Save" button in the Ribbon to save the changes to the table.

9.5.3 Data Validation

Step 1: Set Data Validation Rules (Optional)

- In Access, you can define data validation rules to ensure the accuracy and consistency of the data entered. For example, you can set a rule to only allow numerical values in a field or restrict a date field to a specific range.

Step 2: Add Data Validation Rules

- In the datasheet view, select the field for which you want to set data validation.

- In the "Table Fields" tab, under the "Field Validation" group, click on the "Validation" button.

- Select "Field Validation Rule" from the menu.

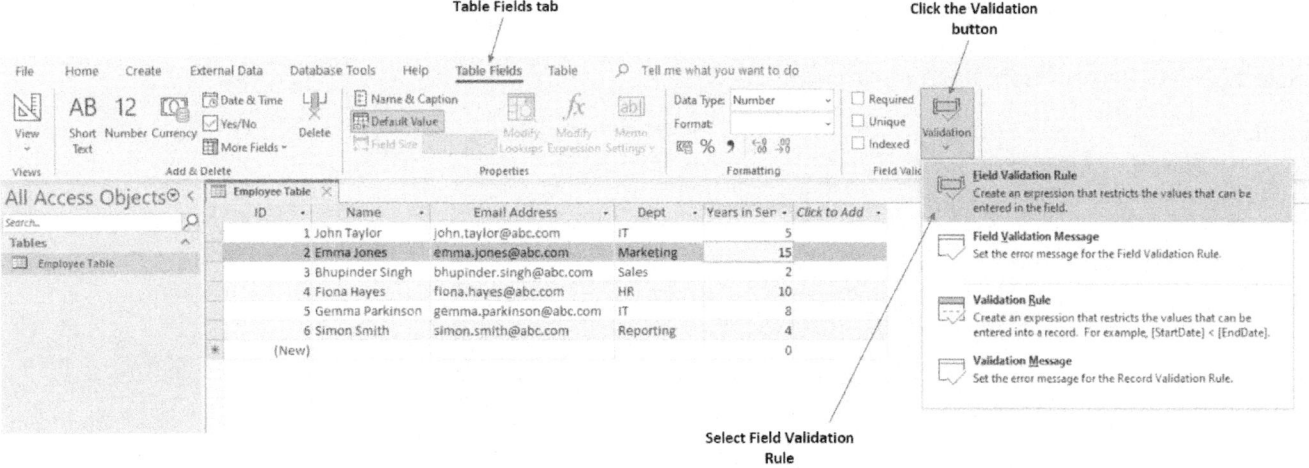

- Use the Expression Builder to create the rule.

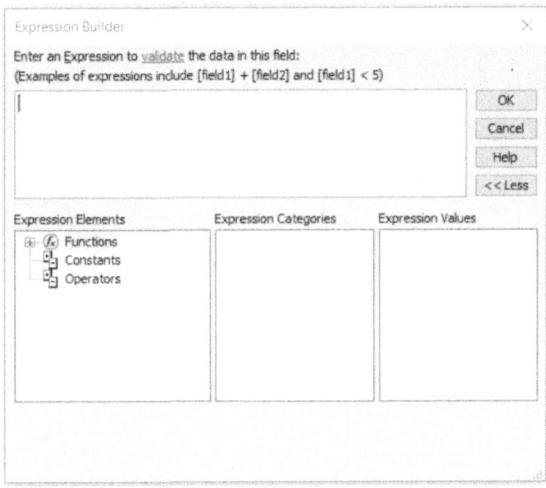

Step 3: Save and Exit Design View

- After setting data validation rules, save the changes by pressing "Ctrl + S" or clicking on the "Save" button in the Ribbon.

9.5.4 Deleting Data from an Existing Table

Step 1: Navigate to the Table

- In the Navigation pane, click on the "Tables" section to see a list of available tables.

- Select the table containing the data you want to delete.

Step 2: Access Datasheet View

- Access will open the table in "Datasheet View," displaying the existing data.

- Locate the record (row) containing the data you want to delete.

Step 3: Delete the Data

- Right-click on the record you want to delete.

- Select "Delete Record" from the context menu.

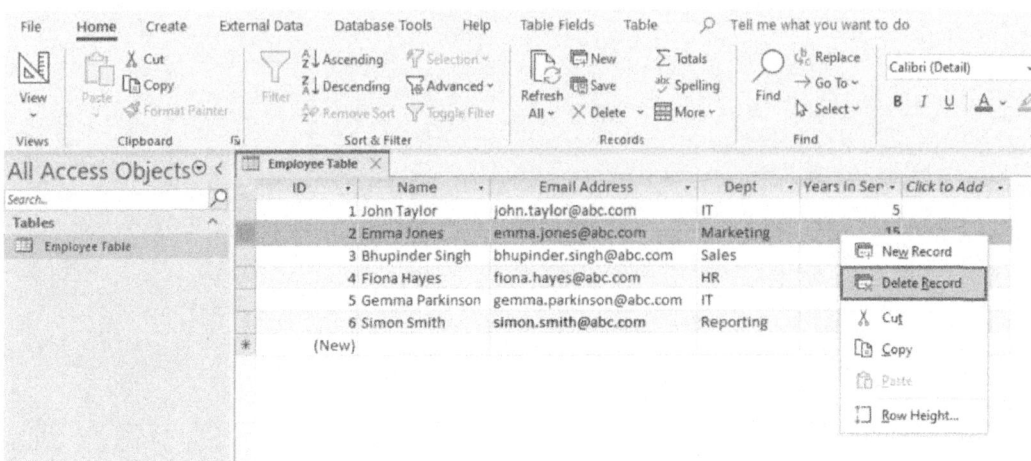

Step 4: Confirm Deletion

- Access will ask you to confirm the deletion.

- Click "Yes" to delete the selected record and its associated data.

Step 5: Save the Changes

- Once you have deleted the data, press "Ctrl + S" or click on the "Save" button in the Ribbon to save the changes to the table.

Entering and editing data in Microsoft Access is essential for maintaining accurate and up-to-date information in your databases. By following the step-by-step instructions provided in this section, users can easily enter new data into existing tables, edit existing data, validate data entries, and delete records when necessary. Understanding these fundamental data entry and editing processes is essential for efficiently managing databases in Microsoft Access and ensuring data accuracy for better decision-making and analysis.

9.6 Building Queries and Reports in Microsoft Access

Queries and reports in Microsoft Access allow users to retrieve, analyse, and present data from the database in a structured and organised format. In this section, we will guide you through the process of building queries and reports in Access by providing step-by-step instructions.

9.6.1 Building Queries in Microsoft Access

Step 1: Open Microsoft Access

- Launch Microsoft Access from the Start menu or desktop shortcut.

Step 2: Open the Existing Database

- In the Access interface, click on "Open" from the left pane and open the existing database that contains the table you want to query.

Step 3: Create a New Query

- Click on the "Create" tab and then the "Query Wizard" button under the "Queries" group.

- Select "Simple Query Wizard" and then click the "OK" button.

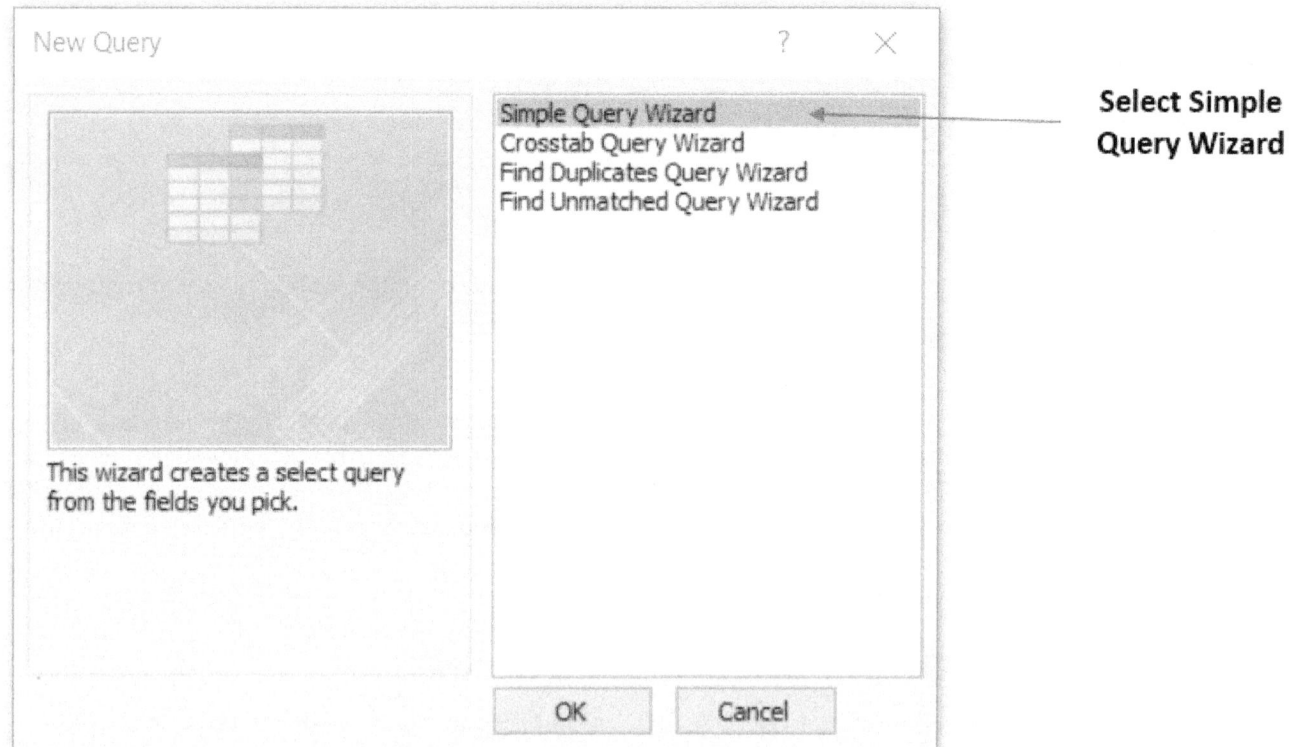

Select Simple Query Wizard

Step 4: Add Tables to the Query

- In the "Simple Query Wizard" dialog box, select the table(s) you want to include in the query under "Tables/Queries".

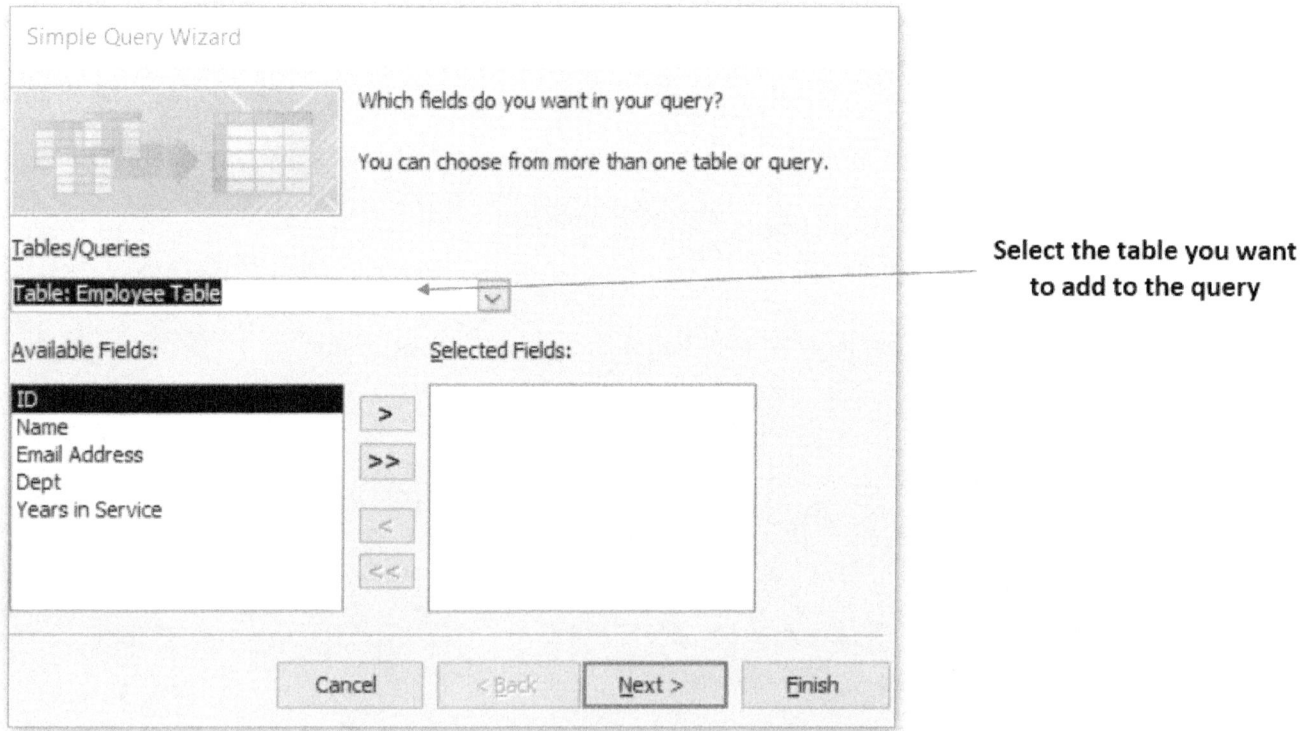

Select the table you want to add to the query

Step 5: Add Fields to the Query

- Under "Available Fields", add the fields you want to "Selected Fields" by selecting the fields and using the arrow keys.

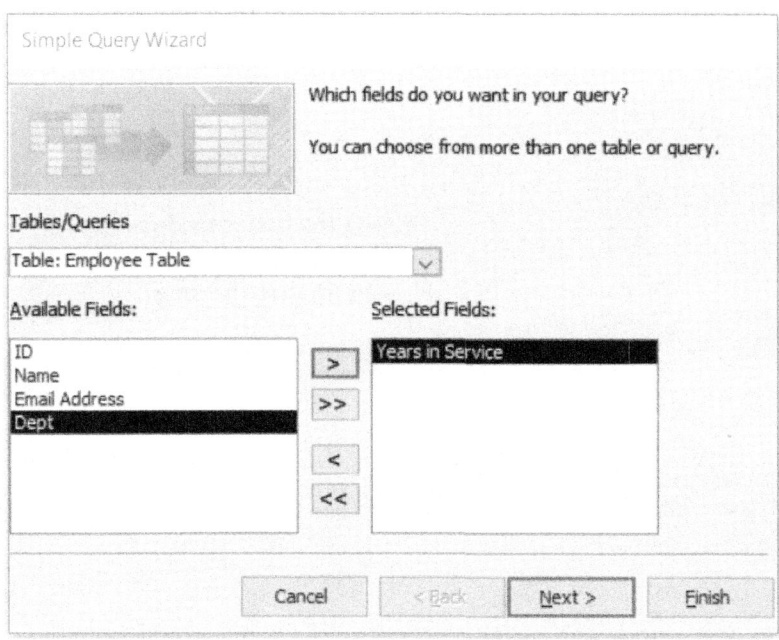

- Click on the "Next" button.

Step 6: Choose a Detail or Summary Query

- If you added number fields, i.e., fields that contain numeric data, then the wizard will ask whether you want the query to return detail or summary data.

- If you want individual records, then select "Detail". If you want summarised numeric data, such as averages, minimum or maximum values then select "Summary" and then "Summary Options".

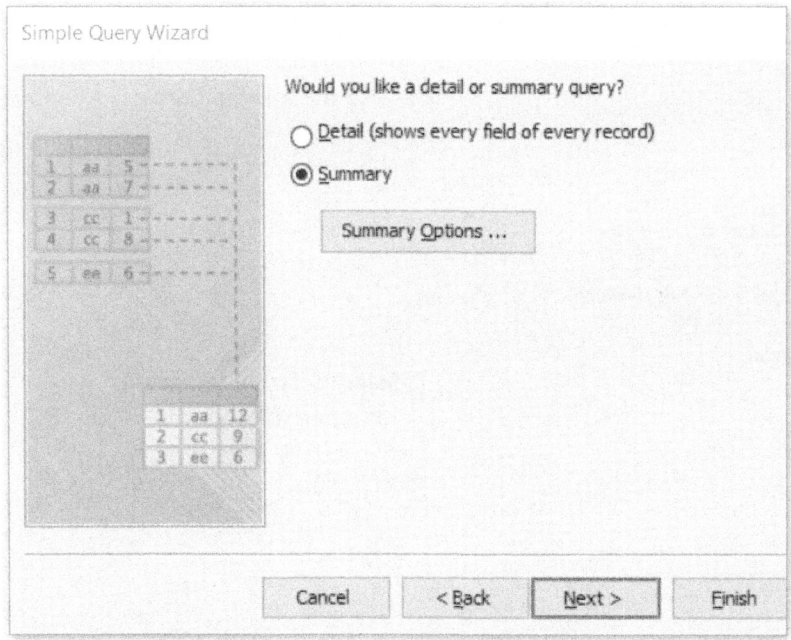

- If you selected "Summary Options", then check the checkboxes to show how you want to summarise the data in the "Summary Options" dialog box and then click "OK".

165

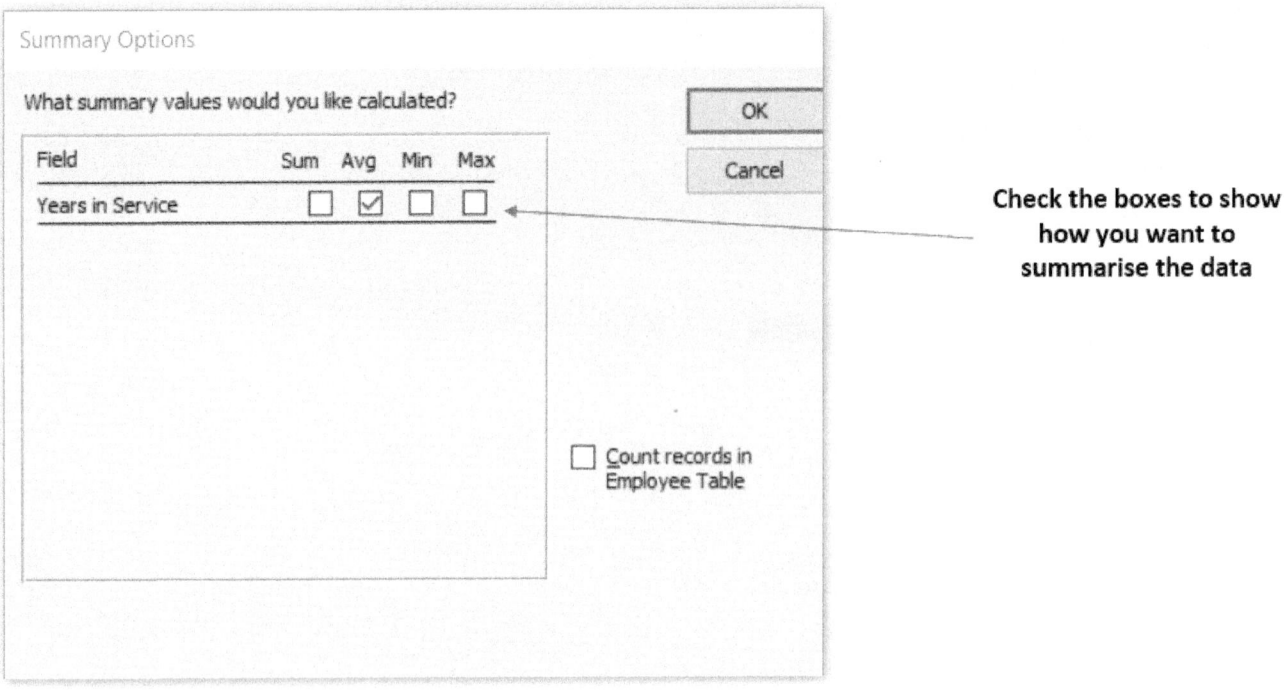

Check the boxes to show how you want to summarise the data

- Click on the "Next" button in the "Simple Query Wizard".

Step 7: Run the Query

- Give the query a title, specify whether you want to open or modify the query, and then click "Finish".

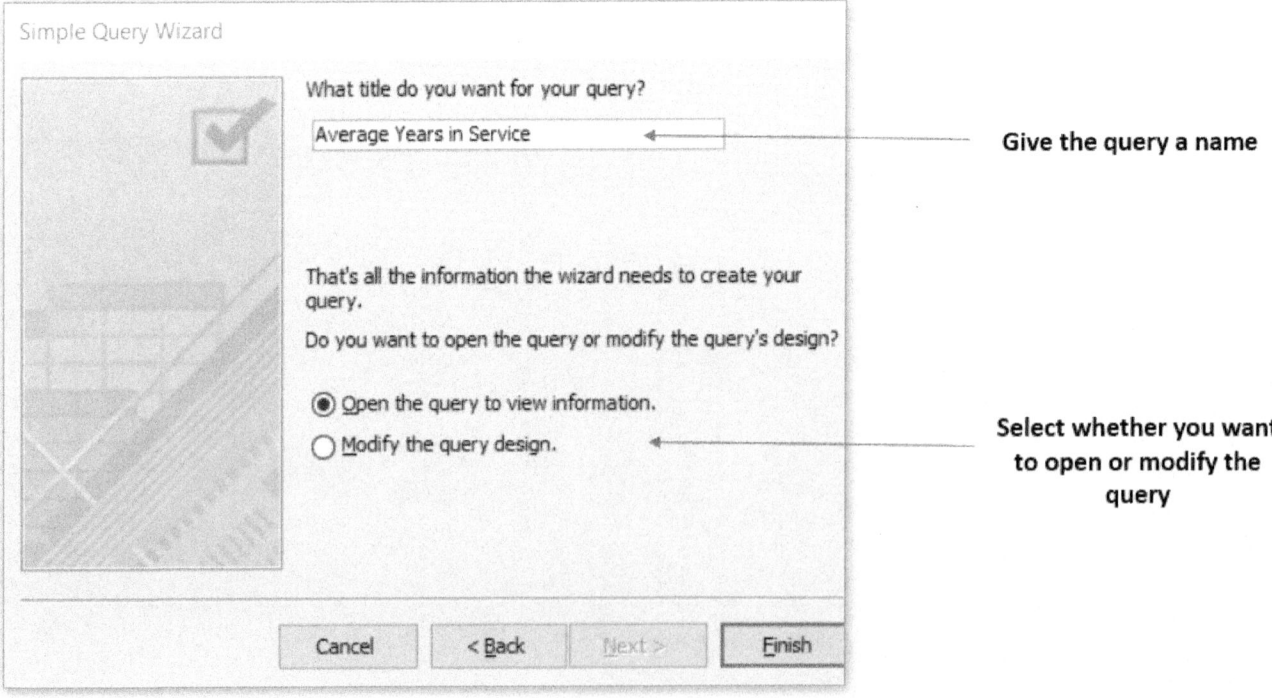

Give the query a name

Select whether you want to open or modify the query

- The query will run and display the results.

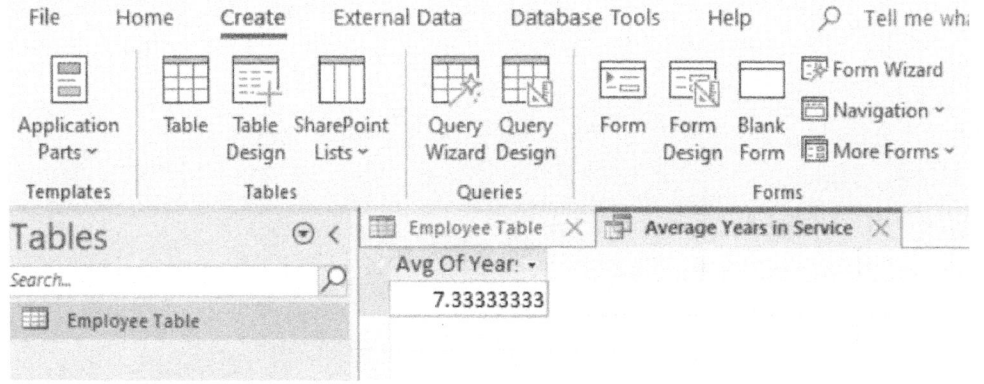

9.6.2 Building Reports in Microsoft Access

Option A: Build a Report using the Report Button

Step 1: Select the Table

- Select the table or query you want to base the report on.

Step 2: Create a New Report

- In the "Create" tab, click on the "Report " button in the "Reports" group.

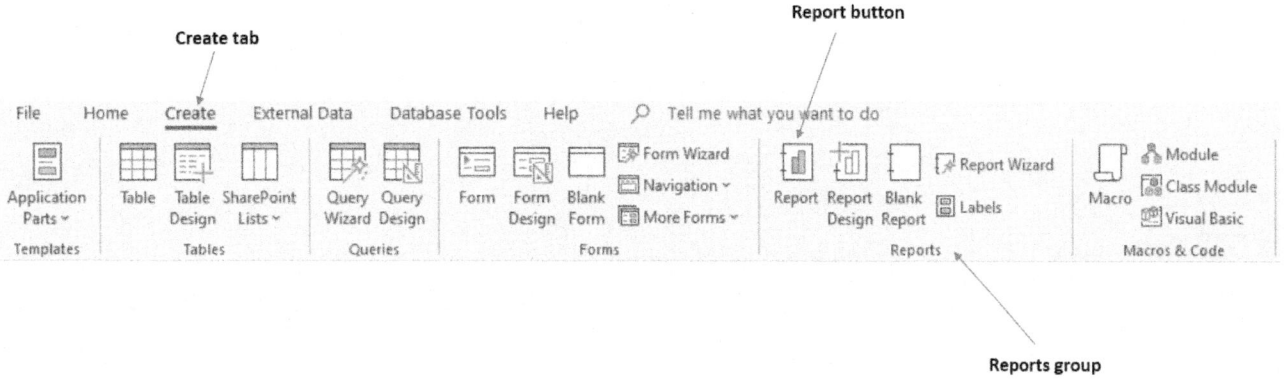

- A report is instantly created based on the active table or query. The report appears in "Layout View".

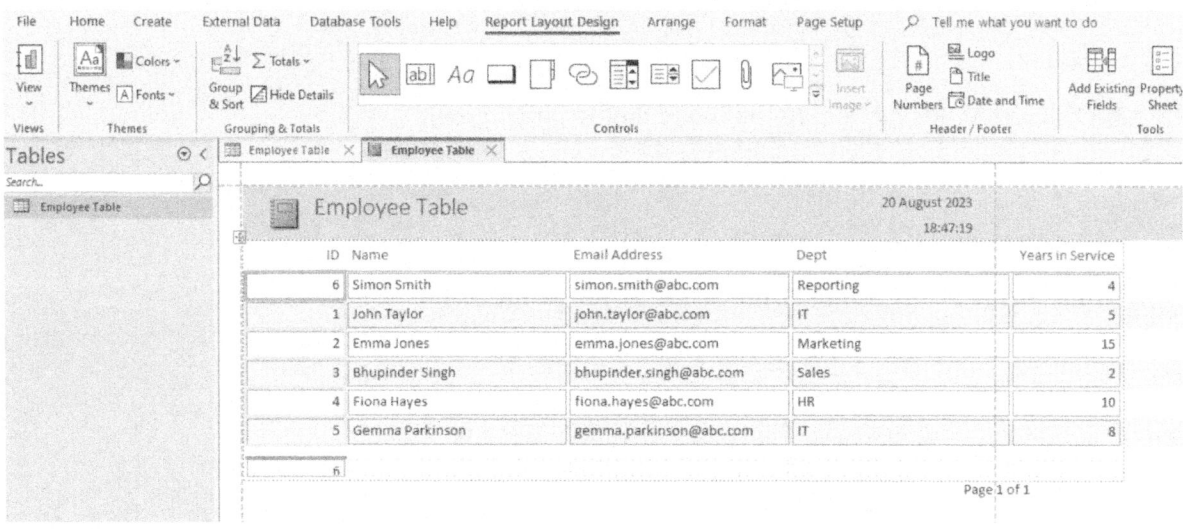

Step 3: Save the Report

- Press "Ctrl + S" to save the report.

Step 4: Name the Report

- Give the report a name and click the "OK" button.

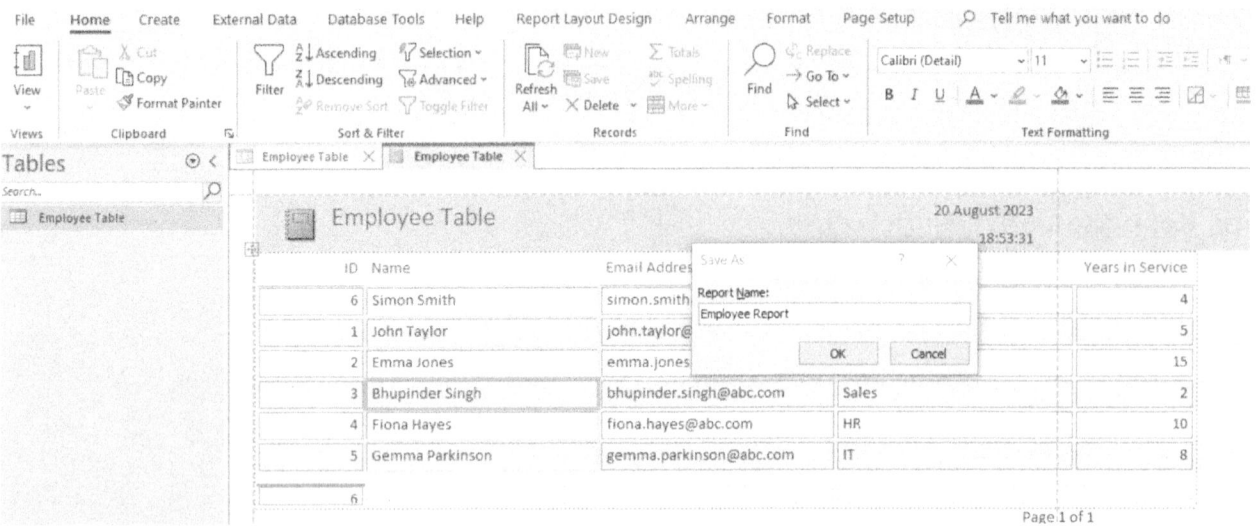

- The report will be saved and will appear in the Navigation pane.

Option B: Build a Report using the Report Wizard Button

Step 1: Create a New Report

- In the "Create" tab, click on the "Report Wizard" button in the "Reports" group.

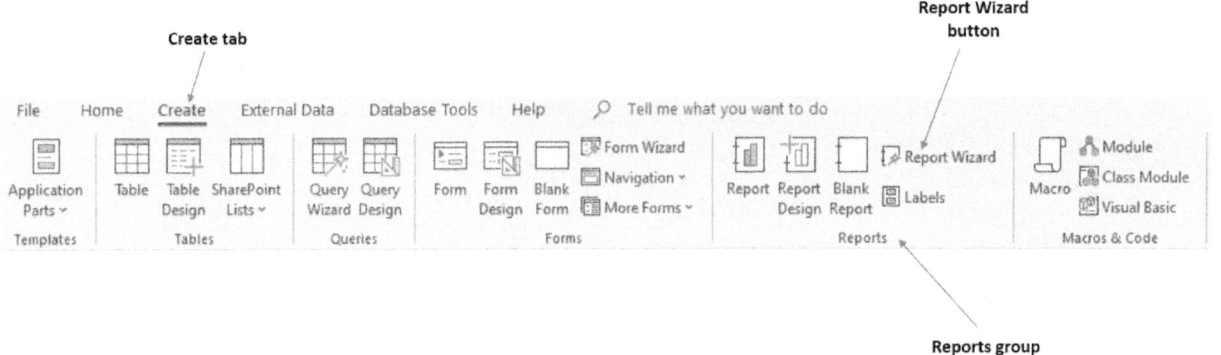

Step 2: Add the Table to the Query

- In the "Report Wizard" dialog box, select the table(s) you want to include in the report "Tables/Queries".

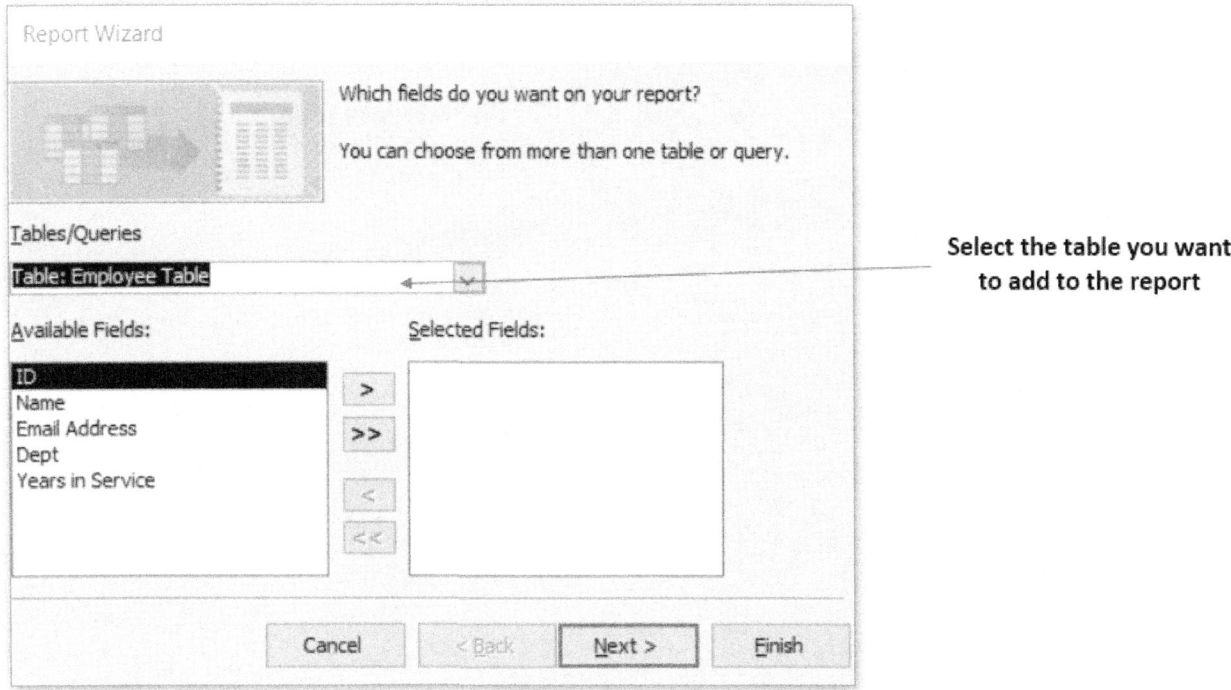

Step 3: Add Fields to the Query

- Under "Available Fields", add the fields you want to "Selected Fields" by selecting the fields and using the arrow keys.

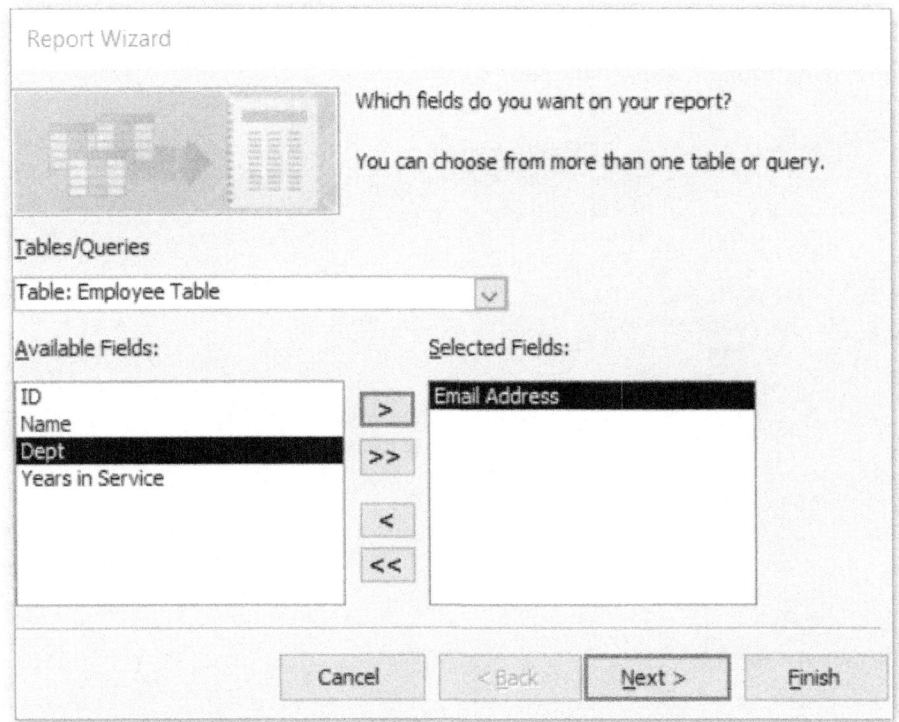

- Click on the "Next" button.

Step 4: Choose the Sort Order

- In the first drop-down box, select the field to sort the records by. By default, records will be sorted in ascending order by the field you select. If you want the field to be selected in descending order, then click the "Ascending" button to change it to "Descending".

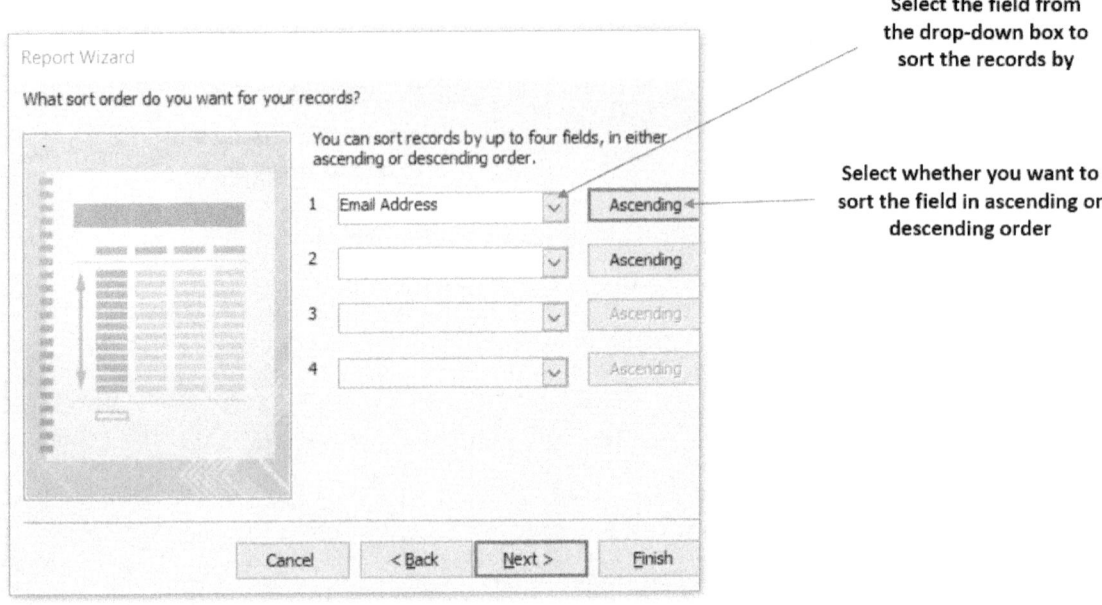

- Click on the "Next" button in the "Report Wizard".

Step 5: Select the layout of your report

- Choose the layout of the report and the orientation and then click "Next".

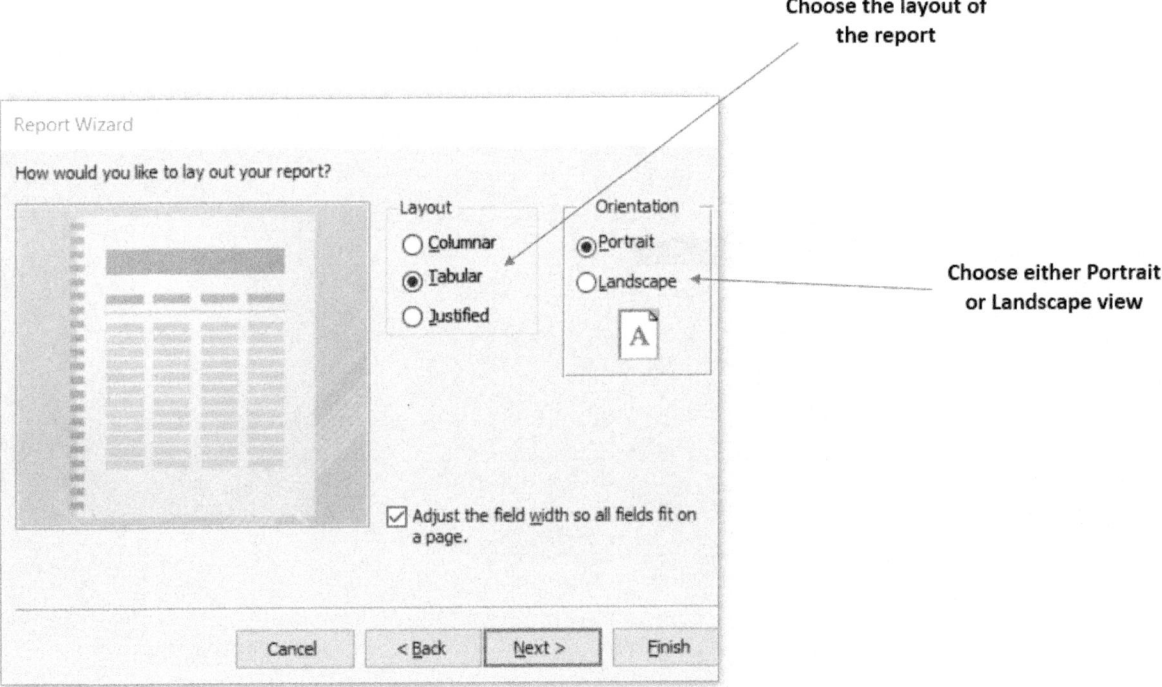

Step 6: Name the report

- Name the report and then choose whether you want to preview it or modify it. Click the "Finish" button.

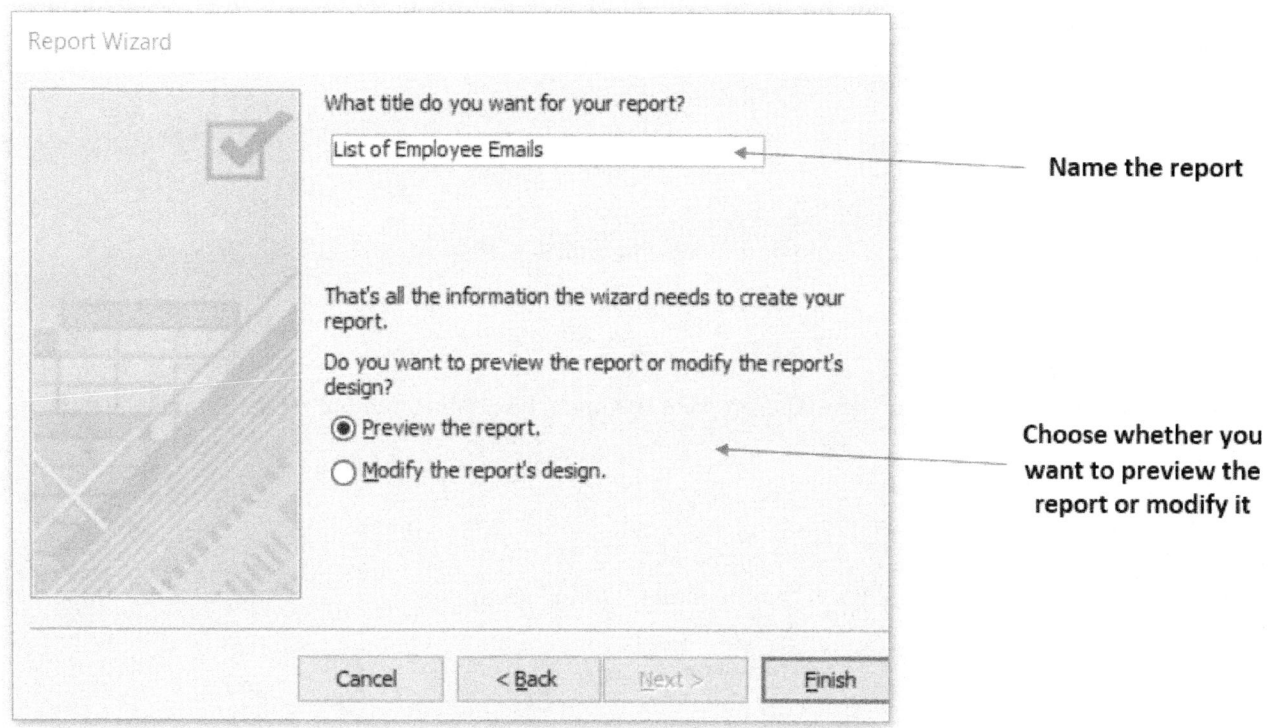

- The Report Wizard will display the report.

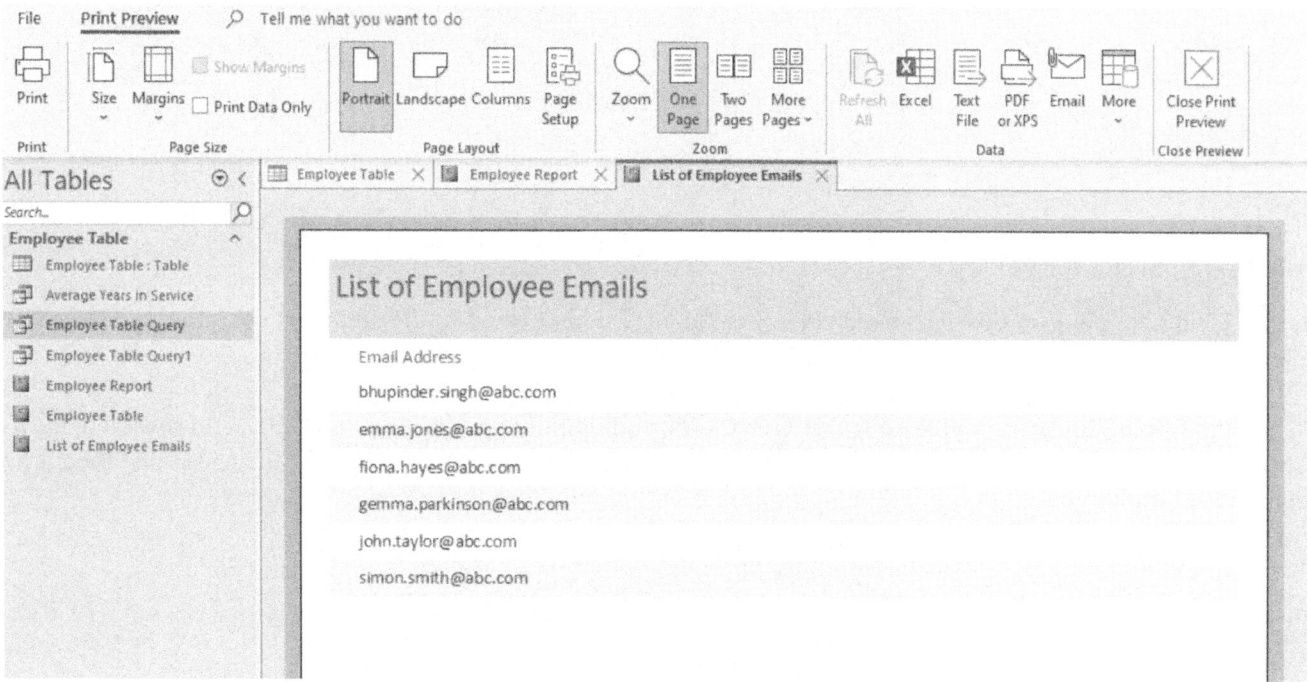

Building queries and reports in Microsoft Access enables users to retrieve specific data from their databases, perform data analysis, and present information in a structured and organised manner. By following the step-by-step instructions provided in this section, users can easily create queries to filter and search data based on specific criteria and build reports to display data with grouping, sorting, and calculated fields. Understanding these essential features empowers users to harness the full potential of Microsoft Access in retrieving and presenting data effectively for decision-making and analysis purposes.

9.7 Designing Forms for Data Entry in Microsoft Access

Designing forms for data entry in Microsoft Access is a crucial aspect of creating user-friendly and efficient interfaces for entering and managing data in your database. In this section, we will guide you through the process of designing forms for data entry in Access.

9.7.1 Creating a New Data Entry Form

Step 1: Open Microsoft Access

- Launch Microsoft Access from the Start menu or desktop shortcut.

Step 2: Open the Existing Database

- In the Access interface, click on "Open" from the left pane and open the existing database that contains the table you want to query.

Step 3: Create a New Form

- In the "Create" tab, click on the "Blank Form" button in the "Forms" group.

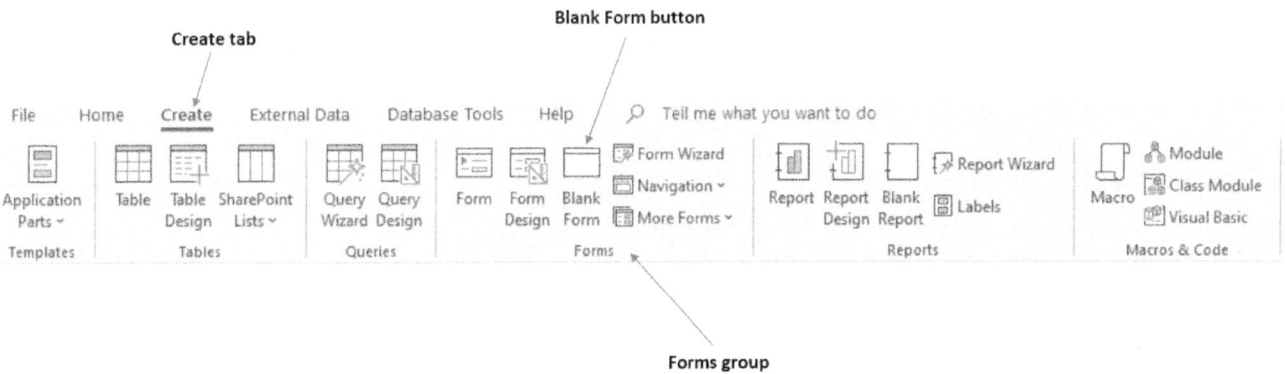

Step 4: Add Fields to the Form

- In the "Field List" pane on the right-hand side, click the plus sign (+) next to the table that contains the fields that you want to see on the form.

- To add the field to the form, double-click the field or click and drag it onto the form screen. To add several fields to the form at once, press the "CTRL" key on your keyboard and then click the fields you want to include and then drag them to the form screen.

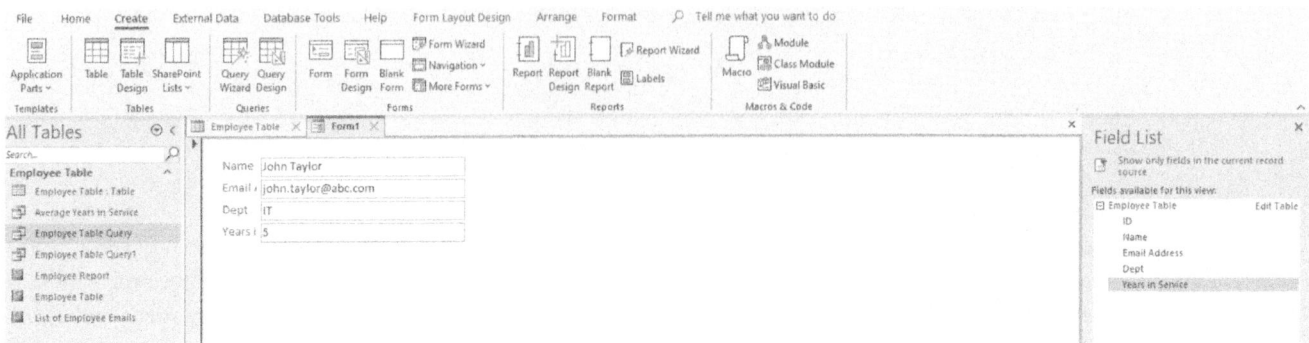

Step 5: Save the Form

- Press "Ctrl + S" or click on the "Save" button in the Ribbon to save the form.

Step 6: Name the Form

- Give the form a name and click the "OK" button.

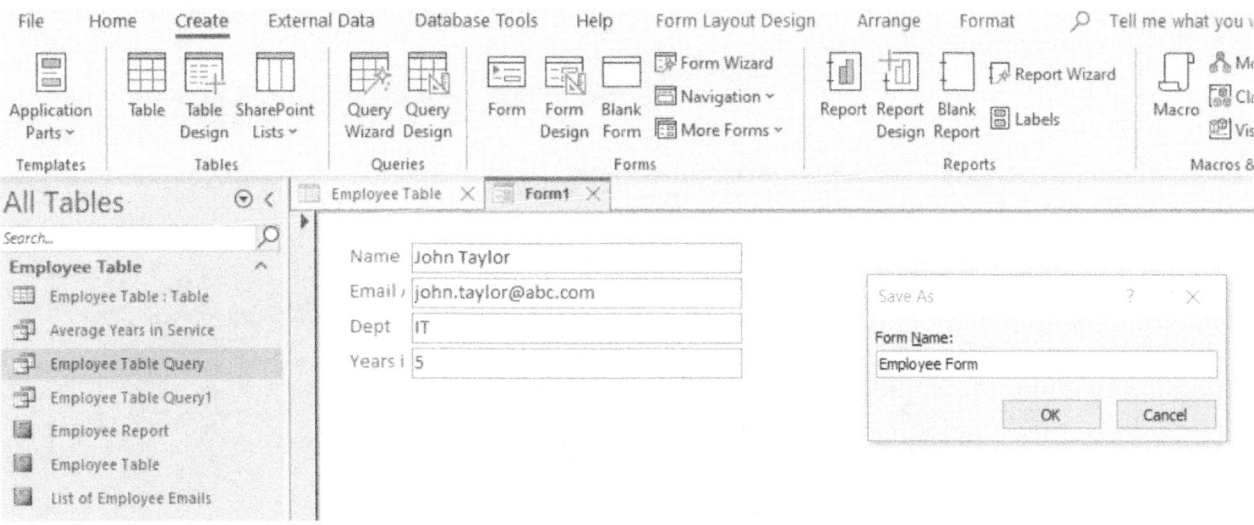

9.7.2 Customising the Data Entry Form

Step 1: Add Labels and Captions

- To improve form readability, add labels and text boxes to the fields.

- In the "Form Layout Design" tab in the "Controls" group, click on the "Label" or "Text Box" button to add labels or text boxes.

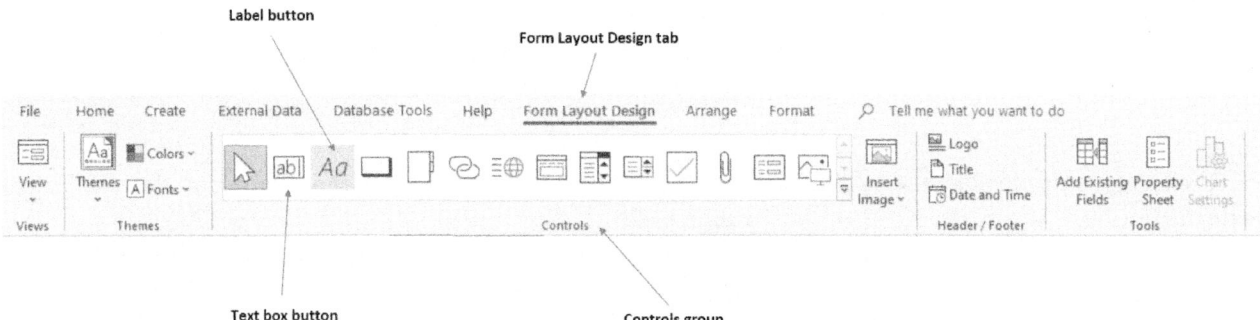

Step 2: Adjust Field Properties

- Right-click on a field and select "Properties" from the context menu to open the property sheet.

- In the property sheet, customise field properties such as formatting, default values, and more.

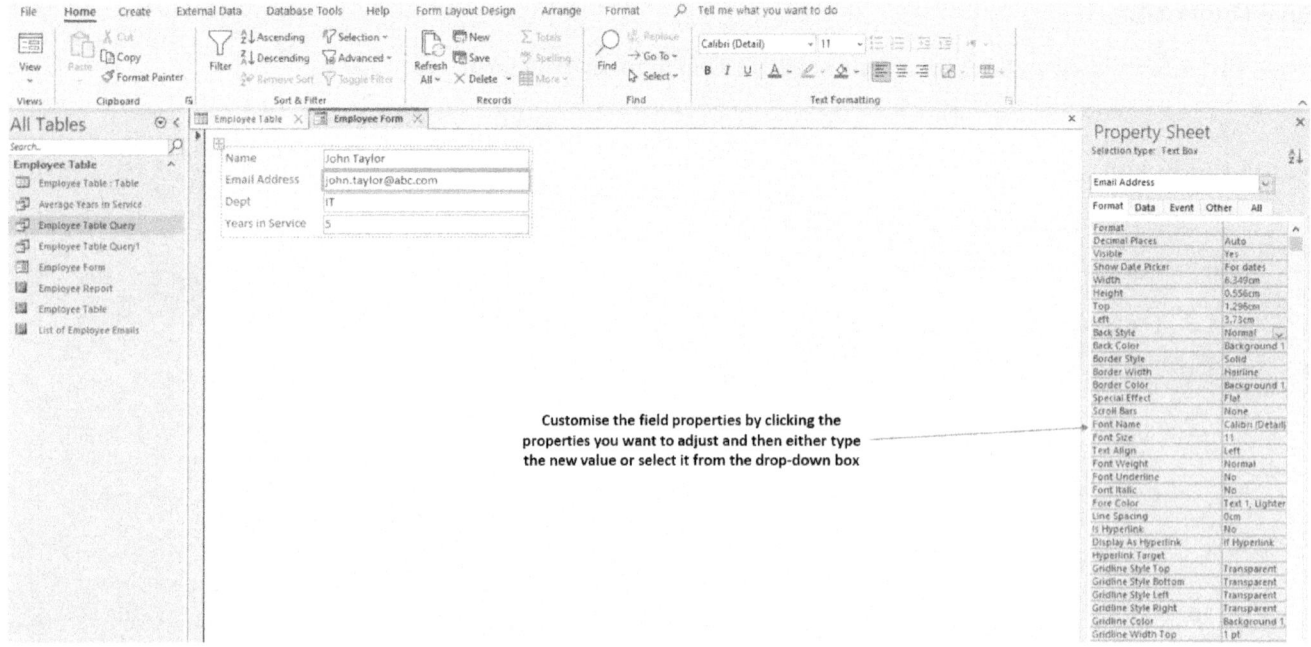

Customise the field properties by clicking the properties you want to adjust and then either type the new value or select it from the drop-down box

Step 3: Add Command Buttons (Optional)

- To add buttons for specific actions, such as saving data or navigating records, click on the "Form Layout Design" tab and then click on the "Button" button in the "Controls" group.

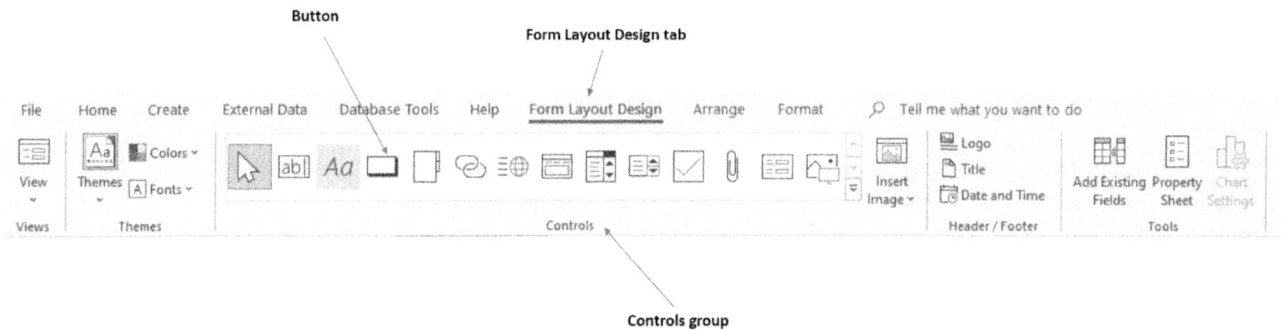

- Click in the forms screen to place the button in the form and then follow the steps in the "Command Button Wizard" to create the button.

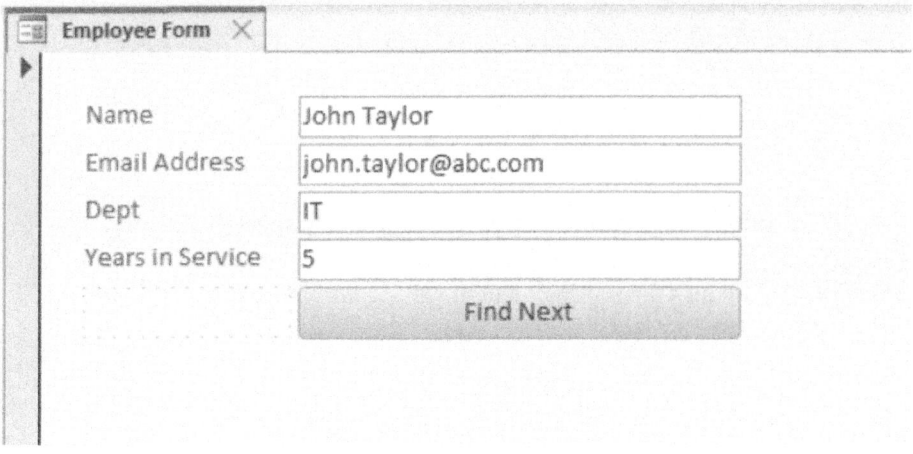

Step 4: Use Form Wizard (Optional)

- If you prefer a guided approach, you can use the "Form Wizard" to create a data entry form quickly.

- Select the "Create" tab and then click on the "Form Wizard" button in the Forms group. Follow the on-screen instructions to select fields and create the form.

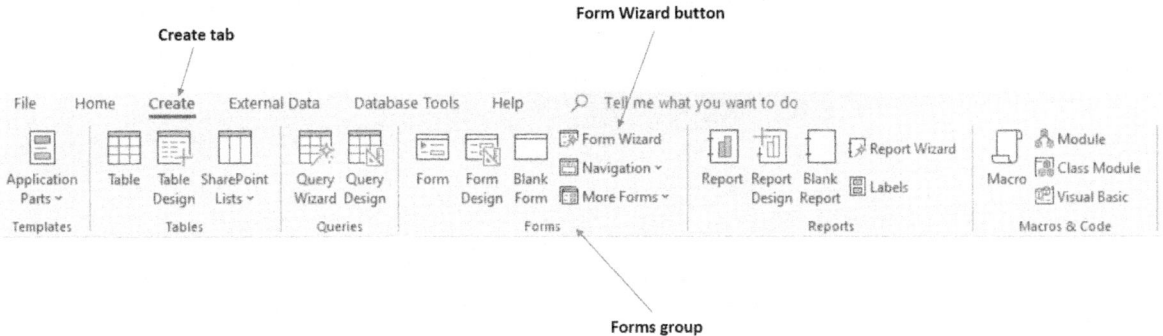

Step 5: Save the Form

- Press "Ctrl + S" to save the form.

9.7.3 Entering Data Using the Form

Step 1: Navigate to the Data Entry Form

- In the Navigation pane, click on the form you created to select it.

- In the bottom right corner click on the "Form View" button to open the form in "Form View," ready for data entry.

Step 2: Enter Data

- Use the form controls to enter data into each field.

- Navigate to the next field using the "Tab" key or the mouse.

- Use the navigation buttons (if added) to move between records.

Step 3: Save the Data

- Once you have entered the data, click on the "Save Record" button (if added), or simply move to another record to save the changes automatically.

Designing forms for data entry in Microsoft Access is a fundamental process that enables users to create user-friendly interfaces for entering and managing data in their databases. By following the step-by-step instructions provided in this section, users can easily create data entry forms based on existing tables, customise the form layout, add labels, adjust field properties, and use buttons for specific actions. The data entry form simplifies the process of entering data into the database, promoting data accuracy, and streamlining data management tasks. Understanding these essential form design techniques empowers users to optimise data entry processes and create efficient and user-friendly interfaces in Microsoft Access.

About the Author

Harjit Suman is a highly accomplished Excel and VBA consultant with a wealth of expertise in Microsoft Office applications. With a passion for simplifying complexities and unlocking the true potential of Microsoft Office, Harjit has become a trusted guide for beginners seeking to master these essential tools.

With an extensive background in Excel and VBA, Harjit has successfully guided countless individuals and businesses in harnessing the power of data analysis, automation, and customisation. Their deep understanding of Excel's functions, formulas, and data manipulation techniques has enabled users to streamline their workflows and make informed decisions.

However, Harjit 's proficiency extends far beyond Excel and VBA. Armed with comprehensive skills in all facets of Microsoft Office, including Word, PowerPoint, Outlook, Access, and OneNote, he has empowered beginners to embrace Microsoft Office with confidence.

Having honed his skills through years of real-world consulting, Harjit possesses an innate ability to empathise with beginners' challenges and tailor his guidance accordingly. His commitment to lifelong learning and staying updated with the latest Office features ensures that his advice remains relevant and impactful in an ever-evolving digital landscape.

Harjit is the founder and owner of the Excel Master Consultant website which offers information on everything about Excel. In his website you will find:

- Lots of free Excel tutorials and blogs to expand your Excel knowledge.
- Online Excel and VBA courses you can buy.
- An online shop where you can buy Excel books in paperback, Kindle, and eBook formats.

Please check out his website below:

www.excelmasterconsultant.com

Please take a visit and drop him a message. He would love to hear from you.

Unlock Your Excel Passion with Exclusive Merchandise and eBooks!

Discover a world of exclusive Excel-themed products at my shop! Elevate your style with our chic mugs and trendy t-shirts, all designed for the Excel aficionado in you. Dive into expert insights with our curated eBooks for a power-packed spreadsheet journey.

Explore our Collection!

- 🍵 **Mugs**: Sip your creativity with every brew using our Excel-inspired mugs.
- 👕 **T-Shirts**: Wear your love for Excel proudly with our fashionable and comfortable t-shirts.
- 📚 **eBooks**: Unleash the power of Excel with our expertly curated eBooks. Elevate your skills and efficiency to new heights.

Why Choose Us?

- 🤓 **Unique Designs**: Stand out with our one-of-a-kind Excel-themed merchandise.
- 📋 **Functional and Stylish**: Our products seamlessly blend utility with style for the modern Excel enthusiast.
- 📚 **Expert Knowledge**: My eBooks are crafted by myself with over 15 years' experience working with Excel, ensuring valuable insights and practical tips.

Don't Miss Out – Excel Now!

Ready to embrace the Excel lifestyle? Visit my shop and discover a world where every click brings you closer to a better, more stylish Excel experience.

☞ **Shop Now**: www.etsy.com/shop/ExcelstoreByHarjit

🔥 Excel Today, Excel Every Day! 🔥

More Books by Excel Master Consultant

Available to buy on Amazon now!

Excel Bible for Beginners Series

Amazon UK: www.amazon.co.uk/dp/B08C4KVFX3

Amazon US: www.amazon.com/dp/B08C4KVFX3

Excel Formulas and Functions Series

Amazon UK: www.amazon.co.uk/dp/B0868RV3D5

Amazon US: www.amazon.com/dp/B0868RV3D5

Excel 365 Bible Series

Amazon UK: www.amazon.co.uk/dp/B0B6WQLMF8

Amazon US: www.amazon.com/dp/B0B6WQLMF8

PLEASE LEAVE A REVIEW
What did you think of this book?

Firstly, thank you for purchasing this book. I know you could have picked any number of Microsoft Office books to read, but you picked this book and for that I am extremely grateful.

I hope that it has improved your Microsoft Office skills and you can now confidently use the Microsoft Office suite for work and personal use. If so, I would be grateful if you could share your experience of reading this book with your friends and family by posting to Facebook and Twitter.

If you enjoyed this book, I'd like to hear from you and hope that you could take some time to post a review on Amazon. Your feedback and support will help me to greatly improve my writing craft for future projects and make this book even better.

Your feedback is very important to me, and I would be very grateful for your review.

I wish you all the best in your future success and happy learning!

Thank you

Printed in Great Britain
by Amazon

44990163R00099